Contents

iii

Modern Languages in the Curriculum

Revised Edition

ERIC W. HAWKINS

Professor Emeritus, University of York

The right of the
University of Cambridge
to print and sell
all manner of books
was granted by
Henry VIII in 1534.
The University has printed
and published continuously
since 1584.

CAMBRIDGE UNIVERSITY PRESS

Cambridge
New York   New Rochelle
Melbourne   Sydney

For
E.M.B.H.

Published by the Press Syndicate of the University of Cambridge
The Pitt Building, Trumpington Street, Cambridge CB2 1RP
32 East 57th Street, New York, NY 10022, USA
10 Stamford Road, Oakleigh, Melbourne 3166, Australia

First published 1981
Reprinted 1984
Revised edition 1987

Phototypeset in Linotron 202 Palatino by
Western Printing Services Ltd, Bristol
Printed and bound in Great Britain at The Bath Press, Avon

British Library Cataloguing in Publication Data

Hawkins, Eric W.
Modern languages in the curriculum.
Rev. ed.
1. Language and languages – Study and teaching –
Great Britain
I. Title
418'.007'1041   P57.G7

ISBN 0 521 34537 5 hard covers
ISBN 0 521 34766 1 paperback

The author and the publisher wish to thank the following for permission to reproduce material in this book:

The British Library for the pages from the facsimile edition, published by Oxford University Press, of Comenius, *Orbis Pictus* on pages 104–7

Oliver and Boyd for the passage and accompanying taped dialogue from *Revision French* on pages 258–9

Preface

Yet another book on language teaching? Is it really necessary? I believe it is, for the following reasons.

We have just passed through a period of ferment in language teaching only comparable to the 'Great Reform' 100 years ago. Then Henry Sweet (Bernard Shaw's Professor Higgins), armed with his phonograph, invented by Edison in 1878, and his new science of phonetics, had announced a revolutionary approach to language study, the 'living philology', which for the first time took the spoken language as its chief concern.

In the 1960s language teachers answered the challenge of another new teaching aid, the tape-recorder, with an enthusiasm worthy of Sweet's generation. Whereas the Great Reform foundered, however, in 1914, with the massacre of so many young teachers who might have carried the movement on, language teachers in the 1960s could look forward hopefully to the opportunities offered by Britain's entry into the European Community. However, just as new methods were being mastered and Britain was negotiating her entry into the EEC, schools had to cope, ill-prepared, with the drift into comprehensive reorganisation. One immediate effect of this on the curriculum was that modern languages ceased to be confined to an elite of 'academic' pupils. By the late 1970s some 85% of pupils in comprehensive schools were starting a modern language. No other subject had to make such an abrupt adjustment. The other main subjects in the curriculum had traditionally been offered across the whole range of aptitude and family background in both selective and non-selective schools. As the comprehensive school enters a period of consolidation there are a number of questions to answer.

The first question is: why a modern language for all? Our attempt to answer this question in Part I leads us to look critically at the justification of the place of modern languages in the secondary curriculum on vocational grounds. The case for modern language study as part of a coherent language education seems much stronger. Since it is impossible to predict, when a pupil is aged 11, which of many possible languages he or she will want in adult life (and here English speakers are in a different position from pupils in European schools who can all be predicted to want English) it follows that the secondary course must be seen as an apprenticeship rather than as the completion of language education. Only when adult needs for leisure or job emerge after adolescence can the learner choose which foreign language to acquire 'for life'. If the right expectations are set up, in the apprenticeship stage, the language of choice can be acquired economically by intensive methods later.

It follows that the selection of the apprenticeship language must be guided by its suitability as an introduction to language learning rather than by guesswork about future national or individual 'needs'. An attempt is made to compare the commonly taught languages from this standpoint.

In Part II we move from 'why?' and 'what?' questions to the question 'how?'. The concept of teaching a language as an apprenticeship, with the aim of facilitating the acquisition of another language later, necessarily raises questions of methodology, but there are other reasons to re-examine methods inherited from the past. One is that an unspoken assumption underlying everything that was written about language teaching in the past was that only a select few, the most verbally able, learned a foreign language. Another is that within the past decade research has given us new insights into the nature of the speech act, the way in which meaning affects the retention of language and the development of communicative competence. We are now able to see why so much that passed for language teaching, since the seventeeth century, has been mere rehearsal, not followed by performance. Rehearsal in the classroom was sometimes followed by performance but only by a select few (by extensive reading of texts whose meaning mattered to the learner or by immersion in the language on study visits abroad). For them rapid acquisition of the language followed. For the great majority, however, even of pupils in selective schools whose contact with the language ended at the rehearsal stage, without performance, results were meagre. It is now suggested that language is acquired most effectively when the learner, having rehearsed, i.e., having learned his lines, an essential stage, otherwise he would have nothing to say, is able to concentrate on the performance, that is on the *message*, which must matter enough to him to divert his attention from the *medium*. Merely relaying other people's messages in obedience to teacher or text-book, as in the exercises tested in the 16+ examinations, does not make the language stick for average learners.

This hypothesis is supported by our survey of the history of language teaching methods. It now seems clear that in the seventeenth century the discipline lost its way, with the disappearance of the immersion learning on which the statutes of the Tudor grammar schools had insisted, and that since then teachers have been engaged in an ever-hopeful quest for a panacea.

Part III attempts to outline the way ahead and at once encounters a further question, hitherto strangely neglected: what ought to be the relationship between modern language study and acquisition of the mother tongue? Until recently writers on modern languages have taken for granted a curriculum in which the foreign language and the mother tongue were taught in isolation from each other, by teachers educated and trained in separate faculties, who enjoyed no dialogue across the curriculum fence and who often used different terms when discussing language with children. Perhaps this mattered less, or seemed to matter less, when the pupils who were learning foreign languages could be assumed to have a good command of the standard variety of English used in school. Now the comprehensive school challenges teachers of English and teachers of foreign languages to cooperate in devising a linguistic education for a wide range of pupils, many of whom do not speak standard English at home. This is specially urgent in schools in urban areas which may receive pupils speaking between them a dozen or more mother tongues. It is no less urgent in schools with pupils whose home language is a regional or social dialect of English or a version of West Indian creole.

The way forward, we suggest, is for teachers of English and of foreign languages to cooperate in planning, and jointly teaching, a coherent language course which would have three elements:
i. study of the mother tongue (generally but not always English)
ii. study of a foreign language chosen for its suitability as apprenticeship in language learning
iii. a course in 'awareness of language' taught in collaboration by teachers of mother tongue and foreign language, and to which

pupils from a variety of language backgrounds could make a positive contribution.

This new twentieth-century 'trivium' (to adopt the name used for their course in grammar, logic and rhetoric by the mediaeval curriculum planners) would be preceded at primary level by a programme called 'education of the ear', designed to give all pupils the tools for verbal learning that so many of them lack. It would be followed at the post-16 stage, when the pupils' career and leisure interests begin to take shape, by the opportunity for rapid acquisition, through immersion learning, of the language of adult choice, and, within each language, the opportunity to concentrate on special registers, e.g. German for the office, etc. Some implications of this programme for teacher training are discussed in the Epilogue.

These proposals may seem difficult to implement, especially at a time when resources are scarce and school rolls are falling. The detailed working out and timing will depend on the support they attract both in and out of schools. They cannot be a complete answer to all the questions raised but I hope they may contribute to charting the ultimate way ahead.

Whatever merit this suggested way ahead may have is due to the many keen and gifted teacher and student colleagues whose example in the classroom has sustained my belief that modern language study has a uniquely valuable contribution to make in the apprenticeship of citizens of a multi-cultural Britain and a polyglot world.

EWH 1980

Preface to the revised edition

The publication of a revised edition of this book makes it possible to up-date to 1985/6 the statistics of teacher supply and of numbers of boys and girls offering the various foreign languages in public examinations at 16+ and 18+. The new figures, unhappily, amply confirm our earlier anxieties. The opportunity has been taken to include new sections (in Chapter 6, now entitled 'The search for solutions'): 'Use of radio and TV' and 'Computers and language learning' as well as some account of the history of the search for 'A universal auxiliary language'.

Interesting progress has been made since 1980 in two areas: new approaches to examining (see Appendix A) and the introduction of courses in 'awareness of language' bridging the gulf that too often separated the English from the foreign language classroom. Both these developments are in line with the argument of this book and it is a pleasure to give some account of them in this revised edition.

The only omission from our previous edition is the detailed syllabus proposed for a course in 'awareness of language'. This is no longer necessary since the ideas outlined there have been developed and improved upon in the widely welcomed series of books for schools under the same title published by Cambridge University Press (see Appendix C). The original syllabus may, however, still be referred to as it was reprinted (as a model that schools might follow) in the DES Report on the Education of children from Ethnic Minority groups *Education for All* (Swann 1985). I would like to record my thanks again to Rosemary Davidson of Cambridge University Press for her never failing encouragement and help, to Elizabeth Bowden for her indefatigable skill as desk editor for this revised edition, and to my friends of many years Anthony Barley, Paddy Carpenter and Alan Moys for their expert advice. May I also thank the many new friends that this book has brought me, both in the UK and abroad, for their messages which have generously rewarded the labour of writing.

EWH 1987

Acknowledgements

I was enabled to write this book by the award of a Leverhulme Emeritus Fellowship for the year 1979–80. I am particularly grateful to the trustees for allowing me to interrupt my fellowship to undertake a teaching assignment in China and to look closely at language teaching there. From that distance some of our own recent anxieties could be assessed more objectively.

My text has greatly benefited from the advice of colleagues who read it in its various drafts, though its many defects remain my sole responsibility. My thanks are due to Geoff Richardson and Nadine Cammish of Hull University and to former HM staff inspector Peter Hoy, Chevalier de la Légion d'Honneur.

Particular aspects of the programme proposed in this book have been clarified for me in discussions with Carl Dodson of Aberystwyth, John Trim, director of the Centre for Information on Language Teaching, and his predecessor George Perren and Michael Salter HMI.

The confidence and encouragement of Eric James made possible the exciting years of experiment at York University. For those years I wish also to thank my friend and colleague Harry Rée; discussions with him on language teaching were always stimulating though we have not always agreed.

I owe a special debt to Peter Green, my successor at the Language Teaching Centre, York University, for his cooperation in so many enterprises and his scholarly advice so generously given. The support and advice, also, of Rosemary Davidson of the Cambridge University Press has sweetened the labour of the writing.

Muriel Woods typed successive versions of my nearly indecipherable text in her scarce spare time with never failing helpfulness.

Finally the dedication of this book to my wife says just a little of my gratitude for her patience and support.

York, 1980 EWH

Part I

Anxieties

1   Euphoria and disenchantment

Great expectations . . .

what will be the effect on language teaching when our daily lives and jobs are enmeshed with our European neighbours at all levels of technology, industry and commerce, not to speak of journalism, entertainment, sport and politics?

Report of Working Party, Incorporated Association of
Head Masters, 1963

When boys and girls equipped with three years of really good primary school French come flowing into the secondary schools they are likely to cause an upsurge of professional vitality and inventiveness, together with an explosive increase of interest in oral work.

Schools Council Working Paper No. 8, 1966

. . . disappointed

in all too many language classes there was an atmosphere of boredom, disenchantment and restlessness; at times this developed into indiscipline of a kind that made teaching and learning virtually impossible

Her Majesty's Inspectorate Series: Matters for Discussion 3,
1977

Suppose that all children learned native-mathematics intuitively at their mother's knee. Let us call it 'M1'. Then suppose that when they reached the age of 11+ their teacher said to them: 'Now you are going to learn the maths they use abroad. It is called M2. I know that you already have M1. It answers all your purposes. I realise, also, that your parents never use M2 at home. When you go for a job your employer will not care tuppence whether or not you have M2. It is true that the universities used to demand M2 as an entrance requirement of all students, but they gave it up in the 1960s. For one thing the university selectors couldn't understand M2 themselves and then M2 was hard. It demanded accuracy and sixth formers preferred easier subjects.

3

None of our leaders in government can handle M2. Nevertheless, you are going to learn M2 in school and persevere with it despite the obvious indifference of the outside world.'

The analogy may not be exact but it will indicate the difficulty of the foreign language teacher's task. The difficulty is aggravated by the rigorous test by which success is measured, a test unique to language learning, namely comparison with the native speaker. In other school subjects the model is always one who has acquired his skills *by the same route that the pupil must take.*

The language teacher's task is not made any easier by the fact that the subject is allotted only 150 minutes (effectively) each week in which the newly acquired skills have to survive in the 'gale of English'. Other complex skills may be hard to acquire, as budding violinists will attest, but, in language learning, the mother tongue actively erodes the new skills between one lesson and the next. In consequence language teachers down the ages have grasped at panaceas. The result has been a lurching, switchback progress. The lurch of the 1960s was as violent as any that language teaching has known.

First there came a marvellous new technical aid, the taperecorder. Almost unknown in schools in 1960, it was by 1970 everywhere in use. The first school 'language laboratory' was installed (in Chorley Grammar School, Lancashire) in 1962; by 1973 there were language laboratories in one third of all secondary schools. The portable film-strip projector was perfected at the same time and audio-visual methods (so-called) became briefly the new orthodoxy. During the decade, also, radio and television began to provide programmes of high professional polish in several languages with which enterprising teachers enlivened their lessons. Native-speaking voices came flooding into classrooms where in the 1950s only the teacher's voice had been heard.

In the early 1960s, too, a series of provocative reports brought language teaching into the forefront of discussion. In 1961 the Hayter Report called attention to the neglect of the non-European languages. In the following year a Federation of British Industries Working Party stressed the need for language skills in industry and commerce and spelled out the case again in a further report in 1964. In 1963 the Nuffield Foundation financed the publication of a booklet (re-issued in enlarged form in 1966) prepared by a group of Merseyside schools: *Modern Languages in the Grammar*

School. It argued for the acceptance of 'communication' as the aim of foreign language study in secondary schools and for a new, more adventurous, approach to reading. It made detailed proposals for the reform of the GCE examinations in modern languages and for the return of a subsidiary examination for non-specialists in the sixth form.

Another seminal contribution was the Annan Report (Annan, 1962) on the teaching of Russian. The Annan Committee went beyond its brief and made proposals for teaching foreign languages in the primary school, for the reform of the 16+ examination, omitting translation into the foreign language, and for the use of new techniques in the classroom. It also recommended the creation of a national languages institute and we owe the creation of the Centre for Information on Language Teaching and Research (CILT) in 1965 largely to the Annan discussions.

New challenge – new materials – new examinations
At the same time the prospect of joining the 'Common Market' of the European Economic Community raised the hopes of language teachers. The Merseyside schools' booklet suggested that: 'The effects upon education that would follow from our joining the Six are at present only dimly perceived. How are we to face the enormous amount of sheer hard, detailed polyglot discussion that . . . this will entail not only on the part of specialist translators and interpreters . . . but of ordinary Englishmen at all levels and in all professions and trades?'

New objectives required new materials. Here the Nuffield Foundation's role was decisive. Its director, Leslie Farrer-Brown, had, as early as 1959, begun discussions about the need to improve standards of performance in foreign languages. It was decided to set up a Foreign Language Materials Project, which began work in Leeds under A. J. Spicer in 1963 on four audio-visual language courses with titles like battle cries: *'En Avant'*, *'Vorwärts'*, *'Adelante'*, *'Vperyod!'*

This Nuffield Foundation pump-priming initiative was followed up in 1967 by the Schools Council, which transferred the project to the Language Teaching Centre, York University, and undertook to continue the new courses up to the level of the 16+ examination. The new materials were part of a wider scheme, jointly conducted by the DES, the Schools Council, Her Majesty's Inspectorate, LEAs and the Nuffield Foundation. This was a bold experiment, unprecedented in the number of schools concerned and the investment of public funds, in teaching French, as Annan had suggested, in the primary school. The pupils concerned in 13 LEAs (and a great many more 'associated areas' which insisted on joining the scheme soon after it was launched) began their French at the age of eight. It was anticipated that when they reached secondary school at the age of 11+ many of them would be ready to begin a second language. It was for them that the Nuffield/Schools Council materials in German, Spanish and Russian were designed. The project caught the imagination of the public as no other curriculum project had previously done and undoubtedly helped to arouse interest in language learning among parents and administrators.

New courses called for new examinations. Here 1963–4 was the 'annus mirabilis'. The Associated Examinations Board broke the log-jam in the 16+ examinations, setting a GCE 'O' level paper without the prose translation into the foreign language. This change, pressed on the Ministry by the Annan Committee, had been resisted stubbornly by the small Modern Languages Panel of the Secondary Schools Examinations Council (SSEC). The year 1962, however, saw the SSEC dismantled. It was replaced first by the Curriculum Study Group and in 1964 by the Schools Council. A series of changes in the examinations followed, many of them prompted by the teams working on the Nuffield project. The coming of the CSE (in 1963) greatly increased school teachers' involvement in examining.

In 1964, too, a number of universities led by Essex, Canterbury and York established Language Centres where language *teaching* as a university discipline could be taken seriously for the first time. New model undergraduate language courses without examination in literary criticism were introduced at York, Bradford, Salford, Bath and Herriot-Watt. In the same year a new association of language teachers, the Audio-Visual Language Association, now the British Association for Language Teaching, was formed. Its rapid growth (membership 990 in 1980) and the liveliness of its journal (circulation 2,400) encouraged experiments in language classrooms. Among such experiments were 'immersion' courses, exploiting intensive methods and breaking away from the pattern of the short daily lesson.

The period was remarkable for the national reputation

achieved by a number of classroom teachers whose individual performance recorded on film and videotape helped to raise standards and inspire imitators on in-service courses in many parts of the country. There was an explosive growth of in-service work actively promoted by an outstanding team of HMI and by a series of distinguished staff inspectors of modern languages. In-service work had a further impetus as more and more LEAs appointed specialist language advisers.

At the same time teachers showed growing interest in getting abroad and in bringing native-speaking assistants into schools. Responsibility for the foreign language assistants scheme run by the DES was transferred (again in the marvellous year 1964!) to the Central Bureau for Educational Visits and Exchanges. The graph shows the explosive growth of the scheme since that date. Towns and even whole counties developed twinning schemes and there began a lively to-ing and fro-ing of citizens of Europe at all levels.

Lasting benefits from the 1960s

So many fresh ideas, so much enthusiasm! So reminiscent of the wave of euphoria seventy years earlier on whose crest the Modern Language Association had been formed (1892) following the Cheltenham conference in 1890 organised by MacGowan and

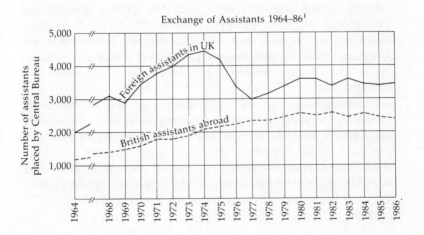

Exchange of Assistants 1964–86[1]

Widgery. Was history to be repeated and the reforming movement to run out of steam?

If there seemed to be widespread disenchantment at the end of the 1970s we should be careful not to overlook the advances made since the Annan Report in 1962. Language classrooms are now undoubtedly more attractive places than they were. Nelson Brooks' appeal (1960) for a 'cultural island' in which to let the foreign language live has been heard by many administrators. There is much more authentic native speech heard now in schools, thanks to tape-recorders, radio, television and videotape. The teaching materials now available to schools show a great improvement in liveliness, richness of illustration and authenticity of language on the course books used in the 1950s. Testing, too, has made giant strides. The needs of the 95% of pupils who do not go on to read a language for university entrance are on the way to being met by examining boards (in the new GCSE), now more responsive to school opinion than in the days of the Secondary Schools Examinations Council.

In the early 1960s there were few, if any, LEA language advisers. Already by 1969 there were 30 with their own association and journal. There are now over 150 with all that this means especially in the support of young teachers on probation and in the provision of in-service training.

Support for teachers nationally has also expanded greatly. In addition to the courses organised by HMI (attended by some 1100 teachers in the four years 1983–87) the Department of Education and Science jointly with the Central Bureau for Educational Visits offers regular refresher courses in France, Germany, Spain and Italy. The Centre for Information on Language Teaching and Research (CILT) also arranges symposia on key issues followed by discussion documents and bibliographies.

The introduction of the compulsory year abroad into most university degree courses in modern languages during the 1960s greatly improved the standard of spoken language of younger teachers, while opportunities for serving teachers to travel abroad have been expanded. In 1967–8 only 39 English and Welsh teachers went on exchange to European countries. Thanks largely to improved maintenance grants this figure had risen to 70 by 1986.

Growing anxiety

Nevertheless, despite the effort put into teacher preparation, the production of materials and in-service training, the impetus of reform slackened in the 1970s. Scepticism regarding the results of so much effort turned, as the decade went on, to mounting anxiety.

The first check to euphoria came in 1974 with the publication of the report by Dr Clare Burstall and her colleagues of the National Foundation for Educational Research on the Pilot Scheme: *Primary French in the Balance* (Burstall et al., 1974). The disappointment caused by the impression that the brave pilot experiment had failed was aggravated by concern about its effects on the study of the 'minority' languages at secondary level. The atmosphere of uncertainty which followed the press coverage of the NFER report contrasted sharply with the positive forward planning of the 1960s.

The new technology, meanwhile, had disappointed the exaggerated hopes pinned on it. In the USA the provision of federal funds through the National Defense Act of 1958, following the trauma of the first Russian sputnik, had led to a vast investment in (mis-named) 'Language laboratories'. (See Chapter 6.) By the late 1960s these costly aids were standing empty and gathering dust in schools and colleges across the United States. A series of widely publicised studies (Keating, 1963; Johnson, 1966; Smith, 1970) seemed to demonstrate that claims made for the language laboratory were unjustified in practice.

At the same time, the theory underlying the audio-lingual method was challenged. This method called for 'mim-mem' or mimicry and memorisation. It was based on a behaviourist model of language learning which had been given powerful theoretical support by B. F. Skinner in *Verbal Behaviour* (1957). In this book, by a brilliant tour de force, Skinner applied to human language learning the concepts of operant conditioning, the fruits of a lifetime's pioneering study of animal learning.

In the late 1960s, however, the pendulum of opinion swung away from 'mim-mem'. Psychologists pointed out that it was not only boring but, if each new speech pattern has to be learnt by imitation, impossibly uneconomical. Linguists also attacked the model of language learning which had been accepted by enthusiasts for the language laboratory. The terrifying figure of Noam Chomsky appeared from what must have seemed to language teachers in the USA and in Britain, untrained in linguistics, the impenetrable fog of transformational generative grammar. He devoured the great Skinner in one terrible 30-page review (1959) and then retreated to the linguistic heights, to descend occasionally (as in 1965 in his address to American language teachers at their Northeast Conference) to castigate the notion that language is a habit-structure to be acquired by practice in language laboratories. There is no doubt that echoes of this classic debate unnerved language teachers in many countries. A coherent methodology expounded for example in Nelson Brooks' widely read *Language and Language Learning* (1960), supported by confident psychological theory and a prestigious linguistic tradition going back to Bloomfield (1933), suddenly seemed to be in ruins, and teachers were offered nothing to put in its place.

Uncertainty among teachers and anxiety about the position of language study in the comprehensive school grew steadily and came to a head in 1977. In that year Her Majesty's Inspectorate published a highly critical survey of language teaching in a sample of 83 comprehensive schools (HMI, 1977) and this followed closely on a conference (November 1976) called by university language teachers to consider 'the crisis in modern langauge studies'.

At the heart of the growing anxiety was concern about the implications of the depressing rate of drop-out from foreign language classes in the new, mixed, comprehensive schools which were increasingly replacing the traditional single-sex grammar schools. Grammar school pupils had seldom been given the option of dropping their language since they were for the most part aiming at university entrance, for which a foreign language was then an essential requirement.

A factor which contributed to the drop-out at fifth- and sixth-form level, but which was not discussed by the university teachers at their 'crisis conference', was the universities' own decision in 1967–8 to give up the traditional requirement of a foreign language qualification for entry to degree courses. They chose to do this just at the moment when Britain was negotiating to join the European Economic Community. Their reluctance to open up debate on this bizarre decision and its effects on pupils' attitudes and expectations at fifth- and sixth-form level is understandable; the universities could scarcely be proud of the way in which they had drifted without any general consultation into such a major change in the curriculum, nor of their failure to take account of its inevitable consequences in the schools.

In the sections that follow we take a closer look at some of these reasons for growing anxiety.

Two set-backs linked

The effect of the two innovations that we have been charting had been to extend modern language teaching *vertically* down the age range in primary schools and at the same time *horizontally* across the (so-called) 'ability range'[2] in the secondary school. The two developments were inseparable. LEAs participating in the Pilot Scheme were required by the DES to offer French across the whole age group *and to continue* this provision when pupils transferred to their secondary school.

The effect of the NFER Report of 1974 on public opinion was to call in question the wisdom of an early start. When, three years later the HMI report (HMI 1977) cast similar doubt on what was being achieved 'across the ability range' in the comprehensive school, the alarm bells rang.

Primary French in the balance?

In fact the NFER evaluation of the Pilot scheme had not been entirely negative. Besides the main excerise of comparing the progress of 8+ beginners with that of beginners at 11+, the report examined other implications of ETML:

1   Does French interfere with other aspects of primary schooling?
2   What methods and incentives are most effective at this age?
3   What organisational problems are posed? etc.

The answers to these questions were by no means negative but they attracted less publicity than the answer to the main question: did the early start result in any substantial gain in mastery? Here the report did not mince words: *'This question can be answered unequivocally in the negative.'* It was this statement that caught the headlines. Typical was the comment in one popular newspaper: 'Le parlez-vous is out!'

The 'fine print' of the evaluation by NFER made less impact:

By the age of 16, compared with those who are taught French from the age of 11, the only area in which pupils taught French from the age of eight consistently show superiority is that of listening comprehension.

'Consistent superiority' in such an important skill might not be a slight gain, one might surmise? Or again:

Where the pupils taught French in the primary school do appear to gain is not in 'mastery' but in attitude. When they have been successful in their efforts to learn French, they do appear to retain a more favourable attitude towards speaking the language than do those who were not introduced to French until the age of 11. (Burstall et al., 1974, p. 243)

Nevertheless the general drift of the NFER evaluation was to confirm what a mass of research elsewhere had established (usefully summed up at the time in e.g. Carroll 1969) that, other things being equal, older learners do make faster progress than younger learners except in the one area of imitation of pronunciation. It is true that the new 'evidence' produced for this common research finding was trenchantly criticised by a number of well-informed observers (see Chapter 6) but their comments, mainly confined to the specialist journals, did not reach the public as the NFER press release had done.

To attempt to redress the negative impact of the NFER report the Nuffield Foundation commissioned its own report *The Early Teaching of Modern Languages* (Hoy 1977), written by the former staff inspector P. H. Hoy who had been closely involved with the later stages of the Pilot Scheme. Hoy's report brought out the many positive advances owed to the scheme:

more authentic materials in classrooms; new model examinations; expansion of in-service opportunities for teachers; increase of LEA support for modern languages, including language advisers with their own association and journal; greater interest among parents in foreign language learning; great interest abroad and admiration for the planning and execution of the Pilot Scheme etc.

Valuable as this corrective was, however, it came too late for the issue of ETML in the UK was being decided not on its merits but because the planners had come up against an insoluble problem, that of teacher supply.

Where to find the teachers?

Already in 1972 the shortage of teachers was acute (Riddy 1972). Even if the NFER report had been positive, the expansion, or even continuation, of primary school French would have been prevented by the lack of primary teachers competent to teach the subject. Only a decision by the colleges of education to include French in the education of *all* students could have met the need.

No doubt the founder-father of the Schools Council and 'eminence grise' behind the Pilot Scheme at its inception, Derek Morrell, had he lived, might have found a way. The problem was beyond lesser administrators.

It is true that the DES launched a scheme in 1970 for intensive ten-week courses in French for teachers concerned with the 8–13 age-group. The take-up, of some 200 annually was disappointing.

By the early 1970s it was becoming clear that problems of teacher supply were rooted in a deeper crisis, to which we now turn, the downward spiral in language provision at both school and university levels, which set in in the mid-1960s.

The spiral of decline

Until the middle 1960s the numbers of sixth formers opting for modern languages had grown steadily, but about 1965 the tide turned. While numbers of girls in sixth forms taking French at 'A' level in fact rose slightly the fall off among boys was catastrophic, from 7,567 passes in 1965 to a mere 4,645 twenty years later. Even the figures for girls give little comfort, however, as the table (page 14) shows. Year by year, the passes of girls in French as a percentage of passes in all subjects went steadily downwards, from 11.6% in 1965 to 6% in 1985.

A striking feature of the table of 'A' level results is the steady worsening over the years of the imbalance between numbers of girls and boys in sixth form modern language classes. The question was asked would it not lead to the eventual disappearance of men from university degree courses and so from modern language classrooms in schools? Other commentators suggested that this may not be the most important question to ask (Rees 1986) and that we should rather be concerned with the overall decline in our subject as a sixth form discipline.

The effect on applications from graduates in modern languages to train as teachers is clear. In 1969, the earliest year for which the Graduate Teacher Training Registry (GTTR) has figures showing separately applications for different subjects, there were in total 3,327 applications from modern language graduates for the Post Graduate Certificate in Education (PGCE) one-year course of initial training. Of these 1,281 were from men (38.5% of all modern language applications). Ten years later, in 1979, applications from men had fallen to 616, a drop of 50% in the decade.

Passes in French, GCE 'A' level, 1965–85
(All examination Boards, England only, Summer exams)
Between 1965 and 1985 the total number of passes at 'A' level (all subjects) rose from 254,788 to 427,619. Girls passes more than doubled, from 90,049 to 200,864. Boys passes rose from 164,739 to 226,755.

Year	Passes in French	Boys	Girls	Total
1965	Number	7,567	10,508	18,075
	% of total passes	3.0% (4.6%)	4.1% (11.6%)	7.1%
1970	Number	6,419	11,630	18,049
	% of total passes	2.1% (3.5%	3.8% (9.5%)	5.9%
1975	Number	5,429	11,490	16,919
	% of total passes	1.6% (2.8%)	3.4% (7.8%)	5%
1980	Number	5,107	12,617	17,724
	% of total passes	1.3% (2.4%)	3.3% (7.3%)	4.6%
1985	Number	4,645	12,075	16,720
	% of total passes	1.1% (2.0%)	2.8% (6.0%)	3.9%

(The figures in brackets show the percentage of passes in French when boys' and girls' total passes are reckoned separately.)

Applications from women had also fallen, though less drastically, from 2,106 to 1,444.

The trend since 1979 gives no reassurance to those anxious about the future staffing of school modern language classes. Latest figures from the GTTR show that total *applications* from modern language graduates for the PGCE course beginning October 1986 in University Departments of Education and Colleges and Polytechnics fell to a record low of some 1,400. (This was, of course, a year adversely affected by the teachers' dispute.)[3] Approximately one half of these applicants withdrew for various reasons and only 687 graduates (all languages) actually embarked on PGCE courses as modern language specialists in the academic year 1986/7, in all institutions, in the proportion of one man to three women.

If the immediate outlook is bleak the more distant prospect is no more encouraging. It is true that comprehensive reorganisation in the 1960s and early 1970s brought one bright ray of light: the encouraging growth in numbers of pupils taking modern languages in the Certificate of Secondary Education introduced in 1963.

Entries for CSE French between 1965 and 1985

Year	Boys	Girls
1965	3,736	4,609
1970	22,563	31,580
1975	43,965	69,338
1980	53,021	94,425
1985	59,860	103,466

(Source: DES, *Annual Statistics of Education* 1965–85)

The growing imbalance between boys and girls is obvious, though less marked than we saw in the GCE 'A' level table. Clearly the figures must reflect credit on very many devoted teachers in comprehensive schools. One contributory factor must be the 'Graded Objectives' schemes now proliferating in many areas (see p. 169), which owe much to the keenness and willingness to experiment of classroom teachers. The new-style papers currently being developed for the General Certificate of Secondary Education should further encourage experiment in this area.

Behind these CSE figures, however, lurk some harsh realities. One is that the devoted teachers now giving these pupils such a good lead may never be replaced. It has to be recognised that CSE (except at Grade I level) has not, in the past provided a foundation on which pupils can advance to sixth form language work. For this a good GCE 'O' level pass is needed and here the picture is very difficult.

We may usefully compare the raw totals of entries for French in GCE 'O' level with those in English Language, a paper taken by nearly all candidates. The results are as follows:

GCE O level: all examining Boards England and Wales, Summer Examinations

Year	Entries	Boys	Girls
1965	French	83,799	79,852
	English	194,776	153,912
	Fr. as % of Eng.	43.0%	51.9%
1970	French	69,632	76,298
	English	173,624	164,188
	Fr. as % of Eng.	40.1%	46.5%
1975	French	67,109	85,028
	English	202,458	222,562
	Fr. as % of Eng.	33.1%	38.2%
1980	French	67,678	94,645
	English	225,961	269,918
	Fr. as % of Eng.	29.9%	35.0%
1985	French	58,962	88,695
	English	242,200	277,484
	Fr. as % of Eng.	24.3%	32.0%

(Source: DES 1965–85)

This is a depressing picture. In the two decades since 1965 the total entries for GCE 'O' level, the ablest section of the school population, rose from some 350 thousand to some 520 thousand while entries for French dropped from some 160 thousand to some 150 thousand.

The figures offer no prospect of arresting the downward plunge of sixth form numbers. Unless quite radical steps are taken there seems to be no escaping from the downward spiral of:

continuing decline (catastrophic for boys, relative for girls) in numbers opting for languages in 6th Forms, leading to:

matching decline in numbers studying languages for first degrees, leading to:

marked fall in applications to train for language teaching with consequent growing shortage of teachers in schools and

disappearance from school timetables of 'minority' languages (see table p. 69) already threatened by falling rolls and staff cuts

Why did the tide turn in the mid-1960s? The question has not been faced and demands a major national enquiry.

In its timing, of course, the downturn coincided with the abandonment of selective secondary schools and the introduction of comprehensive schools. But was this correlation simply accidental and are there deeper reasons than secondary reorganisation? The debate on this question has generated much more heat than light and we lack the data on which to make a judgement.

There are, however, some attendant questions that are worth raising. One change brought with comprehensive reorganisation was the substitution of mixed schools for the traditionally single-sex grammar schools. It is a moot question whether the well-established precocity of girls in verbal skills at the age of 11+ (to which we return later, pages 78 and 186) makes it unsuitable to teach foreign languages in mixed classes at adolescence. The question at least deserves more careful research than it has yet had. Even if we could answer it, however, though it might throw some light on the growing discrepancy between boys' and girls' performance, it could scarcely explain the *relative* decline in numbers of both sexes succeeding in foreign language studies.

Another change introduced along with secondary reorganisation, was the practice of inviting pupils to 'choose' their programmes at the age of 13+ and the removal of the modern language from the 'core' curriculum. It may be worth noting that neither mixed classes at 11+ nor the proliferation of pupils' 'choices' at 13+ are essential elements of a 'comprehensive' school. There now seems to be a growing consensus among informed opinion that, after requiring boys to compete unequally with girls in French classes for their first two years, it is unfair to offer to 13-year-olds the 'choices' that have proliferated in the curricula in many schools. Boys' decisions to drop French are often ill-informed, reflecting the unequal competition of more verbally precocious girls, and later regretted. Girls may well be turned against e.g. mechanics at 13+ for very similar reasons. The insistence of the old selective secondary school on a broad curriculum which included a foreign language up to 16+ was, of course, strongly supported by the policy of the universities in requiring a broad 'matriculation' spread of five subjects for entry on degree studies, and the stipulation that the five subjects must include a language other than English. While the examination system (School Certificate) on which this was based disappeared in 1949, the universities maintained their foreign language requirement until the mid 1960s. How far the abandonment of this requirement contributed to the downward spiral that we have traced is difficult to establish but it must surely have been a major factor.

Trahison des clercs?

Undoubtedly one of the effects of the universities' requirement that all candidates for entry should have a basic command of a foreign language had been to encourage the study of languages in the sixth form by specialists and non-specialists alike. Even if the sixth former opted for a 'main' course without a foreign language, the possibility existed, until 1950, of taking a 'subsidiary' language paper alongside one's main subjects.

The subsidiary paper had been introduced to meet the recommendation of the National Committee of Enquiry (Leathes 1918), that *all* sixth formers, regardless of their choice of principal subjects, should be tested at 18+ in *reading* a foreign language.

Subsidiary level proved a popular target. In 1949, the year in which the paper was set for the last time, before it was axed without consultation, over twice as many sixth formers took subsidiary French as took main French (Schools Council 1970). Despite the disappearance of the subsidiary the universities continued during the next decade to demand a minimum competence in a foreign language from all entrants, and this had the effect of keeping the foreign language firmly within the 'core' secondary curriculum up to the 16+ examination.

The language requirement was dropped in the mid 1960s without proper national debate, still less careful research as to the consequences, in response to a recommendation of the Standing Conference on University Entrance (Letter of November 1965) that: 'passes should not be required in named subjects, except for English' but that responsibility for ensuring that candidates received a good education should 'devolve mainly upon the schools'.

This cant phrase, which took no notice of the great pressures exerted on sixth formers, especially those on the borderline for entry, when faced with university entry demands couched in terms of high grades in only 3 'A' level subjects, can be better understood against the background of the sudden expansion of university provision in the early 1960s. The Standing Conference was in a difficulty. Several of the new universities had, in fact, already broken ranks and given up the traditional broadly based entrance requirements. Something like a competition developed to attract sixth formers, and some universities saw no reason to place inconvenient hurdles in the way of possible applicants for their courses.

Only the most prestigious universities could hold out, and even they were vulnerable. Cambridge, for example, had for centuries demanded of all entrants a qualification in Latin or classical Greek. This requirement was replaced in 1960 by a requirement of qualification in *two* languages other than English. In 1967 the requirement was reduced to *one* foreign language.

Cambridge University's statement on the proposal ten years later to bring back 'ancillary' or 'subsidiary' papers at 18+ in order to widen sixth form programmes (comment on the 'N' and 'F' proposals in *Cambridge University Reporter* 1979) shows how directly even such a powerful university's entrance requirements can be affected by competition to attract applicants:

Cambridge has from time to time tried to ensure some breadth of study by candidates for admission even after 'O' level – for example by the Use of English paper and the language paper in the old Scholarship examination. The university gave up such attempts because they tended to discourage applicants from applying to Cambridge. The University concludes that no university in isolation could afford to impose entrance requirements designed to encourage breadth of study in the sixth form. . . They would, therefore, have to be imposed by the Department of Education and Science.

The key phrase is 'because they tended to discourage appplicants'. It was this that sealed the fate of another attempt to encourage breadth of study, namely the test in the Use of English introduced by the five northern universities in 1964, concerned at the illiteracy displayed by many undergraduates. As soon as the test was introduced, two of the five universities found that they could not fill their quota of places in some science subjects and after two years the test in English was abandoned, not because the university teachers did not think it necessary, but because of competition between the northern universities and others to attract sixth formers. As the Cambridge *Reporter* admits, so long as institutions of higher education compete for applicants, educational arguments regarding entrance requirements cannot prevail.

If incentives to keep up language study in fifth and sixth forms are to be restored it cannot be left to the universities or polytechnics – nor should it. The best hope is that the DES may introduce minimum requirements for award of statutory grants to students. Already minimum requirements (mathematics and English language) are laid down centrally for admission to teacher training courses.

Concern among university teachers about a situation in the schools to which the universities had themselves greatly contributed was echoed by HMI who had already begun a detailed study of modern languages in comprehensive schools.

The HMI survey of 83 comprehensive schools

After the set-back to hopes for French in the primary school the HMI survey *Modern Languages in Comprehensive Schools,* which appeared in 1977, seemed like the *coup de grâce* administered to the optimism of the previous decade. A team of inspectors led by a staff inspector visited 83 (a one in ten sample of the 861) comprehensive schools which had been established at least since 1971, including some sixth-form colleges. The schools were located in 40 different LEAs. The survey had been initiated in 1975 'at a time of rapidly growing concern about the future of language learning in our schools'. The introduction traces this 'rapidly growing concern' to the fact that

during a period (in the '60s) when language teachers were being asked to review the aims of their teaching and to study new approaches, new methods and new techniques, they suddenly found themselves caught up in a process of major educational reform with the introduction of comprehensive secondary schools . . . Most language teachers . . . had experience of teaching only the more able pupils who were likely . . . to be fairly well motivated. Work in a comprehensive school required them to rethink the aims, objectives and content of the courses which they offered their pupils. Few of them found this easy.

The swing towards comprehensive reorganisation is generally thought to have begun with Anthony Crosland's Circular (10/65) 'requesting LEAs to submit plans for the reorganisation of secondary education'. (It is interesting that Crosland's Minister of State, Reg Prentice, pressed for the word 'request' in the Circular to be replaced by 'require' but Crosland stood by the decision not to use legal compulsion, for the time being. The story is told in Maurice Kogan's *The Politics of Education,* 1971.)

In fact, as Kogan has pointed out, reorganisation of secondary education had begun well before the Crosland Circular. Already in 1963 some 90 LEAs had reorganisation plans. By 1965 (the date of the Circular) 12% of children were in comprehensive schools. Public opinion polls in the 1960s showed some confusion about comprehensive reorganisation. In 1967 53% of parents wanted their child to go to a grammar or independent school; 52% were in favour of comprehensive education, while 76% were in favour of retaining grammar schools (!) (D.V. Donnison, 1967 quoted in Kogan, 1971, p. 22).

Parental confusion was matched by lack of preparation on the part of LEAs. The swing to comprehensive schools was quite unresearched. Its likely effects were not studied; in-service preparation of teachers was quite inadequate. Crosland defends the failure to research the question in an interesting passage in his discussion with Kogan. Kogan:

'On the face of it, here was a major change, but the government had done no research on the effects.' Crosland: 'Well this argument had a natural attraction for an ex-academic like myself. But as soon as I thought the thing through I could see it was wrong. It implied that research can tell you what your objectives ought to be. But it can't. Our belief in comprehensive reorganisation was a product of fundamental value judgments about equity and equal opportunity and social division as well as about education.' (p. 190)

Research might not have indicated objectives but it would at last have pointed to the need to retrain the teachers. No research, however, was done: no adequate preparations were made.

Crosland's view reflected a growing public intuition that selection at 11+ is unjustified and the swing to the comprehensive school continued despite the withdrawal of Circular 10/65 by Margaret Thatcher in 1970. By 1978 it was estimated that between 70% and 80% of all secondary pupils were in comprehensive schools, though there was some disagreement regarding the definition of a truly comprehensive school.

For no subject did this reorganisation bring bigger changes than for foreign languages. The other major subjects of the curriculum had all had their place in the timetable of the secondary modern school. Objectives and methods appropriate to the 75% of pupils not admitted to grammar school had been developed over many years. The foreign language was the only subject not previously taught (with a few exceptions) to such pupils. Now, for the first time, the subject was to be offered across the whole range of ability, motivation and home background.

The HMI survey set out to assess the effects of this development in schools with at least five years' experience of it. The inspectors found little for their comfort. If one word must be found to summarise the HMI findings it is lack of 'professionalism', especially on the part of heads of departments concerning matters within their control.

This showed itself in the following ways:

1 *lack of continuity*: only seven secondary schools had held consultations with teachers in their primary 'feeder' schools about transfer at 11+; however, since few of the primary schools encountered were offering French it was at 13+ and 14+ that discontinuity in teaching before and after change of schools took its heaviest toll; there were no commonly agreed criteria for keeping records of pupils' progress
2 *inadequate schemes of work*: the inspectors found only ten 'genuinely helpful' schemes of work; none of the sixth-form colleges visited had a scheme of work
3 *inappropriate objectives for slower learners*
4 *failure to challenge faster learners*
5 *lack of leadership by heads of departments* especially regarding:
      helping colleagues to implement schemes of work
      watching colleagues teach and being seen teaching
      encouraging colleagues to undergo in-service training
      keeping detailed records of pupils' progress
      liaising with feeder and receiving schools
      taking a fair share of difficult classes
      delegation of responsibility to junior colleagues
      setting a personal example of professionalism
      supporting the junior teachers
6 *failure to make effective use of native-speaking assistants*: i.e. inadequate briefing and support (though 21 of the 83 schools had no assistant at all).

The survey listed, in addition, a number of shortcomings for which heads of departments could scarcely be held responsible but which adversely affected pupils' work:

1 *unsuitable teaching accommodation*: in only one in three of the schools were teaching rooms conveniently grouped; in the rest, rooms were scattered and used for general purposes
2 *lack of facilities* such as blackout and display space and adequate acoustics
3 *misuse of facilities*: there were language laboratories in one half of the schools having pupils over 14 but very limited use was

made of them; 10% reported inadequate technical servicing, one laboratory not having been serviced for seven years!

4 *lack of resources*: there was a shortage of readers and library books, reflecting priorities within schools rather than financial stringency

5 *unsuitable timetabling*: the time allocation was 'inadequate' in half of the schools in the first year (i.e. less than 4×40 minutes weekly) and the second and third years were even less well provided; only 60% of fifth-year sets were given adequate time; the tendency to adopt the 'double period' timetable meant that there were often long gaps of up to five days between French lessons.

Whether or not as a result of these shortcomings, two out of three pupils starting a foreign language at 11+ dropped it at the earliest opportunity. The percentage of each age-group in the sample studying languages was as follows:

First foreign language		Second foreign language	
At 11+	89%		
12+	85%	At 12+	9%
13+	80%	13+	14%
14+*	35%	14+	9%
15+	33%	15+	8%

* the year when the language commonly becomes 'optional'

The inspectors commented: 'In all types of schools visited . . . only slightly more than a third of the pupils in this [fourth-year] age group were still engaged [on modern language studies]. The majority of these were girls: in many schools the ratio of girls to boys was two to one, although the proportion of boys was often far lower in abler sets and in the sixth form.'

Her Majesty's Inspectorate has always taken a pride in its positive role of encouraging good practice in schools rather than appearing to sit in judgement. In this spirit the HMI team followed up the survey on a regional basis by a series of confidential in-depth discussions with the Chief Education Officer in which action programmes appropriate for each authority were worked out, followed by no fewer than 80 separate two-day courses for Heads of schools and heads of department, and by similar meetings for LEA advisers. We can surmise that in these discussions an important part of the agenda was provided by Part III of the survey: 'Examples of good practice'. In addition to the 83 schools surveyed the HMI team visited 19 schools 'thought to have interesting features', and examples of good practice from these and from the sample of 83 schools are described.

The HMI report and the discussions with LEAs that followed it stimulated a series of in-service training programmes in many LEAs.[4]

Another consequence of growing disquiet about performance in the comprehensive school was the establishment by the Department of Education and Science of the Assessment of Performance Unit (APU) based on the National Foundation for Educational Research, charged to sample pupil performance in key subjects (e.g. English, Maths, foreign languages) at particular stages in their schooling.

In June 1983 the APU was asked to start a series of annual surveys of the performance of 13-year-old pupils (three annual surveys of French and one each of German and Spanish). The aim was to assess performance across the whole ability range, with emphasis on effectiveness of communication in the foreign language. Two reports on French have so far been published and one each on German and Spanish (DES 1985, 1986a).

The results of the surveys are not reassuring. In some schools high standards were expected and achieved but overall half of the 13-year-olds surveyed could not get the meaning of simple sentences heard or read and were unable to make themselves understood in speech or writing in the foreign language in more than a rudimentary way. The DES statement of policy (DES 1986 b) comments on the APU findings 'these are signs of widespread low achievement'.

It must be said that the reaction of the DES to the growing disquiet seemed to many commentators inadequate. A statement of policy on foreign languages in the curriculum was promised from the Secretary of State for Education (with his colleague in the Welsh Office) but it was repeatedly delayed. When finally, after a consultative draft in 1985, the policy statement appeared in June 1986, it was found to be useful on analysis of the malaise but weak on remedies.

A particular weakness of the Statement was its complete silence on the role of the universities, whose selection procedures have such an influence on sixth form programmes. If non-specialists are to be encouraged not to drop languages at 16+ more is needed than the pious exhortation (para 27) 'We encourage university admission tutors to give full credit for AS level success'. For any reader familiar with the history of the universities' reaction to earlier versions of 'AS' levels (Major/ Minor, 'N' and 'F' etc.) this exhortation must appear quite pointless. The policy statement also failed to give any kind of lead to those who have the responsibility for selecting school leavers for employment, and especially for the Civil Service and the professions, whose procedures and apprenticeship regulations inevitably have a strong backwash effect on the priorities of school leavers.

If reaction to the downward spiral in foreign language teaching from the DES was disappointingly anodyne, many teachers in the classroom showed more determination. We have already referred (page 15) to the explosive take-off of the graded objectives movement. By the mid-1980s over eighty graded objective schemes were operating in some sixty LEAs and the movement was establishing itself as one of the success stories of the comprehensive school. We describe this development in more detail in a later chapter (page 169).

Another positive outcome of the HMI report of 1977 was the three-year research project undertaken by the Language Teaching Centre, York University, funded by the Nuffield Foundation. The project began in 1978. With the help of HMI and LEA advisers, the research team identified some 20 mixed comprehensive schools in urban areas where, despite all the difficulties, there was evidence of effective foreign language teaching (the 'good practice' of the 1977 survey). The team then set about trying to tease out, by means of detailed case studies in the classrooms concerned, the factors contributing to success. The report was published in 1982 (Sanderson, 1982).

But why, after all that had happened in the training and re-training of teachers, in the development of exciting materials and new examinations, should HMI, the Schools Council or the York team have to go about the country – like men with a lantern on a dark night – searching for some evidence of effective language teaching?

Two questions were raised:

1 Had all the effort put into refurbishing language teaching run into bankruptcy and was it worthwhile persisting with the battle to retain a foreign language for all in the curriculum?
2 Were there, despite the endless debates, some still unexamined reasons why English pupils fail to learn a foreign language?

It is to these two questions essentially that the remaining chapters of this book are addressed. We begin by looking at one reaction suggested by the foregoing history of disenchantment. For most school leavers, English, the world vehicle language, will answer all their needs, in business or leisure; therefore, why bother with a foreign language?

NOTES

1 The assistants scheme is now under threat because of the failure of a number of LEAs to fulfil their obligations. There are currently (1986/7) some 32 local authorities not participating in the scheme, in the sense that in order to economise on salary payments they are refusing to make available places in their schools for foreign language assistants. The quality of education offered to their pupils suffers, of course, but this is not the only consequence. These defaulting LEAs continue to benefit from the scheme in that students originating in their schools are still eligible to go abroad as British assistants. There is a basic injustice in this and our European partners have pointed it out and spoken of retaliating against the LEAs concerned.

   The Parliamentary (all-party) Select Committee for Education, Science and the Arts, reporting to Parliament in November 1981, had this to say:

   > it is absolutely vital that pupils should have access to native speakers of the foreign languages concerned. For this reason we recommend that the DES should take on responsibility for the Foreign Language Assistants programme and should make arrangements for this to be funded centrally.

2 Use of the word 'ability' in this context assumes that the 11+ selection procedure discriminated between 'more able' and 'less able' pupils (the latter being allocated to secondary modern schools). In fact, as a series of research studies has demonstrated (e.g. Plowden, 1967, Vol. ii) the factor of 'parental encouragement' is such a determining influence on pupils' performance at primary school level that the concept of a child's ability, divorced from parental influence, loses most of its meaning.

3 The year 1986 was marked by a bitter teachers' dispute. The total of 15,744 applications registered by GTTR for the 1986 course entry in all subjects shows a marked decrease (7.84%) compared with the 1985 total of 17,084 applications. These figures undoubtedly reflect the impact of the dispute on young graduates facing career choices. However the intake of modern language graduates for the PGCE in the previous year, 1985, unaffected by the teachers' dispute, was a mere 742.

4 As this new edition goes to press HMI has issued the latest in its series of papers *Modern Foreign Languages to 16* (DES 1987). In this paper, also based on 'good practice' in schools, HMI argue strongly for the first modern language to be part of the 'core curriculum' up to age 16+ for *all* pupils, with optional second modern languages starting at 14+.

2   Why a foreign language for all?

For the scholar to spend divers years for some small scantling and smattering of tongues – like parrots to babble and prattle, whereby the intellect is in no way enriched, is but toilsome and almost lost labour.
John Webster, *Examination of Academies*, 1654

Beyond all doubt we suffer in competition abroad from ignorance of foreign languages by our merchants, agents, clerks and mechanics.
Royal Society of Arts Journal, 1879 (quoted in *RSA Journal* 100 years later, in 1979)

The legitimacy of studying foreign languages in the schools is being questioned on all sides . . . I am afraid we must say that ours is a failure-ridden discipline.
Dr T. Quinn, Monash University, *BABEL*, April, 1974

Doubts about offering foreign languages to all pupils in comprehensive schools were intensified in the late 1960s by the deschooling debate. In their gloomier moments even some language teachers asked: 'Why not deschool foreign languages?' Why not leave them as an option to be studied by volunteers outside normal school hours, like the violin, or like pony-riding on Saturday mornings (by pupils whose home circumstances do not force them to take a week-end job in the supermarket?).

Some went further: Why not postpone language study altogether until students are adult and able to choose the language needed in their employment or their leisure activities? After all, as adults they would have the motivation and mature concentration required to succeed at the intensive courses which had been shown to be effective in wartime with (selected) adult learners. This was an argument from expediency. Those who advanced it did not reject the role of the school but merely one element in the curriculum. There were others, inspired by Ivan Illich (1971) and Everett Reimer (1971), who opposed the principle of compulsory education itself. Warnings of the dangers of a compulsory curriculum imposed by a one-party state, as in some

27

great powers or in lesser countries in the Third World (where Illich's ideas had been formed), could not fail to strike a sympathetic chord with language teachers who had seen in their youth what the Nazis had done to Germany's once-great schools, or had more recently witnessed the results of compulsory sectarian, segregated schools nearer home.

How far was it appropriate, however, to argue as if the same dangers threatened the curriculum in UK schools with a long tradition of freedom of expression? Here, the deschoolers argued, the danger was a more subtle one. It was the danger of a 'hidden curriculum' reflecting the assumptions of a privileged class. One typical expression of this view saw the school as a sort of prison designed by the so-called 'middle-class' teacher and imposed on children from working-class homes. Again the student of French history, familiar with the grip on power and decision-making exercised by the French bourgeoisie through the *lycée,* must be sensitive to the danger of the state school's perpetuating existing class privileges even in a system claiming (as in France) to ensure *la carrière ouverte aux talents.* But why was foreign language study seen as entrenching privilege through the curriculum?

The argument was that because the study of a foreign language has not previously had a place in the parents' education, any attempt to teach a language to working-class children is unjustified since it challenges, as in some way inadequate, the culture of the home and of the peer group. For some commentators foreign language study came to be cast in the role of the 'sore thumb' in the new, liberated curriculum.

But in a polyglot world, and a European Community, must the curriculum remain static simply to avoid challenging narrower home horizons? No conscientious language teacher would deny that vigilance is needed to avoid unfairness to pupils whose home values conflict with those taught in the school. The presence of immigrant minorities in our schools constantly challenges teachers to be sensitive to home values. Yet are the home values always sacrosanct? Consider (among many similar circumstances that all schools will have met) the home that is exploiting the pupil; the pupil who is being indoctrinated at home or in the youth club in bigotry and hatred; the pupil whose aspirations for a career are being thwarted by parental selfishness, etc. We could prolong the list endlessly. Where is the line drawn between the duty of the community to insist on a pupil's 'inalienable rights' and the right of any given family to set limits to what a child may learn? These are not easy issues. To see through the confusion and half-truths that have characterised the debate we need to ask: What are schools for?

For some the question can scarcely arise. For example the Muslim teacher and his pupil's family take for granted the role of the school as enmeshed in a culture whose rules are revealed in the Koran. The task of the school is to interpret in each generation the revelation of the Prophet and the Book. Ultimately all questions about the teaching programme are answered by reference to the revealed truth. The same must be true to some degree for Christian schools of whatever denomination and for Jewish schools.

The teacher who looks for some justification for the teaching given in school other than divine revelation is forced in the end to make a political decision. Once the political choice is made the educational philosopher can help to clarify the issues, but the political choice must come first.

The view taken in these pages is that education is, in the end, for freedom. This follows from the political choice that our community has made in favour of democracy. It is a choice periodically reaffirmed, as with terrible cruelty and national division in 1649, and one which carries with it the assumption that the individual voter who sanctions the democratic decisions is autonomous. This concept of the autonomy of the individual is crucial. It determines the school's main role, which is to make people as free as they have it in them to be, within the limits of an evolving democracy. If education is for making people optimally free we have to ask: What are the hindrances to children's freedom? A hundred years ago, before children were subjected to what the deschoolers call 'protective detention' in the school system, they were 'free' to work in factories and down the mines. The debates in Parliament on the factory acts of the nineteenth century reveal the way in which the market drove parents to exploit children, sending them into the mines even at the age of five to drag buckets, knee-deep in water, with chains round their waists.

The great army of teachers who have joined in the 'long march' of compulsory state schooling since 1870, in addition to protecting children from such exploitation, have tried to fight more subtle threats to freedom: ignorance, prejudice, the sway of fashion on immature minds, the hidden persuasion of the media on those not armed to recognise it, sheer lack of skills to operate in the environment and all constraints on judgement, taste and understanding.

Our answer then to the question: What are schools for? is that schools at their best are refuges within which freedom from outside pressures is guaranteed and within which the values, skills and *apprenticeship* in citizenship which are required in a democracy can be learnt. In a school so conceived what is the special contribution of modern language study?

Wisdom or skilfulness?

Philosophers of education draw a useful distinction between 'education' and 'instruction'. Both are essential functions of the school and both contribute to autonomy in the learner. Instruction imparts useful skills needed by the individual, and by society, enabling the individual both to lead a full life and to earn a living. Instruction aims to make the pupil as skilful as capacity allows. Education's concern, however, is with making the skilful and not so skilful, pupil a little wiser. Wisdom is the capacity to make the right choices. It is commonly learned by living with the results of wrong choices. Can it be taught? Perhaps the best apprenticeship for wisdom is practice in making apt comparisons. Informed choice (weighing the evidence for and against, including where relevant the transmitted experience of the community and the likely consequences of one's choices for others as well as for oneself) builds on apt comparison and is the essence of judgement. We shall later in this chapter examine some ways in which modern language studies offer unique opportunities for learning to compare the familiar with what is new and challenging. Of course pupils will differ as greatly in their capacity to acquire useful skills as in their capacity to learn wisdom in using them.

There is another way in which pupils will differ which makes innate differences in capacity seem trivial by comparison. It is in the extent to which the home that any given child draws in the great parental lottery is an encouraging or discouraging place. It is now recognised that although the school can make some difference (Rutter et al., 1979) the home influence, both for good and for ill, is paramount. The wise teacher will work with and through the parents the child loves, but the home values are not sacrosanct; the curriculum must respect, but also sometimes challenge, the parochial environment.

What the deschoolers who proposed giving up foreign language teaching in schools failed to see was that their policy would mean a field-day for the fortunate child with good parental support but could only impoverish experience for the child whose home could not help or did not care. If languages were deschooled the children of well-informed and caring parents would be sent along to the voluntary Saturday French class; they would be sent abroad on exchanges and holiday study-visits and would spend terms at European schools. There would be a mushroom growth of fee-paying language schools to cater for such pupils. But with a curriculum determined by the accident of home background, who would ever open the door of foreign language study to the child whose home is a vacuum?

We conclude that there are two questions to answer when we discuss the case for foreign languages in the comprehensive school:

1. are you arguing for foreign language study as instruction or as education; for making pupils skilful or making them wise, or both?
2. are you considering pupils of high academic capacity from articulate, encouraging homes, or pupils from less helpful homes who may be of more limited aptitude for verbal learning?

Failure to answer the first of these questions has led to confusion in the past. It may be instructive to glance briefly at a typical example of a curriculum philosophy based on a shaky premise.

A philosopher's confusion

The wisest philosophers of education accept that it is impossible to define the content of the curriculum on purely philosophical grounds.

I think it is possible to produce arguments to show why some sorts of pursuits are more worthwhile than others . . . to produce some ethical foundations for education. . . . But what I think a philosopher cannot do, qua philosopher, is to pronounce on the relative weight to be attached to such principles, to proclaim that, for example, literature is more important than science. . . . Philosophy has an important contribution to make to practical wisdom, but it is no substitute for it. (Peters, 1973, p. 29)

Not all philosophers have been so cautious and one contribution certainly added to the disenchantment among modern linguists. This was J. P. White's *Towards a Compulsory Curriculum* (White, 1973). In an original and provoking essay he proposed a compulsory curriculum to be confined to the morning of each school day and consisting of 'category 1' activities. These are activities of which 'no understanding is possible without engaging in them'. They are contrasted with 'category 2' activities of which some understanding is logically possible without engaging in them. Those subjects would be relegated to the (optional) afternoon timetable. The first such subject listed is 'speaking a foreign language'. 'Provided one speaks one language, e.g. English', White explains, 'one can gain some understanding of what it is for other people to speak another, even though one cannot do so oneself.'

White's argument is based on a mistaken definition of the discipline he is discussing. He sees the purpose of foreign language study in school as 'producing bilinguals'. It is, therefore, part of instruction not education, merely training in a skill. He fails to see that the educational value of foreign language learning is precisely that it can offer the pupil an experience different from that of the mother tongue and so contribute to an understanding of the polyglot world, and emancipate the learner from parochialism.[1] The person who has never ventured outside his own language is incapable even of realising how parochial he is – just as the earthbound traveller who has never journeyed into space takes the pull of gravity for granted as an unalterable part of the scheme of things.

The danger of failing to challenge pupils to break out of the monolingual straitjacket was wittily expressed by the eminent American linguist Yuen Ren Chao (1968):

Monolingual persons take language so much for granted that they often forget its arbitrary nature and cannot distinguish words from things. Thus primitive peoples often believe that putting a curse on somebody's name could actually harm his person. Persons unused to foreign languages tend to find something perverse in the way foreigners talk. Even Oliver Goldsmith could not get over the perversity of the French, who would call cabbage 'shoe', instead of calling a cabbage 'cabbage'. The story is told of an English woman who always wondered why the French call water 'de l'eau', the Italians 'dell'acqua' and the Germans call it 'das Wasser'. Only we English people, she said, call it properly 'water'. We not only call it water, *but it is water*. (p. 2)

(Later Yuen Ren Chao confesses, naughtily, that when he first heard the story it was a German woman who confused the thing with its name.) The point made by his story, from which curriculum theorists must start, is that the foreign language makes a different contribution from the mother tongue, and one that is complementary to it. This is something which teachers of English, trained almost exclusively through courses in literature with little acquaintance with research in psycholinguistics and language acquisition, may not readily understand.

Parochialism of teachers of English

English and the foreign language should be complementary subjects in the curriculum. In Part III of this book we examine the way in which both subjects might contribute to a coherent linguistic apprenticeship.

The gulf between them hitherto has been wide. In how many schools do teachers of the two subjects even agree on a common terminology for use when talking about language with children? Teachers of English and of foreign languages are generally trained in isolation from each other. Why should we expect them to make common cause when they get into school?

The parochialism of teachers of English was exemplified in the report of a national committee of enquiry set up in 1972 under Sir Alan (now Lord) Bullock. The committee arose from anxiety expressed in the House of Commons and elsewhere concerning existing standards in the use of English. The committee interpreted its brief widely as 'language in education', and its report published in 1975 was entitled *A Language for Life*.

The report made many valuable recommendations for improving English teaching. Some of these (for example, 'Parents should be helped to understand the process of language development in their children and play their part in it') virtually amount to proposing a new dimension in the curriculum, the study of *language* itself. The report also proposed that all teachers in training, regardless of subject, should make a special study of language. We return to these proposals in Part III.

What astonished modern linguists about the Bullock Report was the complete absence from its 600 pages of any reference to foreign languages in the curriculum or to the fact that we live in a polyglot world and that the pupils whose 'language for life' the report describes will, as adults, be brought (in their jobs, their politics, their leisure activities) into ever closer interaction with neighbours whose mother tongue is not English. The Bullock solution, 'language across the curriculum', turned out to mean 'half-way across the curriculum'. It was inconceivable to modern linguists that such a committee could have spent three years studying language in education without once hearing evidence from foreign language teachers or making any proposals for bringing teachers of English and foreign languages closer together. Mistaken views of the nature of our subject can be mischievous but so can failure to recognise its existence!

It may be useful, in order to make a fresh start after so much confusion, to take first the easiest part of our problem, namely the curriculum for the academically able pupil, and begin by considering the foreign language as a useful skill: the argument for foreign language *instruction* for future members of the 'service class'.

The academically able pupil: foreign language instruction

In the debate about the curriculum that followed the 1944 Education Act, the most lucid statement on the education of able pupils was *An Essay on the Content of Education* by Dr Eric James (1949), now Lord James of Rusholme and founder Vice-Chancellor of York University. James had unrivalled experience of teaching able boys as form master at Winchester and High Master of Manchester Grammar School. In his *Essay* he recognises the distinct roles of instruction and education in his suggestion that any subject in the curriculum may be justified under one of three broad heads: 'A study may convey information which is essential to the business of living; it may inculcate valuable skills; and thirdly, it may contribute to the spiritual development of the individual, using the word "spiritual" to include the satisfaction of the highest intellectual, moral and aesthetic capacities.'

His first two heads, essential information and valuable skills, will be served by instruction. James was in no doubt that his able pupils, aspiring to university careers, should at least have a reading knowledge of a language, up to GCE 'O' level. Few university teachers would now disagree though university entrance policies have not helped schools in their difficult task. That an undergraduate who wishes to read for a degree in modern history should have a sound reading knowledge of (at least) one foreign language surely needs no more arguing than does the classical historian's need for Latin and Greek, or the theologian's for Hebrew. Similarly the able musician wishing to study opera had better have reliable Italian. It is for this reason that most universities have been compelled to set up language centres to equip their students with ancillary foreign language skills.

But what of the able pupils not going on to full-time education but into commerce or industry. Do they really need an ancillary language skill? Here the leaders of the great professions, like the leaders of industry, seem to speak with two voices.

The professions

A broadsheet published (March 1979) by the Modern Languages Department of Eton College usefully brings together the views of leading figures in the main professional fields, unanimous in their insistence on the importance of foreign language study in school:

Accountancy: 'I believe that modern languages receive insufficient emphasis in all British schools, and there are no exceptions.' (M. H. A. Broke, Rothschild Investment Trust)

Diplomatic Service: 'Languages are the tools of our trade as diplomats. You can do without them and you can use other people's but you will not be your own master and you will never have the complete feel of the country where you serve.' (Sir Nicholas Henderson, British Ambassador in Paris and in the USA)

Fine Arts: 'Like Norman Douglas, I believe that the trick is to learn *how* to learn languages, and not only for practical reasons. He wrote "They say knowledge (of languages) is power. It is also great fun." ' (R. N. Kingzett, Managing Director of Thomas Agnew and Sons Ltd)

Insurance: 'The City as a whole is short of people who can converse with fluency in foreign languages.' (A. R. Macneal, C. T. Bowring and Co. Ltd)

Journalism: 'In my professional career, command of one or more foreign languages has been a professional necessity.' (Charles Hargrove, *Times* correspondent in Paris)

The list continues, with authoritative statements from leaders in the professions of law, merchant banking, music, stockbroking, and a powerful concluding statement from Sir Oliver Wright, British Ambassador to the Federal Republic of Germany: 'If you are dependent on other people, whether as allies for defence or trading partners to export to or buy from, it is just as well to understand those you depend on. And there is no single better method of insight into people's ways of thought and feeling than their language, and how they use it.'

If an able pupil, whether at public or state school, ever doubted the necessity to equip himself (or herself) with a foreign language, this broadsheet is required reading. The case for foreign languages as a tool, ancillary to every one of the learned professions, is clearly made.

These powerful pleas from the leaders of the professions would carry more weight, however, if the training courses and examinations prescribed by their governing bodies included an ancillary language requirement. Until the aspiring accountant is *required* by his professional body to show evidence of foreign language skills, the exhortations of individuals will count for little. The two voices with which British industry has spoken about foreign language skills are even more discordant.

Industry

In official statements language skills have been rated highly by industrialists. In 1962 the Federation of British Industries Working Party Report *Foreign Languages in Industry* asserted: 'A man who can make himself understood in his own subject with the aid of diagrams, drawings and models and 2,000–3,000 words in the other man's language is a valuable member of the company's staff.' In 1971–2 the Nuffield Foundation/York University Survey (Emmans et al., 1974) followed the careers in industry of 408 modern language graduates who left British universities in 1960, and a sample of 1966 graduates from 'new type' university courses.[2] The survey concluded: 'the general picture that emerged . . . was of foreign language graduates playing only a modest role as foreign language users in industry'. Was this because industry wants languages only as *ancillary* skills (for salesmen, engineers, accountants, etc.)? There was, alas, little evidence in the York survey that industry was doing anything to refresh or add to any ancillary language skills that its recruits brought with them from school.

Some of the largest firms in the UK with extensive business

overseas *had not taken the trouble to record in their files* the language skills possessed by their staff, still less encouraged those with language skills to maintain or extend them.

Sir Peter Tennant commented in the foreword to the York survey: 'older management still tends to treat linguists as potential liabilities rather than assets'. He spoke of management's 'missed opportunities' and of employees 'obviously distressed at having so little use made of their language skills'.

The York survey was made in 1971–2, before Britain entered the EEC. Has the complacency of employers in industry and commerce regarding language skills been altered by the challenge of EEC membership to which modern language teachers so eagerly looked forward?

There are a few signs of it. A survey carried out in the West Midlands by the University of Aston in Birmingham (Ager, 1977) shows a higher level of language demand and use than the York study. A limited survey in the Crawley area of West Sussex carried out by the College of Technology revealed a distinct interest in recruiting staff proficient in a modern language. Of 42 employers approached, 31 replied positively, 24 giving German, 23 French, 12 Spanish and 8 Italian as the languages they considered most in demand (West Sussex, 1978).

Nevertheless a general apathy even at the highest Whitehall levels seemed to persist. Vaughan James (C. V. James, 1979) quotes a significant case (p. 12):

It is regrettable that the House of Commons Expenditure Committee Report on the Civil Service, published in September 1977, makes no reference to a need for British higher civil servants to be able to converse in a foreign language.

A sub-committee of the Committee visited the Ecole Nationale d'Administration in Paris and praised it in the Committee's report for its success in producing first-rate adminstrators. The Ecole has a modern languages department and the study of a foreign language is compulsory for all students. No mention of this aspect of the training of French higher civil servants is made in the Committee's report.

The dismal picture painted by the York report was confirmed in the report of a Study Group chaired by HRH the Duke of Kent which was published in May 1979 under the title *Foreign Languages for Overseas Trade* (BOTB, 1979). The Duke comments in the foreword: 'it has become increasingly clear that the traditional reluctance of the British to learn foreign languages may be seriously affecting our trading prospects'.

The Study Group was set up following a 'crisis' conference 'Does Britain need Linguists?' in May 1978, called by the British Overseas Trade Board, the University of Surrey and the Royal Society of Arts. It reported that 'very few firms are making adequate use of the language training facilities already available . . . there is need of better liaison between firms and educational establishments . . . there is no substitute for the ability to deal with foreign customers in their own language, especially when it is evident that most of our customers are better equipped to do so than we are'.

The complacency of employers has been due in part to a mistaken view of the place of English as the leading world vehicle language. English is spoken as a first language by some 291 millions (second only to Mandarin Chinese) and as a second language by countless millions more. Of the secondary school population in France 84% study English as first foreign language and in West Germany the figure is nearer 100%. English is almost without exception the main foreign language studied in schools in most parts of India and S E Asia; in Anglophone Africa, English is the lingua franca. In China, English is overwhelmingly the chief foreign language studied in schools and universities and 'English by radio' broadcasts (twice daily) are followed avidly by millions of Chinese learners in all occupations. In every part of the globe English is heard daily through (largely American) films, records, television. The use of English in the international control of aircraft further strengthens the position of English as the world vehicle language.

Why not capitalise on this, it is sometimes argued, to set the privileged English speaker free from the tedium of learning foreign languages? The time spent by a German or Frenchman in learning English might be regarded as time we could save?

It is a conclusion which the Duke of Kent's Study Group decided to put to the test. British Embassies abroad were asked whether the use of English was a handicap when dealing with firms abroad. *The replies disposed of the myth that English is universally accepted.*

From France, Britain's second largest market in Europe: 'at the working level of most French businesses including Parisian ones, knowledge of English is very poor and a United Kingdom firm competing in English against a foreign firm using French stands only a very slim chance'.

From Spain: 'It is my impression that less English is spoken by Spanish businessmen . . . than in probably any other major market in Western Europe . . . Any foreign company using English in correspondence, or with literature not in Spanish, starts off at a very serious disadvantage indeed.'

From Germany, Britain's second largest export market overall: 'While a knowledge of the language will not compensate for poor quality or slow delivery, good German will undoubtedly produce a more positive attitude and may well tip the interest scales with a prospective new client.'

From Italy: 'A British firm whose produce does not speak for itself and needs explaining is very unlikely to get any business as a result of letters written in English.'

Even in Sweden, where English is the lingua franca, one firm said its performance had improved noticeably since the staff involved had made the effort to learn something of the language, if only for social purposes.

The Study Group found that 'this message has not yet been understood by many British firms . . . The days when English speaking markets took the bulk of British exports are over. The proportion of British exports going to Western Europe markets has risen from 34% to over 50% in the past 15 years.' (We might add that exports to Arabic-speaking countries have more than doubled.) 'The company interested in competing effectively in major foreign-language markets needs to think seriously about its policy on language training and use. The evidence collected by the Study Group indicates that this is not something which the majority of British Companies have so far done. A more positive attitude towards foreign language skills seems essential. . .'

As to how British industry does manage to solve its language problems (for after all Britain's trade with Western Europe has increased from one-third to one-half in 15 years) the report confirms the impression formed by the York research referred to above, that British firms on the whole are content to recruit English-speaking foreign agents. They rely heavily on them and their very substantial fees add to the price of British exports and make them less competitive.

The Duke of Kent's Study Group raised the further point: that companies may lose out if, by virtue of a lack of linguistic capability, they have no source of market information other than their overseas agents. Learning a language means also learning about the way of life of the people who speak it. For the British on their overcrowded island, importing 50% of their food from overseas, and having to pay for it by sweat and skill, not to make as close a study as possible of their potential customers seems suicidal. We are in fact 'exporting' our language problem, paying the foreigner to do what we are unwilling to do, and our other exports suffer in consequence.

Technicians

Nor is complacency confined to management. The trades unions have a responsibility, especially for the training of the next generation of workers and supervisors.

Technical and commercial education courses are being reshaped by the Technician Education Council and the Business Education Council (BEC) respectively. The BEC is strongly of the opinion that there is need 'for an increased proportion of those employed in business, commerce, and public administration to have a reasonably competent grasp of foreign languages. The Council accordingly wishes to see a steady expansion of foreign language study in further education courses leading to BEC awards' (BEC Circular 1/78, March 1978). In practice, however, in the initial period to 1981, languages are excluded from General (foundation) level courses and only one language may be taken at National level and at Higher National level in any one year, even if the entrant has has two 'A' levels in languages. Not surprisingly the Working Party of West Sussex LEA reporting this 'views with alarm the likely effect of current BEC proposals on modern language study in the further education sector' (West Sussex 1978).

Few things would have greater impact on fourth and fifth formers aspiring to apprenticeships and traineeships than the inclusion in post-school training programmes of a foreign language element, with realistic incentives to reach an appropriate grade as quickly as possible. The prestige accorded to a foreign language skill in post-school courses would soon feed back into school leavers' classes and below. A first step might be, as the Duke of Kent's report suggests, for the government to press for the introduction of languages into the training supported by Industrial Training Boards. It will be an uphill struggle, however, to overcome the complacency of employers and trades unions, which mirrors the parochialism of public opinion.

Our able pupil, then, considering whether or not to work hard at an ancillary language in school, will need to choose between the pious exhortations of leaders in the professions and in industry, and present complacent practice. It seems likely nevertheless that within the coming decade sheer necessity will force those responsible for training courses to give due importance to ancillary language skills. Of the ultimate need for these, whether presently recognised by training boards or not, there can be no doubt.

The academically able pupil: foreign language as education

James (1949) fully recognised the vocational value of instruction in a foreign language. He was less convinced that it contributed to education in a wider sense, except for the few specialists who carry their studies well beyond the sixth form. He quotes Milton (*Tract on Education*, 1644):

the Monsieurs of Paris who take our hopeful Youth into their slight and prodigal custodies and send them back again transformed into Mimicks, Apes and Kicshoes . . . though a linguist should pride himself to have all the Tongues that Babel cleft the world into, yet if he have not studied the solid things in them as well as the Words and Lexicons, he were nothing so much to be esteemed a learned man, as any Yeoman or Tradesman competently wise in his Mother Dialect only. (p. 18)

For James

The cultural effects upon a science student of several periods a week of compulsory French are usually negligible. The language may be a valuable vocational tool, but it is a superstition justified neither by practical experience nor by honest analysis of the theoretical issues to imagine that such hours are automatically cultural merely because they are not specialist . . . a mastery over words and a sensitivity to meaning are essential elements in the education of anyone capable of acquiring them. Undoubtedly, too, one of the most effective ways of acquiring such skills is by learning a foreign language. But the scientist in the sixth form should have spent already four or five years on at least one such language . . . In fact the best way of continuing a linguistic discipline, and certainly the one most likely to secure the cooperation of the pupil, is through the study of his own language . . . we must come to the conclusion that a knowledge of a foreign language, except the bare ability to translate a simple passage as a vocational tool, is not a legitimate demand as part of his general education at the sixth form level. It must be emphasised that this implies no criticism of foreign language as an independent and specialist study. (1949, p. 71)

One vital point that James overlooks here is that 'O' level language skills, earned by five years of hard work, very quickly erode unless kept in use and that this is an important reason why non-specialists in the sixth form must have an incentive not to drop their language after 'O' level. Ancillary language skills which do not count for acceptance for higher education are highly vulnerable. But what of the substantive point: beyond the level of a vocational 'O' level the foreign language is not educative in any real sense for non-specialists?

The foreign language teacher, recalling the excitement and emancipation of his/her own first exploration of the novel, poetry, drama, of a chosen foreign language, might wish to quarrel with James' view. But we should be cautious. His scepticism may be justified.

For the very able linguist, who has spent some time in the foreign country by the time the sixth-form reading is tackled, and already has some feeling for the language, it is probably education in the truest sense to read the great literary works in which the language has been used at its most expressive, which in fact are the language. This experience will only be truly educative however if the young reader is encouraged, while reading, to do two things:

1   To read intensively those English books that can aptly be compared or contrasted with the foreign works. 'Set-books' for examinations should be selected so as to provoke informed comparison of this kind and no foreign language books ought to be set without detailed guidance being given about such supportive reading in English

2   To read extensively in the foreign language about the society and the period for which the set-book was written and its geographical, historical and sociological setting. Again those who nominate set-books have an obligation to give detailed guidance about such background reading. These two conditions have in the past seldom been met. Even the ablest of sixth-form pupils have been thrust unprepared into forming judgements about foreign works of whose counterparts in English they were ignorant, and with only the haziest notion of the expectations that the foreign reader or spectator brought to the literary experience. For the less than outstanding pupil, with a scarcely reliable feel for the language, compelled to consult the dictionary at every line, the dangers are obvious. To encourage such pupils (the great majority of sixth formers) to engage in literary criticism in the foreign language is to encourage hypocrisy. The pupil in his/her uncertainty will grasp at the opinions of teacher or editor in the effort to say the right thing. The comments of critics will receive more intense study than the original works themselves. Scepticism about the value of literary criticism in a foreign language when the readers (and their teachers) lack native-speaking intuition for the nuance of meaning of key words is surely justified.

This is not to suggest that the great works should not be read, and re-read, passages committed to memory, some studied in depth, some rapidly scanned. Together with experience of many other registers of the language (logical exposition, historical narrative, journalism, spoken discussion, technical writing, correspondence etc.) literature is one element of a linguistic apprenticeship leading to that very partial mastery of the foreign language which is all that the non-native speaker can ever aspire to.

There are, however, two other important contributions to education in the truest sense that foreign language study can make in school, for the non-specialist, reasonably able pupil, to which James does not refer. The first is apprenticeship in 'empathy', in seeing how the world looks from someone else's viewpoint.

Emancipation from parochial prejudice

In an earlier section we referred to the way in which empathy declines as puberty approaches, especially among boys. A characteristic of eight-year-olds is their ready sympathy with each other in trouble; their capacity for identifying instinctively with another's expectations. Sadly, with adolescence, especially for boys, comes insecurity, rejection of what is unfamiliar. Colour prejudice is notoriously virulent among adolescents, as is sectarian bigotry.

The relevance of this to foreign language studies may be illustrated by considering the dilemma faced by the teacher in present-day Belfast. What is the school challenged to do in such a tragic situation? For an adolescent on the protestant side brought up to equate 'Rome' and 'catholic' with all that is unclean and hateful, the journey into the Spanish language and literature puts in perspective, as no other study can, the half-truths of home or pulpit or housing estate gossip. When the pupil travels abroad to ask his own questions, trying out the marvellous new linguistic tool his school has given him, foreign language study becomes truly liberating. The writer of these pages cannot be the only protestant schoolboy who learnt from the humane Augustinian Fray Luis de León a view of catholicism very different from that peddled by the rival marchers in Liverpool in the 1920s as in Belfast today. The gentle Fray Luis himself spent the years 1572–6 in Valladolid prison accused of *novedades* (innovations) by the Inquisition, and of having translated the Song of Songs.[3] On the walls of his cell he wrote the famous 'décima':

Aquí la envidia y mentira
me tuvieron encerrado . . .

(Here envy and lies
held me prisoner . . .)

The journey to meet the wise Fray Luis may be, for many such
pupils as our Belfast (or Liverpool) schoolboy, the best way out of
the prison of envy and lies of the slum or housing estate. To go on
to study what destruction those of Fray Luis's faith did to the
Arabic civilisation whose cities they inherited may be a further
step on the liberating journey.

Much of the grace and craftsmanship of the Arabic civilisation
of Seville, Córdoba and Granada was destroyed by the southern
march of the gross, catholic kingdoms. Our schoolboy visiting
Seville is able to contrast the loveliness of the Giralda, the brick
tower of the former mosque, with the mass of the gothic ca-
thedral that sprawls against it, where the delicate arches of the
mosque were razed to make room for it. On stepping inside the
cloister he can read on the wall the comment of a puzzled catholic, the wise and warm Cervantes: '¡Voto a Dios, que me espanta
esta grandeza!' (God! this magnificence frightens me!)

Our protestant schoolboy's able catholic contemporaries who
pursue their German studies into the sixth form may make an
equally 'empathic' voyage, away from parochialism, when they
visit one of the cool, quiet churches of North Germany where
Johann Sebastian Bach sang and taught.

This is not to make exaggerated claims for the discipline of
foreign language study. Of course other subjects are liberating.
History and geography, of their nature, challenge parochialism
and compel comparison across barriers of time and distance.
Only through a progressive apprenticeship in comparison can
judgement be learnt and learning how to make fair judgements is
the beginning of wisdom. But the unique value of the apprenticeship in judgement learnt by able pupils in the foreign
language classroom is that the pupil does not have to take the
teacher's (or text-book's) word for it. The foreign language
teacher says in effect to the adolescent: What we are now learning
in the classroom is in preparation for your journey abroad and
your reading, when the language tools you are sharpening will
be used to answer the question 'What exactly are the differences
between the way of life in the foreign community and the way of

life you know at home?' The language, learnt from text-book and teacher, is also intended to be used to ask: How does the picture of the foreign country learned in the classroom compare with reality? Can other (arts) subjects claim as much?

We are not, of course, arguing that any kind of visit abroad is emancipating. The educational visit must be carefully prepared by reading, including map-reading and history reading. It must be carried through with discipline and should preferably result in a written project, suitably illustrated. It should be followed up in de-briefing discussions during which imbalance in the pupil's impressions can be corrected. (In Chapter 9 we describe some excellent models of such visits.) The GCE 'A' level examination boards could greatly encourage such well-planned study visits by giving credit in the examination for written accounts of modest research projects conducted *in the foreign country* in the course of sixth-form studies.

For the able pupil, who is conscious of a home background which in his own community enjoys low status, there is libera- tion of another kind when he travels abroad. In the foreign language he is judged by what he can do and say, not by where he comes from. It becomes true, as Cervantes said, that 'cada hombre es hijo de sus obras': every man is the son of his own deeds – i.e. not *'hidalgo'* (nobleman), meaning *'hijo de algo'* (some- body's heir).

Emancipation for the school community

A further unique contribution of foreign languages to eman- cipation lies in preventing the school community itself lapsing into parochialism. The language teacher (nowadays), unlike all other teachers in the staff room, has spent a year working abroad. Other teachers may have been abroad on visits or (occasionally) on voluntary service overseas, but only the language teacher will have been required *in the course of his professional training* to roll up his sleeves and earn a living for a year in the foreign community, using the foreign language and getting underneath superficial impressions.

This ensures that there are on the school staff well-informed witnesses who have worked in a different system. Without them, and with doors and windows closed to the non-English-speaking world, school discussion and professional decisions could be even more parochial than they often are. Add to this the fact that the foreign language department invites back into the school speakers of the foreign language (both pupils and staff) to work and play and exchange ideas even with those who never go abroad.

The case then for retaining foreign languages as an important element in the curriculum of able pupils both as instruction and as education is clearly overwhelming. But for all pupils? What of the slower learner who will never point his schoolboy camera at the Giralda nor plan a bike ride in Johann Sebastian's footsteps? Clearly the most difficult part of our enquiry is to establish what place (if any) foreign language learning ought to have in the schooling of the three-quarters of the 11+ age-group previously excluded from the subject and now brought in from the cold, pupils few of whom, by definition, will ever reach even the modest target of GCE 'O' level.

The first question to face is: How strong is the argument for the foreign language *as a vocational skill* for the slower learner?

The slower learner: foreign language instruction

Let us make a bold assumption that, perhaps by adopting the methods proposed in Part III of this book, we could greatly improve the language mastery of even comparatively slow learners. Would we be justified in arguing on vocational grounds for a foreign language for all? A moment's reflection will show that, even if much higher standards could be achieved than hitherto, the argument *purely from vocational need* is extremely flimsy, for two reasons:

1   *A foreign language is not a necessary ancillary skill for many occupations*
    How honest is it for the teacher of slow learning pupils, most of whom will serve behind shop counters, or work at manual jobs, but not aspire to management or to the professions, to pretend that French, German or Spanish will be a useful, let alone a necessary, ancillary skill in their job? What is the prospect of a foreign language being needed by the many school leavers in Liverpool (Birmingham, Inner London, etc.) who are less fortunate and know that they stand little chance of employment anyway? The plain fact is that for them the vocational case for foreign language instruction is a very weak one, unless they propose, as some enterprising non-academic pupils are already doing, to take advantage of the EEC rules to go abroad to earn a living, for example, as bricklayers or lorry drivers. But even for

future migrant workers leaving these islands to seek employment there is a second difficulty:

2 *Which language?*

Even if it were reasonable to hold in front of the slower learner the prospect of using a foreign language in some future employment, can we predict, at 11+, which language will be most needed after school? The future bricklayer, having learnt French, may want to go to Holland. The aspiring lorry driver, especially in the North of England, will know that the busiest routes lead by way of Hull or Newcastle to Europort (Rotterdam) and via the German autobahn to the Brenner. This will call for some phrases in Dutch, German or Italian, rather than French. Similarly, for those who seek office jobs, the particular European language needed by the future linguist/secretary cannot be predicted until she gets her job and discovers which countries her employer has most dealings with. In this we are in a different situation from (say) the Scandinavians or the Dutch who can predict that even their slower learners will need English, the world vehicle language, no matter what job they find themselves doing.

The slower learner: language learning as education

Arguments from vocational usefulness are misleading; they are also ineffective because the slower learner sees through them. If we clear them out of our way we can see more clearly (and ask administrators to accept) the sound arguments for giving foreign language study a central place in the curriculum for all. Regardless of the level of performance this central place is justified on two grounds, one intrinsic and the other extrinsic:

1 Even the slower learner in the earliest stages can enjoy the experience of liberation from the monoglot's 'magical view of language'; it can be a school experience which in itself is fun though difficult and leaves pupils with a sense of achievement, lighting fires of curiosity about the polyglot world which will blaze throughout adult life.

2 The foreign language course, if planned as part of a coherent programme of language education, can do much to awaken linguistic awareness, with all that this means for the whole secondary school experience.

Let us look at these arguments more closely.

Escape from the monoglot's prison: language learning for fun

The slower learner is at least as likely as his faster contemporaries to succumb to what Yuen Ren Chao called 'the magical view of language'. The slower learner is especially vulnerable because he is insecure. The robust, confident intellect is less inclined to equate 'strange' with 'threatening'. Curiosity and tolerance both depend on a measure of self-confidence. This makes it important that the slow learner's experience of the foreign language should build confidence by being enjoyable and rewarding from the outset.

'Reward' is probably the key. There must be a feeling of achievement at each step. Yet the steps must not be so trivial that there is no sense of achievement. It is here that the 'graded tests' of achievement pioneered by working parties of teachers in York, Oxfordshire, Somerset, Lothian and elsewhere may help the slower learner.[4] 'Graded tests' borrow a leaf from the musician's book.[5] They also promise a possible linking, eventually, of language syllabuses in the school system in the UK with the 'unit/credit' concept for adults learning languages which has been pioneered by John Trim and his colleagues for the Council of Europe (Trim et al., 1973). Teachers in many areas have seen a quickening of interest among slower learners as a result of the introduction of short-term grades with immediate, visible rewards (like Boy Scout badges worn on the arm!).

One effect has been to concentrate teachers' attention on defining the content of a reasonable syllabus for the slower learner. Groups of teachers working on materials for the slower learner (a good example is the ILEA working party which is basing its graded tests on the 'Eclair' materials) have devised learning activities which make the syllabus more fun and move at a pace which challenges slower learners without frightening them off.

The first steps out of Yuen Ren Chao's monolingual prison must be absorbing. We have to light fires of curiosity and anticipation that will blaze in adult life. Better no school foreign language experience than one that leaves the feeling: 'I've tried learning a foreign language: but never again!'

Success in the early stages for the slower learner becomes very important. We have to remember that foreign language learning differs from all other subjects in that the native speaker's performance is taken as the criterion. In every other subject the teacher defines success or failure. What is 'failure' for the young historian? How much or how little does he need to know about the French Revolution to 'pass' or 'fail'? The decision is based on a statistical concept worked out by an examining board and ultimately the criterion is 'what roughly 60% of his age-group have in the past managed to learn'. The only comparison any historian faces is comparison with his peers who have (even the professors of history) travelled the same learning path.

In foreign language learning, however, there is the ultimate comparison to be made with the native speaker and his intuitive knowledge arrived at by a road very different from that travelled by the pupil or his teacher. Even if the examiners apply a similar statistical device and call a 'pass' the degree of approximation to native-like performance that is achieved by 60% of candidates, nevertheless the ability to converse with the native speaker, to read the newspaper or the foreign novel, still remains the criterion of performance whatever examiners may say and the learner senses this. He has only to listen to the French radio to be reminded of it.

We can help slower learners by being tolerant of error in performance; by rewarding comprehension and encouraging bilingual dialogue (see Part iii); by teaching them that language learning is a two-stage activity in which apprenticeship (learning how to learn a language) has its proper place, with its own appropriate goals; by devising tests which reward positive attitudes and insight into language at the school stage at least as much as performance. Performance will improve rapidly when the pupil begins to use the language to fulfil real needs, as when he goes abroad or meets a text, or a speaker, with a message that he wishes to understand. For the slower learner this may be a rare experience. The limited role of performance at this level must be frankly faced. There are other criteria by which to judge success or failure in the secondary school foreign language apprenticeship . Reconsideration of the secondary course as the first stage, in a two-stage process, may help us to set more useful objectives for all pupils, but especially for the slower learner.

The foreign language and 'linguistic awareness'
    Discussion in the 1960s and 1970s of the linguistic problems that many slower learners meet in school, and of the value for them of foreign language study, was led astray by the acrimonious and unfruitful controversy over the successive versions of the hypothesis advanced by B. Bernstein (Bernstein, 1971). One widely discussed formulation of the theory implied that some (working-class) pupils had access only to a 'restricted' code, of

largely 'implicit meaning' (i.e. tied to its context), while other (middle-class) pupils had access to this code *as well as* to an 'elaborated' code of more 'explicit meanings', which was the code met in the classroom. This led to widespread discussion of the notion of 'verbal deprivation'. The deprivation notion was denounced by W. Labov (1970) as a myth, and his arguments were documented with recordings made in the negro ghetto in the USA.

The early version of the Bernstein hypothesis was widely accepted, however, among teacher trainers in the UK and the conclusion was drawn by some of them that to include a foreign language in the curriculum for pupils from home backgrounds where only the implicit 'restricted' code was met was unfair and gave an advantage to pupils who had access to a more explicit 'elaborated' code. This was taken further by some sociologists who saw the modern language as part of the 'middle-class' curriculum being foisted on to working-class children.

More recent work by researchers who have listened sensitively to children's speech has offered us a different insight into the handicap from which some pupils suffer when they enter the school system. They have called it 'lack of awareness of language'. Far from suggesting that slower learners in school should be shielded from the impact of a foreign language, their research points the way to an understanding of the special contribution that the foreign language could make in a coherent language education for slower learners.

The concept of 'awareness' of language is summarised by Margaret Donaldson in this way:

In the early stages, before the child has developed a full awareness of language, language is embedded for him in the flow of events that accompany it. So long as this is the case, the child does not interpret words in isolation, he interprets situations. He is more concerned to make sense of what people do when they talk and act than to decide what the words mean. . . . What is going to be required in our educational system is that he should learn to turn language and thought in upon themselves. . . . He must become capable of manipulating symbols . . . the first step is the step of conceptualizing language – becoming aware of it as a separate structure, freeing it from its embeddedness in events. . . . Some children come to school with this step already taken, or at least with the movement already begun. They come with an enormous initial advantage . . . in some homes awareness of the spoken word is greatly encouraged. Some parents talk *about* words to their children, play word games with them and so on. But most talk only *with* words. Indeed a great many children come to school not even aware that separate words exist – that the flow of speech can be broken up into these units. (Donaldson, 1978, p. 88)

Margaret Donaldson's 'awareness' of language is similar to the concept of 'analytic competence' analysed by Jerome Bruner (Bruner, 1975). Its principal feature is 'the prolonged operation of thought processes on linguistic representations'.

Bruner quotes Vygotsky: 'The word, to the child, is an integral part of the object it denotes. Such a conception seems to be characteristic of primitive linguistic consciousness. We all know the old story about the rustic who said he was not surprised that savants with all their instruments could figure out the size of the stars and their courses – what baffled him was how they found out their names' (p. 73).

For Bruner the development of 'analytic competence' is an 'unnatural elaboration of intellectual activity . . . it does not come automatically through language use'.

Primary and secondary language activities
The unnatural dimension of 'linguistic awareness' is stressed by I. G. Mattingley in *Language by Ear and Eye* (Kavanagh and Mattingley, 1972). He describes speaking and listening as 'primary activities' for which we have an innate capability. Reading, however, is a secondary or 'parasitic' activity and is not innate. If the primary activity is underdeveloped this makes the secondary or 'parasitic' activity much harder to learn.

Speech, the primary activity, is highly redundant. Cues to meaning are carried at a variety of levels: gesture, expression, intonation, pauses, and so on, whereas cues in the written form are discrete and at a single level. Once mastered, however, the written form offers great advantages, the most marked of which is speed. The maximum rate of comprehension of spoken language is around 400 words per minute but comprehension of writing can reach 2,000 words per minute. The reader can go directly to a deep level, by-passing the decoding of individual words. The corresponding penalties, in our school system and in our society, for failure to break through the reading barrier, are heavy and cumulative.

Mattingley argues (like Margaret Donaldson) that 'linguistic awareness' has to be learned; it does not develop as speaking (and walking on two legs) seem to do, by maturation. It is, unlike speaking, far from evenly distributed across the population. Some speakers are verbally conscious; they enjoy verbal play. Others do not. Wide variation in analytic competence, or linguistic awareness, contrasts with the relative consistency of primary communicative competence.

Mattingley argues that different writing systems make greater or lesser demands on linguistic awareness. Alphabetic writing, with its complex matching of symbol to sound, demands a higher degree of 'awareness' of language than logographic, or syllabary systems. We could add that the match, or mismatch, of written forms to spoken language (grapheme/phoneme matching) makes learning to read in English harder than in other languages using the Roman alphabet. It has been calculated that it takes English pupils, on average, over a year longer to learn to read than pupils in most other European countries. Spanish linguists have commented on the frequency with which English speakers spell out words to each other in conversation and how rarely one hears this done in Spain. Certainly the existence of possibly 2 million adult illiterates in England and Wales after 100 years of compulsory primary education suggests that reading in English presents special problems. It is often claimed that in languages with a close phoneme/grapheme match (such as Spanish, Finnish, or Japanese) the transition to reading does not pose such a problem.

The work of Donaldson, Mattingley and Bruner helps to explain a feature of reading failure that repeated studies have identified, namely the correlation between reading difficulties and family background. The *National Child Development Study* (Davie et al., 1972) showed that 48% of the children in social class v were poor readers at seven, compared with only 8% in social class i. In a comparative study reported in Bullock (1975) reading comprehension was tested in 15 countries and it was found in all cases that the child's family background gave an accurate prediction of his achievement in reading at age 10 and age 14. The reason why is suggested by Donaldson: 'in some homes awareness of the spoken word is greatly encouraged' but in other homes language remains embedded in the flow of events that accompany it.

When we speak of reading/writing being 'parasitic' upon awareness of spoken language we are not suggesting that the written form of English is simply a recording of spoken language in a visual form. The relationship between speech and writing is more complex. The written form has its own functions: 'once a writing system exists, it takes on a life of its own, becomes partly independent of speech and it is then often writing which influences speech rather than the reverse' (Stubbs, 1980). Some linguists would see speech and writing as two complementary realisations of an abstract language system; others would claim that the underlying language systems themselves differ in significant ways. The evidence seems compelling, nevertheless, that not only do hearing/speaking come before reading/writing chronologically (for all except congenitally deaf children) but the degree of sophisticated awareness that the child develops of his own hearing/speaking determines the confidence with which the next step into the written language will be taken.

For language awareness to develop, it seems that the *quality of the dialogue* with the parent that the child enjoys in the crucial pre-school years is all-important. This is not necessarily predicted by social class. Some middle-class homes do not offer children the precious 'adult-time' that is so necessary for the patient, unhurried exchanges to take place. There is, naturally, less possibility for such dialogue when the home is crowded, the mother is harassed or sick or alone or working, and when the parents themselves lack the precious verbal awareness and the education and imagination that could help them to develop it in their children.

The relevance of this for the teacher of modern languages is obvious. The study of a new language at adolescence, while immersed in English outside the language classroom, relying largely on written materials and tests and using a familiar Roman alphabet with new spelling rules, is obviously parasitic on a great deal of linguistic awareness learned in the acquisition of the mother tongue. It is a parasitic activity but at a further remove. It is dependent not only on analytic competence in the primary activity of listening/speaking, but also to a large extent on the secondary activity of reading an alphabetic script with added inter-language interference problems due to the learner's having already learnt one method of mapping alphabetic symbols onto sounds. One parasitic activity dependent on another but with some lessons to *un*learn!

This recalls, as so often in the realm of thought and language, the pioneering insights of Vygotsky. His *Thought and Language* was suppressed soon after his death in 1934 from tuberculosis at the tragically young age of 36. The work was not published until 1962. In a passage that is very relevant to the present discussion he compares the 'matching of verbal symbols with concepts' to the learning of a foreign language. Briefly summarised, his account is as follows. He distinguishes between two classes of concepts that children must acquire: 'spontaneous' concepts (such as *brother*) and 'scientific' concepts (such as *exploitation*). The spontaneous concept is unconscious, the scientific concept is one which the child is conscious of having made and one which he can discuss objectively and critically. The two kinds of concept interact:

mastering a higher level in the realm of scientific concepts also raises the level of spontaneous concepts. The child becomes conscious of his spontaneous concepts relatively late; the ability to define them in words, to operate them at will, appears long after he has acquired the concepts. . . . The development of a scientific concept, on the other hand, usually begins with its verbal definition and its use in non-spontaneous operations – with working on the concept itself. . . . A child's everyday concept, such as 'brother', is saturated with experience. Yet when he is asked to solve an abstract problem about a brother's brother, as in Piaget's experiments, he becomes confused. On the other hand, though he can correctly answer questions about 'slavery', 'exploitation' or 'civil war', these concepts are schematic and lack the rich content derived from personal experience. They are filled in gradually, in the course of further school work and reading. . . . The influence of scientific concepts on the mental development of the child *is analogous to the effect of learning a foreign language* [our italics], a process which is conscious and deliberate from the start. The child's strong points in a foreign language are his weak points in his native language and vice versa. (p. 109)

Vygotsky probably had in mind a picture of foreign language teaching in which vocabulary was more formally taught than it is nowadays, at least in the early stages. Nevertheless his distinction between the two kinds of concept formation remains substantially valid. The interest for us of his pioneering distinction between the 'conscious' and 'unconscious' matching of verbal labels to concepts is not simply that it presages current interest in linguistic awareness, but that it suggests a valuable, even unique, role for second language learning in a full linguistic education.

Developing 'awareness' of language

In some comprehensive schools experience has shown that, when slow readers are withdrawn from French classes and given 'remedial' reading classes in English instead, they make slower progress at reading English. How could this be explained? The clue is given by Jerome Bruner:

I must report that in my own research and that of my collaborators, e.g. Bruner, Olver and Greenfield [1966], schooling appears to have a profound effect on a large number of mental processes, and I am rather convinced that the chief effect of schooling is to cultivate during development the use of language outside the context of action – and [quoting De Laguna] 'language context comes more and more to take the place of perceptual context'. (Bruner, 1975, pp. 63, 69)

Bruner contrasts the 'analytic competence' required in school with mere 'communicative competence' or Margaret Donaldson's 'language embedded in experience'. Can it be shown conclusively that learning a foreign language helps the pupil to acquire Bruner's 'analytic competence'? It must be said that hard research evidence is meagre. The work simply has not been done.

The NFER evaluation of the primary school French project made some attempt to measure the effect of French on pupils' verbal skills in the mother tongue. The conclusion was that French exerts no significant influence on achievement in other areas of the primary school curriculum. However the research design did not allow any distinction to be made between schools which taught French using audio-visual or mim-mem methods (the majority) and others which set out deliberately in their French teaching to encourage perception of pattern in language, the ability to complete patterns by analogy, or the mapping of spoken sounds onto written symbols. Nor did the NFER study distinguish between schools in which the French lessons took the place of English lessons and those where French was offered without reducing the time given to English.

That teaching French with emphasis on grasp of linguistic pattern and structure can affect cognition is strongly suggested by some research at Leeds University (Lupson, 1977). In a study of pupils in comprehensive schools in Leeds and Liverpool, Lupson showed that at least in one cognitive skill, namely perception of pattern in language and the ability to construct new forms by analogy with perceived patterns, pupils clearly benefited from a year's teaching in French by 'pattern perception' methods. Lupson is scrupulous in not generalising from his limited evidence but his work shows a clear transfer to perception of pattern in another language (Swedish) from skills practised in the French classroom. An earlier piece of research pointing the same way was that of Estacio in Manila (Estacio, 1971). He reported results which clearly supported the assumption that instruction in a foreign language has a direct effect on the development of cognitive processes. Other researches showing clear benefits to mother tongue and cognition generally from foreign language study are those of Skelton (1957) and Lopato (1961). Against these a number of studies are quoted in Burstall (1974) which show neither beneficial nor deleterious effects.

The author's own experience of introducing French and teaching it for eight years in a secondary modern school, all of whose pupils had been rejected at the 11+ examination as unfit for an academic course, left no possible doubt of the beneficial feedback upon other subjects, especially English.

The contribution of the foreign language in the early stages for the slower learner seems to be to offer a new experience of word play, Bruner's 'operation of thought processes on linguistic representations', but in a new medium. At home in the pre-school period something was missing. The slower learner failed to relish verbal play in the primary school because of the initial difficulty with the reading code. Children like doing what they feel confident at. Most primary school mother-tongue programmes reinforce the inequalities of home background. The foreign language offers a fresh beginning.[6] But a beginning at what precisely? The following are some specific ways in which the foreign language can contribute to developing 'awareness' of language:

1   the opportunity to 'recategorise' some areas of experience that the primary schooling has left imprecise, such as the calendar (uncertainty as to which month follows which or how many days are in each month); telling the time; mental arithmetic; concepts of colour, of shape, of texture. Sir Alec Clegg, in Clegg and Megson (1968), reminds us of West Riding five-year-olds who came to school unable to count beyond five and uncertain of the primary colours. Many such children enter secondary school still uncertain of the order and length of the months of the calendar and with other more serious gaps in the conceptual categorising of the universe that the secondary curriculum has to build on. The foreign language offers a neutral medium in which to rehearse such basic concepts without appearing to call attention to the weaker pupils' shortcomings. It is as if children get a fresh chance to read the finer print in the account of the universe they find themselves in, without being branded as needing remedial help.

2   a useful 're-education' of the ear. Children need to learn to listen for meaning and the early stages of the foreign language course can be a very useful apprenticeship and a most enjoyable one, if the listening games are imaginatively developed and really stretch the pupils: see the interesting games designed to promote 'thinking with the ears' in Furth and Wachs (1974).

3   a challenging apprenticeship in matching (new) sounds to written symbols. This 'cross-modality' skill, which underlies confident and enjoyable reading, is one which many pupils have failed to master confidently in the primary school and it is very useful to be able to tackle the problems in a new, neutral medium. The confidence given by growing skill in matching sounds to the regular written spellings of, say, Spanish, feeds back upon reading English.

4   exploration of structures which contrast with English (e.g. new ways of counting, of asking questions or of expressing negatives) which directly promote growing awareness of how language works, while teaching the lesson that English is only one way, not *the* way, in which meaning can be expressed.

5   help in discriminating nuances of meaning in English by exploring alternatives in the foreign language which do not exactly match the English (an obvious example would be learning to understand and to use the two Spanish verbs 'to be', *ser* and *estar*, and later to see how a similar dichotomy distinguishes for example, *saber* (to know) from *aprender* (to learn) (see Chapter 3).

The above observations are supported by a communication received just as these lines are being written, from a teacher-educator in Haifa University who reports: 'I have found that . . . reading skills, often very poor in the native tongue, can also be taught and developed via the foreign language. These youngsters, at the sensitive age of 15–17, reject studies of so basic a nature in their own language (interpreted by them as "childish" and "old hat"). Yet they exhibit quite a degree of receptivity when the vehicle is new, neutral and recognised as a "status" subject of study.'

Need for a new concept of 'language' in the curriculum

We are arguing then for the foreign language seen as part of a continuous education in language beginning in the primary school; for the integration of the foreign language apprenticeship vertically into a language education that is continuous through primary and secondary school, and horizontally as part of the trivium of mother tongue/'awareness of language'/foreign language.

A growing number of schools are experimenting, with foreign language teachers in the lead, with 'awareness of language' programmes of this kind. It is not easy. Teachers of English and of foreign languages have hitherto been educated and trained in isolation from each other. Most English teachers will know little about phonology or language acquisition if their degree studies have been confined to English literature. Very few are capable of reading fluently in a foreign language. Foreign language teachers are equally unaware of what is done in English classrooms. In some schools, however, the teachers of the mother tongue and the teachers of the foreign language have begun to cooperate, the two jointly teaching 'awareness of language' to bridge the 'space between' their two disciplines. (See Appendix C.)

Foreign languages in the core curriculum: conditions for success

Despite the disenchantment of the 1970s the case for including the foreign language in the core curriculum for slower as well as faster learners is irrefutable provided, and the proviso is substantial:

1 we define different foreign language objectives for pupils whose abilities and interests differ
2 we use appropriate methods, materials and *assessments*
3 we prepare pupils by 'education of the ear' and awareness of language in the primary school
4 we integrate foreign language learning in the secondary school into a coherent three-part 'language' curriculum (the new trivium, see Part III) planned as an apprenticeship in learning to be a citizen in a multi-cultural community and a polyglot world.

None of these conditions has so far been fulfilled. To attempt to meet them will call for changes in thinking which some teachers will find hard to accept.

Before we turn to examine these we have one remaining 'why' question to answer: Why should 'foreign language' in British schools necessarily mean 'French'?

NOTES

1 A counter-example of a philosopher who would make a foreign
  language a compulsory element in the curriculum is Raymond
  Williams. In *The Long Revolution* (Williams, 1961) he lists five elements
  which should necessarily form part of a general education:
  1   fundamentals of English and Mathematics
  2   knowledge of oneself and one's environment
  3   study of history and criticism of literature, the visual arts,
      drama, landscape and architecture
  4   the practice of democratic procedures and the study of sources
      of information
  5   an introduction to the study of at least one other culture, includ-
      ing the study of its language.
  It is relevant to add that, without waiting for the philosophers to
  agree, our politicians have already made up their minds. The United
  Kingdom is committed by the rules of the two European groupings
  that we have joined (Council of Europe resolution 1969 and EEC
  report of the Council of Ministers 1974) to aim to offer all pupils the
  chance to learn at least one other Community language.

2 i.e. courses including practical language skills and non-literary
  aspects of 'civilisation' at Salford, Bradford and Surrey Universities,
  Lanchester Polytechnic and Ealing Technical College.

3 It is of Fray Luis that legend tells that on being released from prison,
  and returning to his chair of theology at Salamanca, by way of
  comment on five lost years he quietly began his lecture with the
  customary phrase: 'Decíamos ayer' ('As we were saying yesterday').

4 About eighty versions of short-term graded test schemes are known
  to be operating in sixty local authorities. Their progress is being
  monitored by a committee based on the Centre for Information on
  Language Teaching.

5 The well-known eight grades in piano, violin, etc., widely used by
  teachers of music, motivate young instrumentalists in their long and
  hard climb up the slopes of Parnassus. It is perhaps less well known
  that Trinity College (of Music) has for some years been operating a
  series of graded tests in English as a Foreign Language which are
  increasingly popular with students of English language abroad.
  There are twelve grades, ranging from Grade 1 (ability to exchange
  greetings and answer short questions such as 'what month is it?'
  'what colour is this flower?') to Grade 12 (retelling a story heard once,
  discuss three prepared books, deliver a prepared five-minute talk,
  hold a conversation and retell *in writing* a story heard once).

6 This is of course not to argue that the slower learner starts his French
  level with his verbally more 'aware' contemporaries. Clare Burstall
  (1974, p. 243) dismisses as 'cruelly naïve' those who 'cling to the belief
  that by introducing French at an early age, all children will begin their
  study of the language from an equal standpoint . . . some children
  are highly proficient in the use of their own language – accustomed to
  success – other children have become accustomed to failure, etc.'.

This is well understood by teachers in the classroom who listen sensitively to their pupils. They are unlikely to underestimate the great difference that separates the verbally 'aware' eleven-year-olds from those who can scarcely read. But it is not 'cruelly naïve' to report, as a matter of observation, that, for the verbally unaware, discouraged child with a history of failure, the switch to a new language in which to play verbal games with no previous history of failure can offer a fresh start. Recent medical research by doctors treating the mentally sick by teaching a foreign language supports the idea that getting away from the emotional connotations of the mother tongue may be necessary for some learners. A. Matulis in Detroit found that with schizophrenic patients a foreign language is more neutral and acts as a 'tranquilizer'. He taught German to 23 patients in a locked ward. After six months the patients, at first unkempt, incontinent and shrieking abuse, became calm and began helping each other. 'These patients were able to leave behind the emotionally loaded world of their mother tongue and this finally enabled them to return to their own language and speak more coherently.' (Matulis, 1977)

3   Why French?

French was chosen as the language for the [Pilot Scheme] experiment for a number of reasons. In the first place, although English has supplanted French as the principal international language, French remains clearly the second most widely used international language; on a more practical level, the proximity of France was clearly an advantage and, however difficult it might be to provide the necessary training for primary and secondary teachers to implement an experiment in French, the difficulties presented by any other language would be greater. Moreover, it was felt that the claims of German, Russian and Spanish would be met, to a considerable extent, by the increased opportunities for the learning of a second modern language at the secondary stage, which the experiment, if successful, would open up.

Schools Council Working Paper No. 8, *French in the Primary School*, 1966

Who decides the curriculum?

Let us put ourselves in the position of a teacher who has had the good fortune to be appointed Head of a new 11 to 18 comprehensive school, to be established in an area of planned growth such as, say, the new Selby coalfield in South Yorkshire, surely one of the most exciting challenges that our profession could offer. One of the Head's earliest decisions, before he (or she – we assume 'he' purely to get round the awkwardness of the English syntax) can appoint a nucleus of staff, must be the choice of a first foreign language.

Surprising as it must seem to teachers in other countries, where schools neither possess nor claim such autonomy, the choice of which foreign language to offer and when, like other decisions about the curriculum, is the prerogative of the Head of the school, sometimes advised by HMI, under the general direction of the school governors. The Head's autonomy in deciding the curriculum has been obstinately defended. David Eccles discovered this when, in March 1962, he took a first tentative step into what he called the 'secret garden' of the curriculum by setting up, within the (then) Ministry of Education, a 'Curriculum Study Group' (CSG).[1] In 1964 the 'sadly misunderstood'[2] Curriculum Study Group and the discredited Secondary Schools Examinations Council were merged in the new Schools Council for Curriculum and Examinations.

The Schools Council was routinely attacked, as the Curriculum Study Group had been, by the professional bodies representing teachers and Heads. Fortunately a far-sighted civil servant, Derek Morrell, resisted the clamour and the concept of a national body concerned with the curriculum survived the cries that it threatened fundamental freedoms. Such a national body had, in fact, been recommended exactly 100 years earlier, in 1864, by the Clarendon (Public Schools) Commission. The 'secret garden' was indeed powerfully defended!

Why the autonomy of each individual Head of school in deciding the curriculum should be defended so passionately is difficult to explain. Heads of schools are rarely given training in curriculum planning before appointment. Most Heads on appointment have experience of teaching only their own specialist subject. After success in an interview they are presumed, overnight, to be invested (by magic?) with insight into the value in the curriculum of subjects of which their own knowledge is negligible or years out of date. Those who opposed the Schools Council in 1964, and who now oppose central guidance from HMI, take the view apparently that this autonomy in curriculum decisions given to Heads so ill-equipped for their responsibility is a precious safeguard against central dictatorship. Yet they can scarcely deny that some planning is needed. The Crowther Report (1959) called for 'rethinking the whole basis of the teaching of linguistics in the schools'. A subsequent circular from the Ministry of Education (*Circular* 2/64) spoke of the 'need to bring about a major development in the teaching of languages if this country is to maintain its competitive position in overseas markets'. But whose responsibility is it to re-think or develop? Curricula are in fact shaped in an unplanned, fortuitous way by several powerful agencies which were designed for quite different purposes. The GCE Boards often determine curricula in some detail, yet these Boards are staffed solely for the very different purpose of examining. University decisions about entrance requirements (sometimes arrived at more by drift than by taking thought, as we saw in the story of the language requirement) also powerfully limit the school's autonomy. Is the university don, even if less 'remote and ineffectual' than in Belloc's day, qualified to determine adolescent teaching programmes, especially for the majority of pupils, whom he will never meet because they do not proceed to university, but whose curriculum is inevitably influenced by the selection process? Should it be the responsiblity of the Local Education Authority? Would anyone claim that LEAs are staffed with persons qualified to plan school programmes?

These powerful agencies hover over the schools and, in the vacuum in the middle, school Heads exercise their precious freedom to teach their pupils what they think fit. Each Head's scope for manoeuvre will differ as will his qualifications to make the right decisions. He will take what advice he can get from his senior colleagues. It would be optimistic to expect that the latter would always proffer enlightened views based on acquaintance with the best contemporary practice in this country and abroad. National guidelines from Schools Council or HMI would surely be an improvement on the present chaotic drift. In fact, the Schools Council, dominated by blinkered teachers' unions competing with each other for members, failed to provide the vision hoped for. It has been left to HMI, increasingly outspoken during the 1970s on curriculum matters, to give the most clearly discernible national lead. They will, it is to be hoped, in the 1980s, issue unequivocal national guidelines to be backed by a revitalised Schools Council. Meanwhile, the Head's responsibility in South Yorkshire will not wait. He must trust his own judgement, in deciding which language to choose. At least he has no legacy of existing staffing strengths and weaknesses to pre-empt his decisions, though likely availability of teachers must be a consideration. He will first, presumably, wish to examine the present balance of languages in schools and ask how far it seems justified.

Entrenched position of French

The starting-point must be a realistic look at the entrenched position of French. The Annan Committee, reporting in 1962, had this to say:

French is safeguarded by geography and tradition; it will naturally remain an important language in this country, the more so if Britain joins the Common Market. As France is our nearest neighbour and French history and culture are part of our heritage, French is nearly always the first modern language to be taught. Its choice is not particularly determined by pressure from the universities, for only a few university departments specifically demand French as an entrance qualification with no option. Nevertheless, because of its position in the schools, French is taken by more university students than any other language and this in turn ensures a good supply of teachers in the schools. French enjoys good conditions also in the supply and quality of teaching aids, in ease of contacts with France and in the mass of knowledge derived from experience of teaching it. (Paragraph 56.)

It was not surprising that when the decision was made, in 1963, to launch a national experiment in teaching a modern language in primary schools, French was chosen. The then staff inspector for modern languages, Dr D. C. Riddy, answered critics in the Schools Council Working Paper No. 8 (1966)

'Why French?' The question has often been asked – understandably since it is often said that the country needs more men and women understanding German, Russian, Spanish – why French was chosen as the language for the scheme. The answer is that, other considerations apart, only in French could we have hoped to find the necessary number of teachers. Almost all primary teachers have had at least a five-year course in French when they were at school themselves, and it seemed reasonable to hope that, with additional local courses and the provision of intensive courses, many of them would be able to teach the language in the primary schools . . . if a language other than French had been contemplated, it would have taken many years to get a pilot scheme off the ground.

There are other good arguments in favour of adhering to a single language. The movement of pupils from area to area is one, and the repercussions for the secondary schools, if a diversity of languages is taught at the primary stage, is another. (p. 30)

There is evidence that outside the Pilot Scheme a considerable amount of uncoordinated teaching of French was developing in primary schools in the early 1960s: 'Of 14,000 schools, in 119 areas, which provided information, some 21% were already providing primary French of some kind. Moreover 72% of the LEAs who responded were already providing refresher courses for teachers, and all in French' (Lazaro, 1963).

The Pilot Scheme, then, did not entrench French in the primary curriculum. The language was rapidly digging in before the scheme was launched. On the other hand the outcome of the Pilot Scheme did nothing to encourage the development of the other European languages to which the promoters of the Pilot Scheme had looked forward.[3]

Schools Council Working Paper No. 8 had expressed the hope

'that the claims of German, Russian and Spanish would be met to a considerable extent by the increased opportunities for the learning of a second modern language at the secondary stage which the experiment, if successful, would open up', and stated that

One of the important theoretical advantages of teaching French in primary schools is that, by the time pupils enter their secondary schools, enough evidence should have been accumulated about pupils' linguistic aptitudes to enable a prompt start to be made on a second language [i.e. at 11+]. With longer courses, the development of second languages should be much more satisfactory for both teachers and pupils. (p. 59)

The Nuffield/Schools Council courses in the three 'minority languages' produced for the age range 11 to 16 (*Vorwärts, Adelante* and *Vperyod!*) were intended to encourage the secondary schools to experiment along the lines suggested in the Working Paper.

In practice this did not happen:

Only comparatively rarely (by 1970) had those secondary schools which offer pupils in their third or subsequent year the possibility of learning a second modern language brought this opportunity forward to their first or second year pupils. . . . On the other hand a few secondary schools which had previously offered German or Spanish as a first modern foreign language had changed to French because they now had first year pupils who had already started French. (Schools Council Modern Languages Project, 1970)

This effect of the Pilot Scheme was a great disappointment to teachers of the 'minority' languages because these had, in fact, steadily been gaining ground relative to French.

In Schools Council Working Paper No. 8 Dr D. C. Riddy, HMI, compared entries for School Certificate in 1938 with GCE entries in 1963. Adopting his presentation and updating the tables to include GCE and CSE entries for the years 1965 and 1985, the picture is given in the table on page 66. This shows a steady fall in the percentage of entries for modern languages as a whole coupled with a continuing erosion of the entrenched position of French compared with the 'minority' languages. In 1938 entries for French represented about 13.6% of total subject entries. By 1985 this percentage (taking GCE and CSE entries together) had fallen to 4.9.

Entries for modern languages other than French (and Welsh) represented some 15.9% of entries for French in 1938. By 1965 entries for the 'minority' languages had risen to 31% of entries for French and by 1985 the percentage was 44.2% in GCE 'O' level and 24% in CSE (33.7% overall).

Entries for School Certificate in 1938, 'O' level GCE and CSE in 1965 and 1985

Entries for:	1938 (SC)	1965 (GCE O)	1965 (CSE)	1985 (GCE O)	1985 (CSE)
English language	77,358	346,688	41,487	519,684*	666,125*
French	72,466	163,651	8,345	147,657*	163,326*
German	9,935	32,737	986	42,616	31,855
Spanish	1,338	9,776	235	11,749	6,020
Italian	245	2,895	–	2,389	646
Russian	4	2,374	19	1,375	179
Other modern langs	15	2,539	6	7,142 (incl. Welsh)	934 (incl. Welsh)
Welsh as foreign language	2,886	2,133	152	–	–
Latin	28,735	52,420	20	19,928	5,018
Greek	2,049	2,647	–	1,303	–
Total subject entries	531,445	2,170,019	230,977	3,066,764	3,231,017

* including pupils entered for combined GCE/CSE examinations; thus these figures are slightly inflated

Notes:

1 School Certificate entries give a reasonable picture of the balance of languages studied in secondary schools in the last year before wartime constraints began to have effect. Comparison with GCE entries alone, however, would be misleading. CSE entries must be taken into account as comprehensive reorganisation gathered momentum from the mid-sixties onwards.

2 Many pupils entering for the 'minority' languages also entered for French. These tables do not show how many pupils took a 'minority' language as their sole foreign language.

At 18+, in Higher School Certificate and GCE 'A' level, the pattern is similar:

Entries for HSC in 1938 and GCE 'A' level in 1965 and 1985

Entries for:	1938 (HSC)	1965 (GCE 'A')		1985 (GCE 'A')	
(English is omitted since at this level there was no 'language' paper)					
French	4,752	25,599	(14,378)	22,140	(16,093)
German	899	7,107	(3,535)	7,949	(5,741)
Spanish	138	2,213	(1,016)	2,615	(1,900)
Italian	2	585	(327)	668	(457)
Russian	–	602	(252)	307	(175)
Other MLs					
incl. Welsh	103	422	(189)	1,320	(709)
Latin	2,589	7,901	(3,737)	2,216	(1,305)
Greek	881	1,322	(232)	469	(164)
Total subject					
entries	36,951	370,435	(126,616)	609,215	(288,979)

Note: The figures in brackets show girls' entries alone.

At 18+ entries for French in Higher School Certificate in 1938 represented about 12.8% of total subject entries. By 1965 entries for French had fallen to 6.9%, and by 1985 to only 3.6%, of all subject entries. Of the dwindling total, girls' entries accounted for 56.1% in 1965. By 1985 girls' entries represented 72.7% of the total French entry. Though all languages lost ground relative to total subject entry, none fared as badly as French. In 1938 entries for the 'minority' languages were about 22% of French entries, in 1965 42.6% and in 1985 58%.

Though the 'minority' languages continue to improve their position relative to French, the position of modern languages as a whole, relative to the growth of subject entries, becomes steadily weaker. The numbers of candidates offering the 'minority' languages remains low, in some cases alarmingly so, since very small sixth-form teaching groups are wasteful of resources and vulnerable in times of economic stringency. Falling school rolls further threaten the continuation of sixth-form subjects that attract only small numbers.

To conform or to rebel?

In the light of the national picture, of French strongly entrenched and reinforced by recent developments at primary level but with the minority languages steadily catching up, the Head of school must choose between:

1 Acceptance of the present entrenched position of French as first language
2 Making a bold decision to select one or other of the minority languages as first foreign language
3 Choosing a language to share this position with French if two 'first' foreign languages can be offered in parallel
4 Offering French and another language in alternating years, as some schools do.

The arguments affecting this difficult decision can be summarised under the following headings:

1. Administrative constraints

We consider these first because unless we can staff and administer our curriculum discussion of its merits is academic.

The constraints to consider are:

a availability of staff and prospects for replacement
b accessibility of the foreign speech community (cost and freedom of travel, etc.)
c availability of good teaching materials
d constraints such as needs of pupils moving in and out of school catchment area
e the possible effects on staffing, and on feasibility of options, of the imminent fall in school rolls due to the fluctuation in the birthrate.

2. Extrinsic usefulness

a national 'need' for particular languages (potential usefulness in employment and higher education)
b regional contacts with particular countries
c existing balance of provision of languages within the L E A area (at primary level in feeder schools as well as in other secondary schools).

3. Intrinsic value as 'apprenticeship in language learning'

a value of a particular language in itself as contribution to learner's personal development: suitability as introduction to language learning b relative difficulty (likelihood of pupil experiencing early success and satisfaction)

c interest of the literature, music, art, society to which the language opens the door.

Administrative constraints

The first constraint is availability of staffing. The following table sets out the total numbers of graduate language teachers trained in the five main languages in 1986/7

Main foreign languages offered by graduates following PGCE courses in University Departments of Education and Colleges/Polytechnics 1986/7

	University Departments	Colleges/ polytechnics	Total
French	369	129	498
German	161	30	191
Spanish	18	8	26
Russian	9	0	9
Italian	2	0	2

(Some graduates offer two main languages.)
(Statistics supplied by the Graduate Teacher Training Registry)

The number of graduates trained to teach the 'minority' languages has fallen sharply in the last 12 years:

		1974	1986
Graduates following main courses in:	Spanish	60	26
	Russian	30	9
	Italian	9	2

Italian

The figures reveal to what an extent Italian is a neglected language. In Tudor times Italian was the principal foreign language studied in England. It was replaced by French from the reign of Charles II and has never recovered its place. Italian has much to offer. Modern Italian differs little from the language of Dante, Petrarch and Boccaccio. It also opens up a world of music, opera, painting, sculpture and architecture of incomparable richness, for the student and for the tourist. Italian films and motor engineering challenge the best in the world. Few countries in the world can compare with Italy in beauty and climate which, with the vivacity of her northern city states, made her the cradle of the Renaissance. If modern language studies give to those willing to work at them the key to new kingdoms the Italian key unlocks rich treasures indeed, offering rapid and rewarding progress to the beginner and subtleties enough to engross the specialist.

There is the strongest possible case for building up a supply of teachers of Italian by:

a   beginners' courses in sixth forms
b   'crash' courses at university level and during initial training[4]
c   research and development in teaching materials similar to that promoted by the Nuffield Foundation in the other four main European languages.

For the present, however, the staffing situation alone rules out a choice of Italian as the *main* language in our comprehensive schools.

Russian

The position of Russian is equally disappointing. The Annan Committee (Annan, 1962) made out an overwhelming case for the development of Russian, the lingua franca of over half the population of Europe, at all levels. The Annan Report was followed by a considerable growth in the teaching of Russian, though this fell far short of the Annan recommendation of parity with German. Before 1957 Russian was taught in fewer than 50 schools. The Nuffield/Association of Teachers of Russian survey in 1966 showed that some 485 schools were teaching Russian. A further survey in 1970 showed an increase to over 800 schools. By 1973, however, over 100 of these schools no longer offered Russian (for reasons which we have touched on in our discussion of the Primary French Project). The number of pupils offering Russian has continued to fall. Between 1970 and 1985 entries for GCE 'O' level fell from 3,769 to 1,375. Entries for 'A' level fell from 810 to 307. There was a similar fall in the small numbers of entries for CSE from 232 to 179. This is, of course, an indication of the extent to which the study of Russian is limited to the 'academic' streams in secondary schools. In January 1980 the University Grants Commission proposed the closing of 6 university Russian departments and the phasing out of 13 others as a consequence of the fall in student recruitment. This represents the tragic closing of doors in higher education on one of the great languages and literatures of the world as well as on Russian science, medicine and technology.

It is claimed by experienced teachers that the difficulty of Russian is more apparent than real. The 'barrier' of the Cyrillic script can, they claim, be overcome by gradual introduction of spelling and by playing 'encoding' games in the classroom. Once the alphabet is learned, spelling matches pronunciation well. (Whether St Cyril invented the alphabet or, as some claim, the credit should go to St Clement of Bulgaria, the saintly phonetical work was well done.)

Arguments concerning difficulty, which we must pursue when considering French and Spanish later, are academic, however, in this connection, because the choice of Russian as our main first language in the secondary school is ruled out for geographical reasons. It is an essential requirement of our 'apprenticeship language' that we must offer all our pupils the chance to visit and get to know well the country whose language they are studying. Until Russia becomes much more accessible, with fares within most families' means, and communications and publications are freely exchanged, Russian must remain a second language.

For administrative reasons of staffing and accessibility, then, we must rule out Italian and Russian as first 'apprenticeship' languages. The remaining three languages, French, German and Spanish, pose fewer administrative problems, French being obviously of the three the easiest to staff and easiest of access. Three other administrative considerations argue for retaining some French from 11+:

1   mobility of families across LEA boundaries in the 1980s will require that schools make provision for pupils entering in mid-course. Statistics warn us that the vast majority of such entrants from other schools will already have started French
2   despite the decline in the early teaching of French, the language is still begun below the age of 11+ in some 20% of schools (Hoy, 1977). The expectations set up in feeder schools cannot be disregarded
3   falling school rolls will entail reductions in staffing, making it more difficult to provide courses in several languages. This can only strengthen the considerations in 1 and 2 above.

Within our administrative constraints what can be said about our other two criteria, 'national need' and 'intrinsic value as apprenticeship'?

National 'need'

The concept of national 'need' for a particular language is elusive. It is necessary first to distinguish between 'real needs' (e.g. language skills of which employers in industry and commerce have need, did they but know it!) and 'felt needs' (i.e. needs of which employers are aware and which in practice they attempt to meet). In the Nuffield Foundation three-year study of the use of languages in industry carried out at York (Emmans et al., 1974), most of the firms investigated showed a high degree of complacency concerning the language skills of their work force. Even among the top dozen firms in the *Times* annual list of 1,000 with the biggest turnover, including firms with wide international ramifications, there were personnel directors who told the York investigators: 'We should like to help you – by distributing your questionnaire to members of our workforce who possess language skills – but we keep no such records! We simply do not know, and it will take us weeks to find out, which of our employees has, or has not, any language skills.' Clearly a firm with such a bland approach to the polyglot nature of the world with which it was doing business could not be expected to know what industry's real needs are in language skills. It could only report its own felt needs, which were minimal.

If the felt needs of employers for language skills do not reflect real national needs, how could the latter be assessed? Some tentative indication might be given by the size of the potential markets for our exports, since our island, importing as it does every alternate spoonful of food that its people eat, can survive only by exporting goods and services in return. A mere count of the number of speakers in the speech communities to which we export is less significant than the consumption per head of the goods we can offer. Nevertheless, total numbers of speakers are a starting-point. The following table shows the 22 most widely spoken languages, with approximate numbers of mother-tongue speakers. The first ten languages listed account for some two-thirds of the population of the world.

Measured by number of speakers, French barely gets in the top dozen, with Russian, Spanish and German speakers greatly out-numbering French. Merely counting heads, however, may be a less useful measure of potential national need of language skills than counting numbers of customers for U K exports. This gives a very different picture.

Main languages of the world and mother-tongue speakers

1.	(Chinese) Peking Dialect (Mandarin):	515 million
2.	English:	300 million
	(plus hundreds of millions of non-native speakers)	
3	Spanish (Spain and America):	225 million
	(including the Ladino spoken in Turkey and Israel)	
4.	Hindi:	180 million
5.	Russian:	150 million
	(plus some 42 million who speak it fluently as second language)	
6.	Bengali:	125 million
7.	Arabic:	120 million
	(plus many millions who have some knowledge of it)	
8.	Portuguese:	103 million
	(including 3 million Gallicians)	
9.	Japanese:	100 million
10.	German:	100 million
11.	Bantu:	100 million
	(there are more than 100 Bantu languages)	
12.	French:	75 million
	(including creoles, plus many speakers familiar with French)	
13.	Italian:	60 million
14.	(Chinese) Cantonese:	55 million
15.	Korean:	51 million
16.	(Chinese) Min dialect:	50 million
17.	(Chinese) Wu dialect:	50 million
18.	Javanese (Indonesia):	45 million
19.	Telegu:	45 million
20.	Tamil (India and Sri Lanka):	45 million
21.	Urdu:	35 million
	(plus some 45 million who speak it as second language)	
22.	Ukrainian:	35 million

(after Kenneth Katzner, *The Languages of the World*. Routledge and Kegan Paul, 1977)

Britain's trading position in a polyglot world

Over the period 1967–83 the percentage of Britain's exports going to English-speaking markets fell sharply, as shown on p. 74.

If these figures suggest anything it is that Britain's market for exports in the near future will increasingly involve buyers whose native language is not English. The increase in exports to French-

UK exports to major English-speaking markets:	Percentage of total UK exports:	
	1967	1983
USA		
Canada		
Australia	28.2%	19.2%
New Zealand		
S. Africa		

Exports to our EEC European partners:	Percentage of total UK exports:	
	1967	1983
Exports to all EEC countries	26.6	43.6
Exports to Germany and GDR	5.6	10.1
Exports to France, Belgium and Luxembourg	7.7	13.5

The greatest percentage increase was to the 19 oil-exporting countries (mainly Arabic speaking):

	1967	1983
Exports to 19 oil-producing states	5.1	10.1

Exports to other countries changed little:

	1967	1983
Exports to USSR	1.2	0.7
Exports to Japan	1.7	1.3
Exports to Spain and five major Spanish-speaking S. American states	3.5	4.2
Exports to Italy	3.0	3.7

speaking countries, to Germany and to the Arabic-speaking countries, is marked.

A related question is how far school provision of language skills determines the felt needs of employers. The York study (Emmans et al., 1974) analysed the use of languages in a representative sample of 40 firms, on the eve of Britain's entry to the EEC. Part of the York study was a survey of 4,258 advertisements for jobs mentioning a language requirement in four national newspapers in the 12 months ending May 1972. In all, 29 languages were mentioned. The majority of these, however, were mentioned fewer than ten times. Some advertisements mentioned several languages. French was mentioned in just over half the advertisements with German not far behind (51% and 40% respectively). The following table shows the languages asked for as first (or only) language:

	Percentage of advertisements
French	45.0
German	22.5
Spanish	5.6
Italian	3.0
Russian	0.8
Other European languages	9.9
Middle and Far Eastern languages	1.1
Unspecified languages	12.1

It is impossible to say how much the employers were influenced, in framing their advertisements, by their expectation of finding applicants with the language skills specified. Presumably few employers waste money on advertising for skills which they do not expect to find.

On the other hand the York team found little evidence of employers attempting to supplement the existing school and university provision of language skills. There were only 80 instances of language graduates in industry (some 10% of the total of graduates contacted) undertaking language training at the suggestion of employers. The languages studied on the initiative of the employer were:

Language	Number of times mentioned
German	13
Italian	12
Russian	12
French	10
Spanish (and S. American languages)	9 (+2)
Arabic	6
Polish	2
Portuguese	1
Rumanian	1

Language	Number of times mentioned
Swedish	1
Asian languages	6
Other European languages	4
African languages	1

It is interesting that the York team's analysis of all employees' use of languages in the sample of 40 firms surveyed showed the same order as the survey of advertisements:

French   used by 79.9% of all employees using a language in their job
German used by 54.9% of all employees using a language in their job
Spanish used by 22.6% of all employees using a language in their job
Italian   used by 13.3% of all employees using a language in their job
Russian used by 5.4% of all employees using a language in their job

In both of the above tables the position of French may reflect the substantial output of French from the formal educational system. If we are to attach any weight to the elusive concept of 'national need' it would seem, from the export figures and from the York survey, that though the balance of numbers studying French and German respectively may not be quite right, yet these are the two languages in greatest demand.

What we can never predict, however, is that the particular pupil who learns French at school will need French (and not German or some other language) in adult life; any balance between language provision in the school system and national 'need' could only be a paper balance. It would be possible to have the balance exactly right, yet discover that all or most of the pupils who studied German in fact later took jobs or developed interests in which French was required and vice versa.

The argument from vocational need is further weakened when we reflect that the majority of our pupils in the comprehensive school, destined to drive tractors, serve in shops, or work in mines or factories, even if they escape unemployment, will rarely need a foreign language as an ancillary skill in their job and it would be dishonest to pretend otherwise. The case for the foreign language as an ancillary skill for pupils who stay on in sixth forms or go on to further education courses is obviously much stronger since they can make a meaningful choice of

language in the light of the career possibilities opening up for
them. If, instead of looking at vocational needs, we considered
regional interests or links with particular countries as a guide to
choice of language for the majority we might be on stronger
ground. Whatever job a particular pupil was destined for, the fact
that, for example, the district of Humberside has growing contacts with Holland, Germany and Scandinavia might be a reason
for introducing Dutch, German and Swedish into Humberside
schools. At least then we could be sure that the school's choice of
a foreign language would be supported by interest in the locality
among parents, civic leaders, employers (even possibly among
trades unions?).

Where no clear regional interest can be detected a valid extrinsic criterion would be the maintenance of a balance of language
provision between schools within a given area. This would serve
both to keep the task of FE establishments within reasonable
bounds and to offer parents, especially parents moving into a
new area, a choice of foreign language courses. This was the
solution proposed by the Sussex/CILT Colloquium of five LEAs
in the South East (Bearne and James, 1976): 'The present unplanned predominance of one language should be replaced by a
system of agreed variation of first foreign language . . . a group of
up to six schools might form a suitable number for agreed variation of first foreign language.'[5]

The conclusion from all this, for the Head of school planning
his curriculum, must be that arguments from national, vocational
need for any particular language are hard to sustain. What of
intrinsic considerations?

Apprenticeship: learning how to learn languages
If the school experience is seen as apprenticeship and if we
grant that the language learnt at school may not be the one later
needed, if one *is* needed, in employment, we are at once on more
solid ground.

We can ask: what is it that makes a language suitable as apprenticeship in language learning in school? Probably the overriding
criterion is that the experience shall be an enjoyable, because
successful, one. This means that the language chosen for school
study should not be excessively difficult.

Difficulty is itself an elusive concept. Experienced teachers have reported that many adolescent (self-conscious) boys show embarrassment when asked to imitate the sounds of French (especially the nasal vowels and the tonic stress on final syllable, etc.) although they are willing to copy German or Spanish sounds. This vague impression may simply be the reaction of boys in mixed comprehensive school classes studying French alongside girls of their own age who are, on average, much more verbally and psychologically mature. Many girls in mixed classes rapidly leave most boys behind and the subject itself tends to be dubbed a girls' subject, in consequence. Boys, as Burstall showed (1974), perform much better at French in single-sex schools.

We are on firmer ground if we approach the question of difficulty by considering the two chief sources of error in learning a foreign language:

1 the contrasts between languages which lead to 'inter-language' interference
2 the 'intra-language' interference or overgeneralisation from rules met in the course of the early journey into the language.

The errors caused by the first of these have been called 'transfer errors'; errors due to the second are 'analogical errors' (Corder, 1974). It seems to be agreed by the authorities on error analysis that nearly all learner's errors come into these two categories. Pit Corder would add a third category: 'error induced by the teacher or the materials used' about which, he accepts, very little is known.

Recent work by psychologists interested in the effect of memory on language learning helps us to understand how the two kinds of interference, both 'inter-language' and 'intra-language', work.

In everyday thinking, we assume that to 'remember' something is like playing back a tape, even though the tape may have gaps and static on it. . . . It is only partially true. In remembering we do get back some features of the original experience as though from a tape. But another large part of the process consists of *generating a new image* that contains elements from that 'tape' and then recognising whether that new image is like the original . . . Judgment about whether the generated image is like the original depends on the criteria *which already existed* within the individual. (Stevick, 1976, p. 23)

So when we recall an item in the foreign language from memory, the item is not played back automatically like a recording; we have to re-create it and in the process it is reshaped by expectations set up by experience both of the mother tongue and of previous learning of the foreign language. Nor is this true only of recall. It applies to recognition memory, also. Of these two main sources of error, both due to interference from previous experience, we consider first 'inter-language' contrasts. Do these give us a measure of difficulty?

Inter-language contrasts

'Contrastive analysis' has had a chequered history. It had a great vogue following Robert Lado's *Linguistics Across Cultures* (1957). For Lado the clue to ease or difficulty in learning a foreign language lay in a close comparison of its points of contrast with the learner's mother tongue. Teaching method, choice of materials and testing he suggested, ought to be based on 'contrastive analysis'.

In fact the problem turned out to be more complex than the early enthusiasts suspected. What exactly was to be compared? Were there common features (universals?) in the 'deep structure' common to all languages which could be compared? But if these were, in fact, common features would they not be identical? How else could they be linguistic universals?

One suggestion was that the common features compared might be notional or semantic features in the deep structure, whose surface realisations we could compare. (See Van Buren, 1974, for a detailed discussion.) Unfortunately we do not yet possess grammars based on 'generative semantics'. As Van Buren comments ruefully, 'the lack of a theoretical model of grammar which is adequate for the performance of some practical task is a common situation in applied linguistics'.

In the absence of a grammatical model which can meet the demands of rigorous contrastive analysis, applied linguists have shown interest in the more pragmatic and less rigorously scientific concept of 'linguistic distance'. Already in 1967 Francis Mackey in Quebec could claim to have produced a 'calculus or overall formula for measuring linguistic distance' (Mackey, 1967).

Mackey's pioneering concept has been carried further by Vaughan James (James, 1979). He offers a tentative comparison of the distance from English of the five commonly taught European languages at five linguistic levels: phonological, grammatical, lexical, orthographic and spelling. James expresses degree of distance from English as a five-point scale (1= closest to English, 5= most distant). His estimate of distance at the various levels is as follows:

Levels	Degrees of distance				
	1	2	3	4	5
phonological	Italian	German/ Spanish	Russian	French	–
grammatical	–	French/ Italian/ Spanish	German/ Russian	–	–
lexical	French/ Italian/ Spanish	German	–	Russian	–
orthographic	French/ German/ Italian/ Spanish		(German gothic)	Russian	–
spelling	Italian/ Spanish	German/ Russian	–	French	

Expressed globally James' distances are as follows:

French	12	
German	10	(12 if gothic script taught)
Italian	6	
Russian	16	
Spanish	7	

James' overall order of distance which he, in a necessarily condensed and introductory essay, equates very roughly with difficulty for the English-speaking learner is thus from easier to harder:

Italian, Spanish, German, French, Russian.

A complication in computing distance between two languages is that it may be easier to cross a given linguistic distance in one direction than in another, just as movement between two camps on a mountain climb is easier in one direction than the other, though the same distance is covered in each direction.

To take an example: the distance between the English verb and the Chinese (Mandarin) verb is considerable. Chinese has one (invariable) verb form, used with all persons. The Chinese speaker learning English, therefore (in this limited part of the grammar), may face more difficult problems than the English speaker learning Chinese. (Chinese, needless to say, poses other problems to the English-speaking learner!)

Similarly, to take an example from nearer home, learning the present tense of verbs in Danish involves memorising a single invariable form – used with all persons:

(to be)	(to have)	(to write)	(to love)
jeg er	*har*	*skriver*	*elsker*
du er	*har*	*skriver*	*elsker*
han/hun er	*har*	*skriver*	*elsker*
vi er	*har*	*skriver*	*elsker*
I er	*har*	*skriver*	*elsker*
de er	*har*	*skriver*	*elsker*

Not only does the Danish speaker learning English have to learn to use appropriately several English forms:

I write (I do/don't write)
I am writing

where Danish only has:

jeg skriver (ikke)

but he must learn inflections:

I write
he writes
I am writing
he is writing

where the English speaker learning Danish has the one invariable form to remember:

jeg skriver (I write)
han skriver (he writes)

We must be careful not to oversimplify. The interference of 'I am writing' may cause the English learner to produce* *jeg er skriver*, despite the apparent simplicity of the Danish verb. The difficulty of a simple comparison such as we sketch above is that it fails to include other problems (for example the fact that the English 'you' is the correct form of address for singular and plural as well as informal and formal contexts whereas the English student of Danish must learn to select between at least three possible second person pronouns. This may prove harder than inflecting the verb appropriately). All the relevant language contrasts must be added together if we wish to compute 'distance'. Nevertheless, impossible as the total computation must be, for particular parts of the grammar and the lexicon, linguistic distance in a particular direction can obviously affect limited bits of the learning.

A further complication is that degree of distance does not always coincide with degree of difficulty. Sometimes learning is facilitated by a clear and consistent, even though large, difference between mother tongue and foreign language. Learning difficulties may be caused more by confusion and bewilderment due to inconsistency (not magnitude) of linguistic differences between foreign language and mother tongue. Vaughan James in his pioneering paper (1979) adds the reminder that cultural distance between speech communities may be a source of greater learning difficulty than purely linguistic distance. With all these reservations made, however, James' analysis suggests that, of the five commonly studied European languages, French and Russian should present most difficulties for the English-speaking learner, and Italian and Spanish fewest, judged by the linguistic distance to be traversed on the journey.

Intra-language contrasts

What of our other criterion, intra-language inconsistencies which lead to analogical errors? Here we are in virgin territory. The work has simply not been done. No complete comparative analysis has been made of the analogical, internal contradictions that beset the learner of the various European languages. Yet most experienced teachers would probably agree that the learner's confidence is undermined far more by intra-linguistic than by inter-linguistic interference. To take a simple example from French, very few English learners experience any difficulty with: It's hot – *il fait chaud*. The difficulty comes when the learner meets: It's hot (coffee) – *il est chaud* – and having skirted round that analogical pitfall goes on logically to produce: He's hot – **il est* *chaud*. Similarly teachers of French will recognise as an old friend the form: **il fait pleut* (analogous with: *il fait chaud*).

But if analogical error is the main bugbear, as we suspect, and more common than transfer error, what advice can we give to our Head of school who is anxious to offer his average and slower learners early satisfaction in their language learning? Whatever answer we give can only be tentative since no detailed comparison of analogical errors in the various languages has yet been made. We should also stress that we are considering only the early stages (the first four or five years?) of the school course. Some languages reserve their subtlest 'intra-language' problems until advanced work is reached. Spanish may be an example. A student of Spanish may move easily through his course up to 16+ only to discover that years of study lie ahead before he can read *Don Quijote* with pleasure or appreciate the loveliness (even grasp the meaning) of such a poem as Góngora's *Angélica y Medoro:*

> En un pastoral albergue
> que la guerra entre unos robles
> lo dejó por escondido
> o le perdonó por pobre . . .

(The phrases *'lo dejó'* and *'le perdonó'* go beyond 'O' level grammar!)

Is French, in fact, more fraught with analogical inconsistencies, even in the early stages, than Spanish or German? Experience of learning these three languages and attempting to teach two of them suggests that French comes first in order of analogical inconsistencies. Spanish certainly has strong claims to be considered easiest in the early stages, with German second.

Matching speech to writing

Let us consider how this affects a problem which for many young learners proves an insurmountable hurdle: the transition to writing. The teacher faces a dilemma. If he tries to shield the learner from the written form of the language, relying solely on the ear, the pupil is deprived of any support for the growing load on the memory. Pupils with limited STM capacity have no means of reinforcing *ear* learning by *eye* learning in which at least half of an average class will be more confident and proficient. Learning can take place only during the short class exposure to the teacher's voice or tape recording: without writing or reading, homework or private study is ruled out.

Yet, if the teacher does introduce writing from an early stage, analogical errors, especially in French, abound. The great Henry Sweet (1899), facing this problem, proposed to circumvent it by phonetic spelling, to which we return in Part III.

It is the nature of the match between the spoken and written language that causes difficulties. Consider, in French, the variety of spellings used to represent the two common vowels [e] and [ɛ]

[e]	[ɛ]
é	è
et	ê
ai	est
ez	ais
er	ait
ed	ell
ef	ett
(ais	enne
(ait for some speakers)	ess
	mer(ci)
	(jou)et

or the problem of the 'mute' ending:

[lɛv]   spelt   *lève, lèves, lèvent*
[dy]   spelt   *du, dû, due, dus, dues, dut, dût*

How many learners, even university students, has one heard uncertain how to pronounce the names of persons and places which are household terms in French:

Camus (*s* pronounced as in   [kamy] (not as in *Fréjus*)
   Fréjus?)
Boulez (*z* pronounced?)   [bulɛz]
Saint Tropez (*z* pronounced?)   [trope]
Mendès-France (*mend* as in   [mɛ̃ndɛs] (*en* pronounced *in*)
   vend?)
Saint-Jean-de-Luz (*z* pronounced   [lyz]
   s or *z*?)
oignon (*oi* as in *moi?*)   [ɔɲɔ̃] (*oi* not as in *moi*)
linguiste (*guiste* as in *guise?*)   [lɛ̃ngɥist] (*guiste* not as in *guise*)

le Lot	} *t* pronounced?	[lə lɔt]
le gros lot		[lə gʀo lo]
le Doubs (*bs* pronounced?)		[lə du]
un os/deux os?		[œ̃nɔs / døzo]
un oeuf/deux oeufs?		[œ̃nœf / døzø]
un boeuf/deux boeufs?		[œ̃ bœf / dø bø]
le cassis?		[lə kasis]

Double consonants constitute another inconsistency in French spelling, especially when words cognate with English words are concerned. For example

if *addition* why *adresse*? (Eng: address)
if *commission* why *comité*? (Eng: committee)
if *litanie* why *littérature*? (Eng: literature)

A related source of error is the pronunciation of the vowel before the double consonant. For example

immédiat [im]
but *immangeable* [ɛ̃] (sometimes [im])

Spelling rules found logical enough by specialists nevertheless confuse young learners.

And what of Spanish and German? Have their spellings no inconsistencies? Of course they present some problems but most teachers of these languages agree that the match between speech and writing is close and consistent. (Other languages commonly quoted as having a good 'grapheme/phoneme' match are Finnish, Japanese, Serbo-Croat, Swahili.) Spanish is particularly well served: there is one spelling for each sound; tonic stress is clearly indicated by the written accent whenever simple stress rules are overridden; double consonants are clearly pronounced as such. German spelling is almost equally helpful to the young learner. With so many pupils leaving primary schools lacking confidence in reading English (Bullock, 1975) we want if possible to offer, in the first foreign language, an apprenticeship in matching sounds to written symbols that will build confidence. The pupil's growing confidence will feed back positively upon reading in the mother tongue.

As an apprenticeship, then, in the transition from speaking/hearing to reading/writing in a foreign language, there seem to be good reasons for preferring either Spanish or German to French. Moreover if we consider another difficulty that plagues slower learners, namely gender, we shall see that Spanish has clear advantages over both of the others.

Grammatical gender

English enjoys the advantage over all other major European languages of having adopted 'natural' in place of 'grammatical' gender. Old English had grammatical gender like other Indo-European languages. The loss of its three grammatical genders in the Middle English period (broadly the twelfth to fourteenth centuries) seems to have been a consequence of the decay of the inflectional endings of (strong) adjectives and demonstratives. In Old English these inflections showed, at least in the singular, whether a noun was masculine, feminine or neuter. As the inflections were reduced in the Middle English period to a single ending for the adjective and fixed forms for 'the', 'this', 'that', 'these' and 'those', the support for grammatical gender was removed.

Exactly why the adjective endings were lost the historians are less sure. Was it due, indirectly, to the Norman Conquest? By making English the language mainly of uneducated people the Norman Conquest probably made it easier for grammatical changes to go forward unchecked. However caused, the fortunate loss of grammatical gender has made English more accessible to the foreign learner and may be a decisive factor in the emergence of English as the world vehicle language. Conversely, the English-speaking pupil, meeting the complications of grammatical gender for the first time, finds this the greatest single contrast with his English-based expectations of how language works. Unless the gender of every new noun is solidly learned, the pupil is unable to select the correct article whether definite or indefinite; he cannot use the correct adjective form; a correct pronoun cannot be substituted for the noun; in French the perfect tense, perhaps the commonest verb form in the language, cannot be correctly used.

Of the Romance languages, there is little doubt that French offers most possibility of analogical error in the memorising of gender. At the same time the role of grammatical gender in signalling the 'constituents' of a sentence, that is, the way in which groups of words belong together and thereby facilitating the processing of incoming messages, should not be forgotten.

Grammatical gender is not simply to be dismissed as a nuisance to the learner! The difficulty of recognising and recalling gender for the learner on a 'drip-feed diet' in school arises from the paucity of gender clues given in the classroom context, compared to the bombardment of redundant signals of gender received by the native-speaker in childhood. Even given this bombardment of signals, however, primary teachers in France spend a great deal of time correcting children's genders. Our English pupil, enjoying a comparatively slight and intermittent exposure to the foreign language, needs all the help we can give him.

In French the very common 'e' (mute) ending, deriving from both masculine and feminine endings in Latin, is a most misleading signal of gender. Spanish signals gender by spelling much more consistently.

The following tables of common nouns, which could be extended easily by the most cursory leafing through the dictionary, illustrate the nature of the difference between the two languages in this respect:

French *Gender not signalled by spelling*	Spanish *Gender clearly signalled by spelling*	
	masculine	feminine
cigare	⟵ *cigarro*	
charge		*carga* ⟶
commerce	⟵ *comercio*	
coude	⟵ *codo*	
douane		*aduana* ⟶
disque	⟵ *disco*	
livre (book)	⟵ *libro*	
livre (pound)		*libra* ⟶
silence	⟵ *silencio*	
théâtre	⟵ *teatro*	
troupe		*tropa* ⟶
groupe	⟵ *grupo*	

In the case of each noun in the above list, typical of very many more, the clearly signalled gender in Spanish gives the clue to the gender of its cognate in French. Thus a pupil whose introduction to Romance languages began with Spanish would later have no difficulty recognising the gender of the French cognates and the reverse would not apply. Vaughan James, in the paper on linguistics distance referred to earlier, discusses the concept of 'clusters' of cognate or related languages as an element in curriculum planning: 'The idea of using one language in a group as a spring-board for access to others is undoubtedly a useful one.' For access to gender in Romance languages a start with French is scarcely helpful, but a start with Spanish could be.

It is not only the mute *e* ending that causes trouble as we see in the examples below:

French		Spanish	
Spellings which do not signal gender		Gender clearly signalled	
		masculine	feminine
eau	(f)		agua ⟶
morceau	(m)	⟵ pedazo	
maison	(f)		casa ⟶
flocon	(m)	⟵ copo	
douceur	(f)		dulzura ⟶
malheur	(m)		desgracia ⟶

Of course there are exceptions in Spanish and problems for slower learners such as the Spanish use of *el* before feminine nouns beginning with stressed *a* or *ha*:

el ala	(f)
el hambre	(f)

Most teachers who have taught both languages would agree, however, that uncertainty about gender in French is a major cause of loss of confidence. From the very first dialogues in the classroom uncertainty about gender inhibits the slower pupil:

— *Paul, où est votre dictionnaire?*
— *Le voici monsieur* (or is it *'La' voici monsieur?*)

As soon as adjectives are met there may be up to five forms to master (*nouveau, nouvel, nouvelle, nouveaux, nouvelles*), and if the pupil has the least doubt about the gender of the noun his choice of adjectives is a matter of guesswork.

The introduction of writing is often the *coup de grâce*; not only is there the need to make the adjective accord with the noun, for example

la nouvelle radio (f)

but similar sounds must be spelt differently:

> *la nouvelle radio*
> *le nouvel observateur*

In German the problem is further complicated because there are three genders to manipulate. As in French, spelling of German nouns does not give any consistent signal of gender, although some approximate rules can be formulated to help the learner. Nor does meaning give many clues:

> *Sonne* (sun) is feminine
> *Mond* (moon) is masculine

exactly the reverse of the Romance genders – while *Kind* (child), *Mädchen* (girl), and *Weib* (woman) are all neuter.

German, it is often claimed, presents its hardest problems early on: mastery of its four cases, with inflection of articles, adjectives and pronouns and selection of accusative, dative or genitive case after propositions. It therefore has fewer complications to unfold in the more advanced stages. In this respect it could be said to contrast with Spanish.

The verb

There is a further reason, however, for the choice of Spanish rather than French as the apprenticeship language. It is that the form of the Spanish verb in the present tense corresponds closely to the English while the French is disconcertingly different and this causes difficulties at the very outset of the course. Teachers of French will be familiar with the transfer errors which are caused by the economy of the French present tense:

1. (*Tous les jours*) *je regarde la télé* (*après le repas du soir*)
      'I watch the "telly"' (every day after supper)
2. (*– Qu'est-ce que tu es en train de faire?*)
    – Je regarde la télé
      'I am watching the "telly"' (at the moment)

This leads pupils to produce (by transfer from English):

> * *Je suis regardant*, etc.

In Spanish the (so-called) 'progressive' tenses (present and past) match the English:

I watch	*Todos los dias (yo) veo la televisión*
I am watching	*(Yo) estoy viendo la televisión (en este momento)*
I was watching	*(Yo) estaba viendo . . . (cuando ella llegó)*[6]

This close parallel between Spanish and English in the progressive forms of the verb, usually the first to be met by the beginner, reinforces the strong case that has emerged from our discussion in favour of Spanish as the first 'apprenticeship' language.

The position of German

We should not jump to a conclusion about Spanish, however, without considering the position of German.

The GCE 'O' level statistics show how German has steadily strengthened its position by comparison with French. Entries for German, expressed as a percentage of entries for French, increased as follows:

1938	School Certificate	German entries 13.7% of French
1965	GCE 'O' level	German entries 20.0% of French
1985	GCE 'O' level*	German entries 28.8% of French

* entries for French in 1985 were somewhat inflated by inclusion in the statistics of pupils entered for the experimental joint GCE/CSE 16+ papers which were set in French but not in German.

The figures for boys are specially interesting. Between 1965 and 1985 the number of boys entering for French *fell* from 83,799 to 58,962 (down 30%) (despite the inclusion in the figures of pupils entered for the joint GCE/CSE papers in French but not in German).

In the same period the numbers of boys entering for German *rose* from 15,941 to 16,128.

The picture at GCE 'A' is similar (DES, 1965–85). Entries for German as a percentage of entries for French were:

1938	Higher School Certificate	German entries 18.9% of French
1965	GCE 'A' level	German entries 27.7% of French
1985	GCE 'A' level	German entries 35.8% of French

The contrast between boys and girls entry figures is striking: between 1965 and 1985 the number of boys entering for German 'A' level fell from 3,572 to 2,208 while girl entries rose from 3,535 to 5,741.

It is not known, of course, how many of the pupils taking German offer it as a second foreign language, in addition to French. Some indication is given, however, in a study carried out in the county of West Sussex. This is an LEA in which German is more strongly established than in the country as a whole as *second* foreign language. Out of 276 teachers offering foreign languages, 163 offer French only, 18 offer German only, 4 offer Spanish only; all 45 schools offer French as FL1 to 'O' level. About 13% of pupils learn German as FL2. Of the 276 teachers engaged in language teaching, 221 (80%) spend most of their time on French. A significant number of teachers are qualified in the minority languages but cannot make use of their qualifications (West Sussex, 1978). In another local authority in the south with one of the most rapidly increasing school populations in the country, the language adviser considers that there is a strong case for offering pupils a choice between French and German. His view is that a choice between French and Spanish would be less acceptable to parents. If the case for German seems so clear to advisers in LEAs on the south coast, might not the case for German seem even stronger to the hypothetical Head of our new school in the Yorkshire coalfield, given the close links with Germany via Hull and Newcastle?

Five other points might be made, all strengthening the case for German:

1 Studies of language use in industry, such as the York study (Emmans et al., 1974) show German strongly challenging French and quite outdistancing Spanish.

2 Experienced observers comment on the greater readiness of adolescent boys to imitate the sounds of German than those of French

3 Germany is more accessible geographically than Spain; far more visitors, school-exchange parties and native assistants find their way into British schools from Germany than from Spain; inter-school links with Germany have hitherto flourished, while those with Spain for a variety of reasons (some of them historical) have languished.

4 The argument that the complex German case system is an insuperable barrier, especially for less able pupils, is challenged by many teachers who claim that careful planning of the introduction of vocabulary can considerably delay the need to become too much concerned with inflections

5 With regard to staffing it seems clear that the position in German must be easier than in Spanish. In 1986, some 191 graduates in training in University Departments of Education and polytechnics/colleges had German as their main subject, compared with only 26 in Spanish.

Summing up

Obviously there can be no easy solution for our Head of school. Considered purely as a linguistic apprenticeship, offering pupils of all abilities the prospect of rapid initial progress in learning genders, mastering verb forms and making a confident transition to the written form of the language, Spanish has clear advantages. Equally clearly, German is strongly established as the principal second foreign language; recruitment of staff is easier than for Spanish and the opportunities for imaginative study visits and for developing school links are probably better than for any other country, including France.

At the same time, French is entrenched in many areas in feeder schools, and there is the further problem of pupil transfer across LEA boundaries. This makes it essential to retain some French teaching. The impact of falling school rolls on school staffing is bound to make it increasingly difficult for schools to make special provision for pupils who transfer in mid-career.

A possible solution (as suggested in West Sussex, 1976) might be to organise local consortia of schools, each of which offered a different language. This would be disliked by some administrators because it gives parents one more argument to use in support of their preference of one school over another.

Would a better solution be to introduce two first foreign languages in parallel, half of the year group taking (say) French, the other half Spanish or German? Many schools operate such a scheme. Some advisers consider that it can only operate successfully in large (eight-form entry?) schools, if viable sixth form sets in both languages are hoped for.

Finally there is the possibility of offering different languages across the whole year group in successive years, for example, French to this year's intake, German to next year's. This has the disadvantage that pupils entering in mid-course with (say) French may well find themselves in a German year.

What advice can we give, in the absence of a nationally agreed policy? It can only be to choose the course that has fewest disadvantages for a particular school. Ideally we would welcome the dual first foreign language pattern, with French offered every year to cater for the intake from feeder schools committed to French and late entries already embarked on French and in recognition of the present availability of French staffing. The choice of the second language in each year must lie between German and Spanish. It might be possible to offer German one year and Spanish the next as the language for half the intake. This would be the best solution if staffing and falling rolls permit. It is, however, most important in all this not to exaggerate the finality of whatever language choice a given pupil will make. The decision is not a life-or-death affair. We should keep in mind the role of the foreign language in the secondary school. It is an apprenticeship only. Nobody can predict, when the pupil is only 11 or 13, which of the world's languages he or she will need in adult life. Pupils and their parents must be constantly reminded of this. The objectives of the secondary school apprenticeship are to gain insight into language, to learn how to learn a language, to sharpen the tools of learning while relishing the experience so that after school further language learning will be something to look forward to. It will be the school's business to explain this fully and often to parents *and to the staffs of feeder schools*. The proposed provision at 16+ of a wide choice of languages for adult use must also be explained.

The 'apprenticeship language', once started, should be continued by all pupils for the full five years of the secondary course, as part of a coherent 'language' curriculum with three elements:

1 foreign language
2 mother tongue
3 linking study:'awareness of language'. (See Part III: 'The Way Ahead.')

For a very few slower learning pupils out of a full ability intake – perhaps 15% in any year – the foreign language element in their course might, after year 2, merge with the 'awareness of language'. This would mean that more and more of the practical language activities in the 'language' course would take place in the mother tongue. Meanwhile investigation of life in the foreign country would continue by means of comparative studies of aspects of the foreign community that slower pupils can judge, such as cost of living surveys comparing the UK with our European neighbours or comparative projects in home economics involving foreign study visits. The possibility of handing over a greater or lesser part of the foreign language area of the curriculum of slower learning pupils to 'awareness of language' in years 3 and 4 is one of the advantages of the approach to language across the curriculum described later.

It is not suggested that there may not be other and better curriculum patterns than the ones outlined. Local interests, size of school, close links with a particular teacher-training institution may suggest other solutions. Much more important than the initial choice of French or Spanish or German is the way we teach the apprenticeship language.

NOTES

1 This was seen as a 'significant change in the organisation of the Ministry' in the letter from the Permanent Secretary, Dame Mary Smieton, to L E As and teacher organisations. It had the job 'of fore-seeing changes before they become apparent on the ground' (Kogan, 1971, p. 170).

2 Maurice Kogan's phrase (ibid.).

3 It is estimated that prior to the impact of the Pilot Scheme some 12 – 15% of secondary pupils took a *second* foreign language (either Latin or German/Spanish/Russian), generally beginning at age 13+ or 14+.

4 For 10 years (1968–78) all language graduates following the Post-graduate Certificate Course at the Language Teaching Centre, York University, were required during their training year to learn Italian from Dr Trudie Berger from scratch and take it intensively up to approximately G C E 'O' level. Many subsequently continued their studies in the vacation at Perugia. By this means some 300 graduates were sent into schools with a taste for Italian as a subsidiary subject and a 'head start' enabling them to initiate Italian classes as sixth-form options. See also the discussion of conversion courses (p. 290).

5 The idea of 'area curriculum committees' planning language provision across school boundaries was first put forward in 1963 in *Modern Languages in the Grammar School* (I A H M, 1963) para 49, where it was suggested that such committees might also facilitate closer links between primary and secondary provision.

6 This parallel between Spanish and English goes much further. In both Spanish and English all verbs fall into one of two classes:
   (i)   those verbs whose meaning is 'perfective', that is their meaning contains an implication that the activity they describe is going to stop sometime;
   (ii) verbs of 'imperfective' meaning carrying no such implication.
Typical of the first class would be: to jump (*saltar*), to think (*pensar*); typical of the second: to know (*saber*). Spanish even has two verbs 'to be', one 'perfective' (*estar*) and one 'imperfective' (*ser*). There are also 'perfective' and 'imperfective' verb forms: I am -ing (I was -ing), etc., generally called 'progressive', are in fact, by implication, 'perfective' forms, because they imply that the activity will cease. The simple present is 'imperfective'. This explains why, in both English and Spanish, verbs of 'imperfective' meaning cannot be used in the ('perfective') progressive tenses. One cannot say: *I am knowing, etc. (*estoy sabiendo*), but both languages allow: I am jumping, thinking, etc. (*estoy saltando, pensando*).

Part II

Lessons from the past

Lessons from the past

4   Immersion or gardening in a gale?

French should be talked into the child . . . Grammar is only for those who have the language already.

John Locke, *Some Thoughts Concerning Education*, 1690

A Frenchman, a man of learning, is arrived in London from Paris in order to teach the French language, Fables, Poetry, Heraldry, French philosophy and the Latin tongue without exacting any study from his scholars, all study being an obstacle to his method . . . a simple method and one shorter than any which hath been hitherto practised . . . enquire at Mr Bezançon's Snuff Shop in Little Earl Street, the Black Boy by the Seven Dials.

Daily Advertiser, 29 June 1752, quoted in John Hooper
Hartnoll, *Exposure of the Hamiltonian System*, 1823

The great empirical philosopher and the charlatan in Mr Bezançon's snuff shop both offered versions of 'French without tears'. The prospect is alluring and down the centuries language teachers have dreamt of finding a panacea to lighten their labour. Workaday reality, however, has always disappointed their dreams. It is not hard to see why.

Picture the foreign language teacher's daily task. The class arrives for its lesson babbling excitedly in English about the day's doings. The teacher shuts the door on English speech patterns, enclosing the pupils within the 'cultural island' of the language classroom, and for 40 minutes strives like a keen gardener to implant in the recalcitrant soil a few frail seedlings of speech patterns in the foreign language. Just as the seedlings are taking root and standing up for themselves, the bell goes and the class is dismissed into the English language environment.

For the next 24 hours the pupils are swept along by a gale of English, listening to different teachers, reading specialist textbooks, asking for more custard with the lunch-time pudding, surviving amid the playground witticisms, shouting on the games field, gossiping on the bus going home, relaxing in front of the 'telly'. Even in bed the English speech patterns shape the weird logic of dreamland.

Next morning the foreign language teacher finds yesterday's tender seedlings of French, German or Spanish lying blighted and flattened by the gale of English. She (he) gently revives and waters them but, just as they reach the condition they were in yesterday, the bell rings again and the gale of English sweeps in to destroy all, or nearly all, the patient gardener's handiwork. Some schools 'block' the four weekly periods into two sessions each of 70 or 80 minutes. By this method four or five days of English can elapse between two foreign language lessons, possibly the worst of all worlds, as the HMI survey of 1977 suggests. It is no wonder that after five years of this wasteful method only one in ten of 11+ starters reach the modest goal of GCE or its equivalent.

One reading of the history of language teaching has been to see it as swinging like a pendulum between two extremes of method, as teachers have searched for a solution which has always eluded them. Sometimes the pendulum has seemed to swing between learning grammar rules and 'direct method'. At other times the swing has been from learning by ear to learning through reading. A more recent swing of opinion has gone from emphasis on perception of structural patterns to drilling in new linguistic habits in a language laboratory (and back again).

There are useful lessons to be learnt from some of these ever-optimistic lurches of the pendulum in the nineteenth and twentieth centuries and we examine them in our next two chapters. We begin by looking at a quite fundamental change in language teaching, which dates from the seventeenth century. Its significance seems to have been overlooked in much that has been written about language teaching. Not until the second world war and the threat to national survival did the truth of what had been frustrating language teaching in schools for three centuries sink in.

Immersion learning (IL) *v.* foreign language (FL) learning

Teachers of English distinguish between English as a *second* language (ESL) and English as a *foreign* language (EFL). ESL teachers operate in environments where their pupils can expect to meet English outside the classroom (for example, the Pakistani pupil in Bradford who learns ESL in school must use his English on the bus going home) and thus 'formal' (classroom) learning and 'informal' learning are combined. EFL teachers, on the other hand, operate in classrooms which are cultural islands. Outside their classrooms English is not normally met (for example, in France or in China). Little 'informal' learning takes place. English teachers refine their terms further. They distinguish between ESL in Bradford and ESL in (say) Anglophone African countries where English is the lingua franca of commerce and higher education. There are other possible refinements of the definition. Teachers of modern languages working in the UK have not needed to make this distinction between second language and foreign language learning. There is another distinction to be made, however, in our discussion of teaching method. It is close to the ESL/EFL distinction, though not identical. We distinguish between: the language lesson which is accompanied by use of the target language outside the classroom for everyday activities (as with Latin in the Tudor grammar school or French for the seventeenth century aristocrat's child with private tutor or, nowadays, French learnt in a French family or on an intensive 'reciprocal' course with equally matched numbers of French and English students); and the language lesson which takes place in an otherwise English context and is the pupil's only experience of the target language ('gardening in a gale').

To avoid inventing unnecessary new terms we will call the second 'FL' as our English colleagues do; so SFL = Spanish taught as a foreign language, in the formal classroom only. The first we will call 'IL' (or immersion learning); so SIL = Spanish taught by formal study plus immersion as on a reciprocal course. IL will share some, though not all, of the characteristics our English colleagues associate with second language (SL) learning. (The 'immersion' component may have to be contrived where our English colleagues can take it for granted.) Our FL/IL distinction is fundamental if we are to understand how language teaching lost its way after the seventeenth century. It also underlies the hypothesis on which Part III of this book is based.

The seventeenth century: a turning-point

In the switch from IL to FL, the seventeenth century was the turning-point. Throughout the Middle Ages languages were learnt by immersion. Latin was an essential vocational subject for clerks and administrators; learning by use was widespread. It was only towards the end of the Middle Ages, when classical

Latin was studied as a dead language, that 'deduction', construction of sentences from rules, was erected into a method by some teachers and they were sharply rapped on the knuckles by enlightened authorities. Both Luther and Melancthon protested against burdening pupils with too much formal grammar. Immersion was the method favoured also with *modern* languages in the few schools that offered them. In 1573, schoolboys at Southampton Grammar School under Adrian à Saravia were compelled to speak French at meal times. 'He who spoke English, though only a sentence, was obliged to wear a fool's cap at meals and stand aside and watch the rest eat' (Watson, 1909). Saravia was one of the many foreign teachers who came to England as religious refugees. There were, by 1622, sixteen protestant schoolmasters in London teaching their native language.[1]

It was exceptional, however, for modern languages to be taught in grammar schools in Tudor times. Modern language teaching mostly took place outside the grammar schools.[2] The practically useful subjects like navigation, astronomy, bookkeeping, languages, essential skills in Tudor and Stuart times, when London was taking over from Venice as the capital of the world's maritime trade, were left to the private academies.

Here, and among the private tutors engaged by aristocratic families, immersion in modern languages had powerful advocates. In 1633 Sir Robert le Grays, requesting appointment as tutor to the prince (later Charles II), promised not only

> to render Latin his *linguam vernaculam*, not clogging his memory with tedious rules after the common pedantic fashion but by a way much more easy: so that if Sir Robert lived until the Prince was 7 years old the nimblest Latinist should find him his match . . . but also to make French, for Her Majesty's respect, his first learned tongue, and the Italian and Spanish also, so as he shall be able to read with or discourse therein. (Watson, 1909, p. 483)

John Locke, the father of empiricism ('knowledge depends on perception via the senses') in the seventeenth century, was firmly committed to the principles of inductive learning which Francis Bacon had proposed instead of the Aristotelian, rationalist deduction from given premises. He applied inductive theory to language learning and this was the method he claimed to have used as Latin tutor to the 3rd Earl of Shaftesbury. In *Some Thoughts Concerning Education* (1690) he advocated learning by 'roat':

a man who does not speak English or Latin perfectly by roat, so that
having thought of the thing he would speak of, his Tongue of course
without thought of Rule or Grammar falls into the proper Expression and
Idiom of that Language, does not speak it well, nor is Master of it. And I
would fain have anyone name to me that Tongue that anyone can learn,
or speak as he should do, by the Rules of Grammar. Languages were not
made by Rules of Art but by Accident, and the Common Use of the
People. And he that will speak them well has no other rule than that; nor
any thing to trust to but his memory and the habit of speaking after that
fashion learnt from those that are allowed to speak properly . . . which
in other words is only to speak by roat. (§ 168)

The same method should be used with modern languages:
'French should be talked into the child . . . Grammar is only for
those who have the language already.'

John Locke wrote as a former private tutor to an aristocrat. He
assumed an environment where the learner would have the
constant companionship of a native-speaking tutor and friend,
and could expect to be immersed in the foreign language because
of family connections and responsibilities. He was therefore
arguing for a method of IL acquisition rather than FL learning.

In the early part of the seventeenth century, at least, the same
could be said for Latin teaching in the grammar schools.

Immersion in Latin

So long as Latin remained the lingua franca of Europe it was an
essential vocational tool for any youth aspiring to further education or to work in the public service. It was taught in the grammar
schools by a mixture of 'grammar/translation' and learning by use
(IL). It is true that practice varied from school to school. There
seems, too, to have been a swing towards FL teaching in the
course of the century. Even late in the seventeenth century,
however, many grammar schools expected pupils to use Latin for
all school dialogue once the rudiments had been acquired, just as
Montaigne (1533–92) and his brothers had had to use only Latin
in the nursery: 'nor man nor maid-servant were suffered to speak
one word in my company except such Latin words as everyone
had learned to chat and prattle with me' (Montaigne, 1580).

The charter of King James Grammar School, Knaresborough,
North Yorkshire as late as 1657 stipulated that after the first three
years in the school, any boy caught using English, even in the
playground, was to be beaten by the headmaster. In Tudor times
this had been the rule:

Boys were not taught Latin, they were taught *in* Latin; they were not allowed to utter a single vernacular word whilst at school . . . No teaching of any kind in the vernacular existed anywhere before 1550 or thereabouts . . . If Shakespeare crept unwillingly to school he did so because there he would be confronted by a Master who spoke nothing but Latin and would birch him if he spoke an English word to another boy. (Goldschmidt, 1950, quoted in Charlton, 1965, p. 119)

Oundle statutes (1556) insisted that boys speak Latin to each other 'as well in the school as coming and going to and from the same'. At Rivington (1566) it was prescribed that 'In the school they that can must speak nothing but Latin.' Many similar statutes could be quoted. (It is significant that the Jesuit order, to this day, insists that its novices, learning to use Latin as the lingua franca, must use Latin even when doing menial tasks such as cleaning the lavatories.)

It is true, as K. Charlton (1965) argues, that the difficulties of implementing these statutes in schools must have been enormous and 'already . . . at the beginning of the 15th century English was used in grammatical texts . . . the prohibition of English speaking in Tudor school statutes must be put in context, and interpreted as referring to those hours of school life devoted to the speaking of Latin and not as an absolute prohibition'. Immersion in Latin in the sixteenth and seventeenth centuries was perhaps increasingly in the shallow, rather than the deep, end of the pool. Nevertheless the assumption of constant use of the language outside the classroom was there until the second half of the seventeenth century which can be seen as a turning-point in the history not only of Latin teaching, but of language teaching. The colossal figure of Comenius bestrides this period and his own development symbolises the change from IL to FL.

John Amos Comenius (1592–1671)

The greatest in a long line of protestant, migrant language teachers, John Amos Comenius[3] was the exiled leader of the Moravian church. He was one of the greatest Latin scholars and educationists of the age and spoke four languages fluently. He and John Locke met in Holland when both men were in exile from their own countries. In 1641 Comenius spent a short time in London (it was the year of Thomas Wentworth's execution when London was temporarily safe for heretics). Comenius' *Janua*

Linguarum Reserata (The Gates of Tongues Unlocked and Opened) was published in London in 1631. It was originally a text-book in Latin and German intended to improve the teaching of Latin. The English edition was in Latin, English and French. It offered 'a short way of teaching and thoroughly learning within a yeare and a halfe at the farthest, the Latin, English, French (and any other) tongue, together with the ground and foundation of Arts and Sciences, comprised under a hundred titles and a thousand periods'. (Its title recalls the Jesuits' *Janua Linguarum Silinguis* originally published in 1611, 'for teaching Latin to Spanish youth'.) The book was in effect a vocabulary arranged by centres of interest. It was intended as a general education as well as a language text-book. In other words Comenius anticipated that it would be read in schools where Latin, or whatever other language the teacher chose, was used outside the narrow limits of the language classroom. Comenius had a dream of universal knowledge, 'pansophia', which would be acquired as the language learning progressed. At the same time the language would be acquired by use or immersion (IL).

Merely to rely on immersion, however, was not enough. Comenius gave detailed attention to method in the classroom. His *Didactica Magna* (1632), not translated into English until 1896, proposed eight rules for teaching a plurality of languages including: the mother tongue must be mastered first; modern languages before Latin and Greek; languages are easier learnt by practice (and by actions) than from rules; reference should be made to what is already known of previous languages and subject matter that is familiar (e.g. the Catechism which children know by heart). Four stages of text-books are necessary: the *Vestibulum* – a few hundred words in sentences for infants; the *Janua* – 8,000 words in sentences for boyhood; the *Palatium* – discourses for maturer youth with paraphrasing rules; the *Thesaurus* – selections from classical authors for manhood with translation of idioms. Putting into practice the ideas of the *Didactica Magna* and anticipating modern learning theory, Comenius in *Methodus Linguarum Novissima* (1646) proposed a 'visual method' of teaching Latin since 'pictures are what most easily impress themselves on the child's mind, to remain lasting and real . . . children need to be given many examples and things they can see and not abstract rules of grammar'. In 1659 an English edition of the work he is perhaps best known for, among modern linguists, his *Orbis Sensualium*

IOHAN-AMOS COMENIVS,
MORAVVS. Æ. ÆTAT 5...04...

Joh. Amos Commenii

ORBIS

SENSVALIVM

PICTUS.

Hoc eft,

*Omnium fundamentalium in Mundo
Rerum, & in vitâ Actionum,*

Pictura & Nomenclatura.

JOH. AMOS COMMENIUS'S
Vifible WORLD.

OR,

A *Picture* and *Nomenclature* of all the chief
Things that are in the world; and of
Mens Employments therein.

A Work newly written by the Author in
Latine, and High-Dutch (being one of his laft
Effays, and the moft fuitable to Childrens
capacities of any that he hath hitherto made) & tranflated into Englifh.

By CHARLES HOOLE, Teacher of a
Private Grammar-School in
Lothbury, LONDON.

For the ufe of yonng Latine-Scholars.
Nihil eft in intellectu, quod non priùs fuit in fenfu. Arift.

LONDON,

Printed for *J. Kirton*, at the *Kings-Arms*, in
Saint *Paules* Church-yard, 1659.

(270)

CXXXIII.

Ludus Pilæ.

Tennis-Play.

(271)

In a Tennis-Court, 1.	In *Sphæristerio*, 1.
they play	luditur
with a Ball, 2.	*Pilâ*, 2.
which one throweth,	quam alter mittit,
and another taketh,	alter excipit,
& sendeth it back with	& remittit
a Racket ; 3.	*Reticulo* ; 3.
and that is the sport	idq; est Lusus
of Noble-men	Nobilium (ris.)
to stir their body.	ad cõmotionem corpo-
A winde-ball 4.	*Follis* (pila magna) 4.
being filled with air	aëre distenta
by a means of a Ventil,	ope *Epistomii*,
is tossed to and fro	sub dio
with the Fist 5.	*Pugno* 5.
in the open air.	reverberatur.

Pictus (Picture of the Visible World), was published in London (illustration). It was a development of his 'Gates of Tongues Unlocked'. It was originally issued in Latin and 'High Dutch', and translated into English by Charles Hoole, a teacher at a private grammar school in Lothbury, London. This most attractive text-book 'for the use of young Latine Scholars' pioneered many ideas that later became common-place: teach the language directly using visual aids (numbered pictures illustrating everyday activities); use a reduced, maximally functional vocabulary; trust to multiple examples rather than abstract rules; induce rules from examples rather than deducing sentences from rules ('The exemplar should always come first; the precept should always follow'); set out the mother tongue and foreign language side by side in complete sentences. Comenius also suggested that pupils should copy the pictures in his text-book and even colour, in their own copies, the etchings illustrating the lessons, a device that teachers of slower learners have exploited in our own day.

Already, however, Comenius was aware of the changes that the seventeenth century was bringing, especially the decline of Latin as the accepted lingua franca. Indeed it was the lack of a lingua franca suitable for the dissemination of the new scientific ideas that caused him to sympathise with the dream which preoccupied many of the most lively seventeenth-century minds, such as Bishop Wilkins of the Royal Society, namely the construction of a universal language. He recognised that, for good or ill, the age of Renaissance monarchies in Europe had installed national vernaculars as the media for education and even for works of advanced scholarship intended for the international community of scholars. (Isaac Newton was the last great English scientist to issue his magnum opus in Latin in 1687.) Already in 1632, Comenius had argued, in the *Didactica Magna*, that modern languages should be taught before Latin. He probably made the same assumptions about the conditions under which they would be learnt, that is, immersion learning, as John Locke was to make. His views on teaching method, however, underwent a change as the century progressed.

Kelly (1969) warns against exaggerating Comenius' support for inductive methods: 'In Comenius's early writings, the grammatical rule was a prop to learning but in later years it was imitation that became a prop to the rule.' For Comenius, as the years went by, understanding of the 'precept', the grammatical principle, assumed increasing importance and his later work marks a transition to the Latin teaching of the eighteenth and nineteenth centuries.

The decline of Latin

Nothing should detract from the attractiveness and innovation of Comenius' text-books, especially the *Orbis Pictus*, but it is not difficult to see why his ideas made so little impression on the grammar school classrooms.[4] New methods could not be used without ecclesiastical and Privy Council authority; the grammar school curriculum had to be 'safe'. New methods also called for teachers trained to use them and there was no response from the universities. This indifference by the universities was to be repeated in the early twentieth century when the Great Reform collapsed for lack of interest in language teaching as a discipline in its own right. Comenius had no base from which he could train teachers to use his text-books.

As the seventeenth century unfolded, as Comenius had foreseen, Latin became less and less a vocational subject. Foster Watson dates the decline in the vocational use of Latin in England to the restoration of Charles II (1660). 'In spite of the fact that Charles II married a Portuguese wife, his court brought in the French language so effectually that it is from this time that Latin was dislodged from its position as the secretarial language and French became the English diplomatic language' (p. 530).

The grammar schools, constrained by their charters, ecclesiastical visitors and the terms of their benefactions, did not reflect this change in vocational requirements for some 150 years. Latin retained its position but it had to be justified on other grounds. It survived in the eighteenth century only because 'authority' approved. Scientific papers and text-books were now written in English.

Language teaching in the eighteenth century

There is a generally accepted view of the ancient universities in the eighteenth century: 'a university in which professors had ceased to lecture, where tutors regarded an enquiring student as a nuisance and where work was the last thing expected, the chief cause being the disappearance of the poor scholar, his place being taken by the gaming, drunken, extravagant sons of the aristocracy'. This view is challenged by Nicholas Hans (1951). From the *Dictionary of National Biography* he studied the careers of 3,500 men of repute born between 1685 and 1785. Although he agrees 'schools and institutions free from religious control formed the main current of modern education in the 18th century, nevertheless Oxford and Cambridge trained 34% of all English pioneers of science in the 18th century and 80% if medicine and technology (not taught at Oxbridge) are left out'. Hans claims: 'the eighteenth century was perhaps the most interesting period of English education . . . as brilliant schemes and philosophical works as the 17th century . . . also a period of actual realisation of modern education' (p. 46). How much of this excitement spilled over into language teaching? Alas, very little. In 1724 two professorships with supporting lectureships and 'King's scholarships' were established at Oxford and Cambridge to encourage the study of modern languages. In the climate of the time, however, they quickly lapsed into sinecures.

Meanwhile in the grammar schools 'tradition offered passive resistance to any subject unrelated to religion or the languages of religion: Latin, Greek, Hebrew' (Watson). In exceptional schools such as Christ's Hospital, Manchester Grammar School and Hull Grammar School advances were made in mathematics, experiments with the telescope, botany, geography and history. There were even some schools which experimented with new methods of teaching Latin – isolated examples of Comenius' seeds finding a fertile soil.

Hans finds no evidence, however, of progress in modern language teaching in the grammar schools. Only in the private academies which educated 10% of 'leading men' (Hans) was the curriculum unfettered and advances could be made towards modern studies. 'The direct method was known to them', says Hans. They were, of course, encouraged, just as the academies in Tudor times had been, by an influx of native-speaking refugee teachers. Towards the close of the eighteenth century, the French Revolution provided England with scores of first-class French scholars. 'Florian, for instance, staffed his Academy at Bath with French scholars who had previously taught at French universities. Not scholars alone; almost every exiled aristocrat, and later the republican opponents of Robespierre, resorted to giving private lessons as a living' (Hans, 1951, p. 188).

The nineteenth century: the search for panaceas

At the turn of the century the impact of the agrarian and industrial revolutions and the cataclysmic events in Europe shook even the complacency of the grammar school governors. The traditional curriculum, based no longer on a useful and living vernacular tool, Latin, as in Tudor times, but on the safe conning of the three 'languages of religion', began to be questioned. The school charters and the terms of their endowments, however, stood in the way of change.

In 1805 the governors of Leeds Grammar School wished to employ trust funds for the teaching of modern languages. Lord Eldon's famous judgement in the chancery court (reaffirmed 20 years later) stipulated that trust funds could be applied to Latin, Greek and Hebrew alone; to draw upon them for instruction in French, German or other modern studies would be misappropriation.

It was not until the Newcastle Commission 1858–61 on the education of the poorer classes, the Clarendon (Public Schools) Commission 1861–4 and the Taunton (Endowed Schools) Commission 1864–7, that reform of the curriculum was taken seriously. In his *Outline of English Education*, J. W. Adamson, while acknowledging the pioneering ideas of Butler (Shrewsbury), followed by Arnold (Rugby), remarks that 'no public school ventured of its own motion to reform the curriculum . . . the first steps in a real reform of courses . . . were taken by the early Victorian foundations, chiefly proprietary, such as Cheltenham, Liverpool, Marlborough, Rossall, Brighton, Radley and Bradfield'.

Modern languages in the grammar school: FL not IL

When the modern language breakthrough came it was German that led the way, thanks partly to the prestige of German thought (Humboldt's psychology, Kant's and Hegel's philosophy, Froebel's educational ideas) and German science and technology, not to speak of the repute of the literary giants, Schiller and Goethe, and the impact of such great musicians as Haydn, Mozart, Beethoven.

Political unrest later enriched English (and American) life by sending abroad, especially after 1848, a stream of German-speaking refugees. In the USA, the result was that by the end of the nineteenth century, German became the predominant language in the High Schools (see Appendix A). Though French remained the chief foreign language studied in English schools, German was a close second, quite out-distancing Spanish and Italian.

By the middle of the nineteenth century, however, the conditions that John Locke and John Amos Comenius had taken for granted when teaching either Latin or modern languages no longer obtained. Latin was not now a necessary vocational tool. It was not in common use outside the classroom. The modern languages which were being introduced alongside Latin, and which would in course of time take the place of Latin, were similarly confined to four or five short weekly lessons in the cultural island of the language classroom. Language teachers in schools were gardening in a gale of English. Curiously, the significance of this was not generally appreciated. One or two perceptive observers saw that language teaching under such conditions posed entirely new problems which had not faced the Tudor grammar schools teaching a vocational subject by IL methods. For the most part, teachers of both Latin and modern languages battled on doggedly, heads down to the gale. The methods they adopted were the only ones they could adopt in such conditions.

French and German were at first taught either by the classics masters as an extra subject, or more often, as in Tudor times, by immigrant native speakers. The classics teachers naturally used the 'construe' methods that they knew. The native speakers preferred more active, oral methods but found control difficult in the robust conditions of the nineteenth-century classroom and in self-defence resorted to construe and reading.

Public examinations (for example for Army and Civil Service, the Oxford and Cambridge Local Examinations and London Matriculation) stressed knowledge of grammar and philology. The available text-books also encouraged 'grammar/translation' methods. A typical example was de Fivas' *The New Grammar of French Grammars* which went through more than 50 editions between 1840 and 1890. 'Part 1 contains the accidence . . . chapters on each part of speech . . . in complete isolation; Part 2 deals with the syntax in a similar order . . . with disconnected sentences in English for translation into French' (Gilbert, 1953, p. 3).

H. G. Ollendorf, *A New Method of Learning to Read, Write and Speak the French Language in Six Months* (which also ran into about

50 editions from 1843 to 1890) was some improvement on this. At least accidence and syntax were not separated and the parts of speech were not learnt in isolation. The English sentences were graded so that structures learnt earlier were utilised in later sentences. However, the sequence of grammar followed by disconnected sentences for translation into the foreign language was unchanged. Two other very popular grammars (Ahn, 1834 and Plötz, 1865) were similar, with the addition of disconnected sentences for translation into English. There was little or no attempt to teach pronunciation. The language was treated as if it existed only in written form.

This method was strongly supported by establishment opinion. Giving evidence to the Clarendon Commission in 1864, the Taylorian Professor of Modern Languages at Oxford (Max Müller) advised: 'I would aim principally at securing an accurate knowledge of grammar and secondly a sufficient amount of reading – but I should not attempt fluency in conversation.' In 1868 the Schools Inquiry Commission deplored the fact that 'parents demanded facility of conversation and correspondence, not a sound grammatical knowledge'. In girls' schools, French was taught in a 'superficial' manner. 'It is certainly rare to find girls whose minds the study of French seems to have done anything to strengthen or train', although French was better known by girls than by boys (Gilbert, 1953). The 1868 Report also condemned French teachers of French who 'dwell too much on idiomatic usage, rather than on grammatical principles . . . – the French lesson is too frequently conducted in the French language' whereas 'at Newcastle Grammar School French is taught precisely in the same way as the ancient languages – the method is sound; grammar, not vocabulary, being first considered. . . . In some other schools [in Northumberland] the results are worthless. . . . The conversational system is the one most in favour and few boys if any can conjugate the auxiliary verbs' (quoted by Gilbert, 1953, p. 2).

So strong was 'establishment' opinion that even a loyal supporter of modern language studies such as H. W. Eve, Headmaster of University College School, felt obliged – at the Headmasters' Conference 1879 – to defend modern languages as a mental discipline equal to the classics and to claim: 'Your first object is to discipline the mind; your second to give a knowledge of French or German.' This was an interesting comment because in echoing the similar justification advanced for Latin when it ceased to be a vocational subject, it tacitly acknowledged that, when the modern language is taught in normal classroom conditions, claims based on vocational usefulness for the average pupil cannot hold. Other justifications ('mental discipline') had to be invoked, to make headway against those who opposed the introduction of French and German into the curriculum. One of the most confident and closed minds on the subject was Gladstone's. Giving written evidence in 1861 to the Public Schools Commission (he was then a member of the Government), he stressed the need to 'limit and restrain without scruple' the claims of subjects such as 'pure science . . . modern languages [or] modern history', which compete with the 'paramount classical training'. The latter was ordained by divine providence to be 'not a mere adjunct but (in mathematical phrase) the complement of Christianity . . .'. Faced with this kind of polemic from such a powerful source, Mr Eve may well have felt the need to claim moral advantages for language studies.

Not all those who questioned the place of French and German in the curriculum were as reactionary as Mr Gladstone. There were perceptive commentators who saw that the conditions under which the pupils of Locke or Comenius had acquired their second languages were very different from those of the nineteenth-century school classrooms.

Appointed inspector of schools in 1851, the enlightened Matthew Arnold (whose father Thomas, head of Rugby School 1828–42, had, following Shrewsbury, introduced modern languages into the regular timetable), while he campaigned to awaken England to the defects of public education, yet did not consider that instruction in speaking foreign languages was school business (Adamson, 1925). Similarly John Stuart Mill in his famous Inaugural Address at St Andrew's in 1867 which 'raises the discussion about education to a level which controversies seldom reach' (Adamson, 1925) would not have modern languages, history or geography taught in secondary schools; the first should be learnt abroad, the other two by desultory reading. (Mill, a child prodigy who had begun to learn Greek at the age of three, possibly overestimated the effect of 'desultory reading' for average pupils!) In practical terms his proposal to shift all modern language study abroad is unworkable for all our children.

There are ways, however, discussed in later chapters, in which all pupils can be helped to acquire a language by IL and Mill had perceived the limitations of the FL methods. For the next hundred years, successive generations of teachers were to rediscover the truth of his observation, as they sent their fifth and sixth formers on exchanges and study visits abroad and saw their French and German progress by leaps and bounds. 'Immersion' (as the old grammar school charters had insisted) was essential. Yet for a hundred years teachers grasped at one panacea after another, in the hope of finding some way round the truth that John Stuart Mill had glimpsed. The story of that search, often exhilarating and led by teachers of great distinction, is the subject of our next two chapters.

NOTES

1 'Renaissance England had within it the seeds of a truly explosive expansion of grammar school education, both in provision and in content and method. Instead, the sovereigns of the period, faced with religious atomism, political danger and economic dislocation, saw the schools as an important instrument with which to maintain public order and achieve political and religious conformity. Instead of acting as breeding grounds for humanist ideas, a distinct possibility at the beginning of the period, the grammar schools became instruments of national policy, a means of strengthening the state against religious innovation. The grammar schools of Renaissance England had become to the nation what the voluntary elementary schools of the nineteenth century were to their various denominational sponsors – instruments for maintaining the *status quo*.' (Charlton, 1965, p. 130)

2 Indeed in post-Elizabethan times following the Gunpowder Plot (1605) the magistrates in some areas regarded modern languages as potentially subversive and language teachers (mostly from abroad) as likely papist spies. Watson quotes the stringent statutes in Bury St Edmunds (1607) to prevent 'the infectings of youth in Poperie by schoolmasters' which were specially aimed at 'teachers of English, Latin, French, Italian or Spanish tongues'. Annual inspections and licences were required. Watson points out that the grammar schools were controlled by authority; teachers had to be licensed; text-books were prescribed by the King and Privy Council; the statutes of the founders could not easily be altered. Only the education of the higher classes or those who could afford the academies was 'as free as the wind'. (Watson, 1909, p. 523)

3 His name is spelt 'Commenius' on the title page of his books but historians have adopted the simpler spelling.

4 An exception was Rotherham Grammar School where Charles Hoole
   taught Latin following Comenius' methods. Hoole later moved to
   Lothbury where he ran a private school. He translated Comenius into
   English (1659) and published in 1660 '*A New Discovery of the Old Art of
   Teaching School* in which Form I reads, among other books, Comenius'
   Orbis Pictus and Form III the *Janua Linguarum*. Hoole comments
   (Vol. II, p. 6) that the *Orbis Pictus* was too expensive for school use
   owing to the cost of printing the illustrations! (quoted in Kelly, 1969).

5   Reform and counter-reform

The number of grammars upon the French language etc. . . . . pretending to remove its difficulties, has become so great that any new production of the kind may be termed a nuisance. Yet every day brings forth some new grammatical 'chef d'oeuvre' . . . notwithstanding . . . the study of languages still continues to be a slow and tedious affair.

C. le Vert, *An Analytical, Comparative and Demonstrative Mode of Tuition*, 1826

The awakening for modern languages came in the heyday of Victorian times. Some historians have depicted a sudden revolt signalled by the trumpet call in 1882 of the young Wilhelm Viëtor's pamphlet, *Der Sprachunterricht muss umkehren* (Language teaching must about-turn).[1] In fact Viëtor, a lecturer from Marburg teaching at University College, Liverpool, was only giving expression to ideas that had been current for many years in England, Germany, Scandinavia and France as well as in the USA.

As early as 1823, controversy was provoked by the Hamiltonian method. This was a course in 48 lessons based, its author, James Hamilton, claimed, entirely on the way he had himself learned German, using the Gospel of St John with interlinear translation and no grammar. Had he perhaps been reading John Locke's correspondence? In a letter to his French friend Nicolas Thoynard, dated 20 September 1679, the philosopher had written: 'Quand vous aurez la fantasie d'apprendre la langue Angloise vous n'avez qu'à suivre ma méthode en lisant tous les jours un chapitre du nouveau testament et en un mois du temps vous deviendrez maistre' (quoted in Ollion, 1912, p. 37).

Hamilton claimed great success for his method (600 satisfied pupils!). He was challenged and outfaced in a series of public debates by John Hooper Hartnoll (*Exposure of the Hamiltonian System*, 1823). In 1826 C. le Vert produced his *Analytical, Comparative and Demonstrative Mode of Tuition with Ocular and Mechanical*

Demonstration. Another intriguing development was Mr Pemberton's *Philosophical Model Infant School for Teaching Languages, Native and Foreign, on the Natural or Euphonic System* (1857).

Interest in methods of language teaching was unflagging in the nineteenth century. In 1875, the Reverend R. H. Quick published his *Account of Celebrated Methods* in which he reviewed a succession of 'panaceas' down the ages from R. Ascham (1570), who used a model book of Cicero's letters to teach Latin with stress on retranslation into the foreign language, to J. Jacotot (1826), who also advocated basing the teaching (of French) on a single book, *Télémaque*, always starting each lesson from the beginning and going a bit further each day.

For Quick the two most important nineteenth-century innovators were Robertson and Prendergast. Quick's account is not referred to by Gilbert (1955) who briefly mentions Robertson as 'improving' the Hamiltonian method in the early forties. Theodore Robertson lived at Bellevue, near Paris. His *Nouveau Cours pratique, analytique, théorique et synthétique de la langue anglaise* ran into many editions in the forties and fifties. His *Practical Lessons in French* (1853) applied his method for English schools but he remained chiefly known (Quick tells us) in France. His method was similar to the method developed by Langenscheidt in Germany. It relied on a model book which introduced all the main 'roots' in the French language. Each lesson consisted of a text from the model book with three translations: 1. a literal, interlinear translation; 2. a fair English version; 3. a phrase-by-phrase translation in parallel columns for practice in retranslation. Then came 'variations' on the text followed by lexicographical and grammatical commentary.

Thomas Prendergast (*The Mastery of Languages*, 1864) similarly relied on learning not words but 'sequences'. The learner had a book containing a number of idiomatic sentences in the foreign language with translations into good English, covering all the main constructions. The basis of the Prendergast system was learning by heart, as John Locke had proposed, followed by 'variations' in which language previously learnt was practised.

Four ways to reform

Quick's review is useful but it leaves out some of the most interesting forerunners of the Great Reform, who helped to break down the barriers to change. He was also too close to events to disentangle the main themes of the reform. There seem to have been four main themes, one of which, the 'reading method', surfaced briefly and was then forgotten, except in the USA, where it became the orthodoxy of the 1920s. The other three themes were: 'direct method' (banish the mother tongue); 'natural method' (imitate the child); 'phonetic method' (teach via a phonetic alphabet).

Reading method (teach via the written form of the language)

The pioneer of the reading method was Claude Marcel, French consul in London. After his early advocacy of learning through reading he moved to the USA and lent his weight to the 'natural method' advocated by French writers such as Lambert Sauveur and François Gouin. His early impact on reform in the UK was through his book published in London in 1853: *Language as a Means of Mental Culture and International Communication*. Marcel advocates a reading approach. Although he begins with translation his originality is to aim at 'mental reading . . . without the interposition of the native words . . . thinking in a foreign language . . . immediate association of signs and ideas'. He regards translation and teaching of grammar rules by rote as an obstacle to comprehension. 'Grammar should be learned by induction.' Gilbert (1955), to whose researches on this period our indebtedness in the following paragraphs is gratefully acknowledged, remarks on the similarity between Marcel's 'mental reading' and the views of Michael West in the 1920s (West, 1926).

Reading was also the key to success for C. Colbeck of Harrow. In his *On the Teaching of Modern Languages in Theory and Practice* (1887), based on lectures given to students in Cambridge, he argues: 'For use in actual life we all wish to be able to read foreign languages . . . [therefore] . . . we should not begin with conversation . . . The eye is incomparably swifter than the ear.' It was the proponents of learning through the ear, however, who had most following in Europe[2] until the 1920s.

Direct method (banish the mother tongue)

An early advocate of the direct method was the classics teacher, J. S. Blackie. In 1852 in two lectures in Aberdeen (the second one in Latin!) *On the Studying and Teaching of Languages* he set out what Gilbert considers to be the first detailed 'direct description of a method'. In opposition to C. Marcel, Blackie would trust mainly to the *ear*. 'The teacher must speak readily and pronounce well.' Anticipating the German reformers by a generation, Blackie advocates 'direct association of objects with the foreign word' to break the 'evil habit of continuing to think in the mother tongue'. Finally, for Blackie 'grammar is only . . . a continuous running comment on the daily practice of hearing, speaking, and reading'.

Natural method (imitate the child)

The natural method is associated chiefly with the French reformers, notably Gouin, to whose seminal book *L'Art d'enseigner* we shall return.

Phonetic method (teach via a phonetic alphabet)

Finally a number of distinguished phoneticians, A. J. Ellis, *Essentials of Phonetics* (1848) A. Bell, *Visible Speech* (1865); Henry Sweet, *Papers to the Philological Society* (1874 and 1876); and A. Sayce (1879), gave phonetics an unquestioned place in the prospectus of reform, later consolidated by the monthly journal initiated in 1886 by Paul Passy, *Le Maître Phonétique*, which became the organ of the International Phonetic Association.

The prospectus for reform was largely complete, then, before Viëtor wrote his famous pamphlet. His 'trumpet call' was scarcely a new tune. Why had the profession not responded to earlier, home-made, summonses?

The weight of establishment orthodoxy on the side of mental discipline is part of the answer, especially the conservatism of the universities. As in the seventeenth century, the reformers got little support from university teachers. Sweet, the Reader at Oxford, denied a professorial chair according to George Bernard Shaw (preface to *Pygmalion*) by the small-minded jealousy of his colleagues, was almost unique among English academics of distinction in taking language *teaching* seriously. He did have one ally at Oxford, the great Jowett, Master of Balliol, whose intellect did not need to shelter behind received opinion. Addressing the French teachers of French in 1887, Jowett advocated an oral approach: 'Nature taught us to begin with the ear and not the eye.' This provoked a considerable correspondence in the *Journal of Education*. However, the Oxford Honours School of Modern Languages, set up in 1903, did not – still does not? – reflect Jowett's openness to Sweet's plea for 'the living philology'!

A second factor delaying reform was the low status of modern languages in the schools. With no lead coming from the universities, reform could only come from school teachers, but modern language teaching was a new discipline and it was some time before it developed its own professional standards, organisation and journals.

Gilbert quotes from the Clarendon Commission report (1864) to show how low the prestige of the subject was in schools:

'It is a complete impossibility to teach French at Eton' (headmaster)

'The French instruction has been a failure. The masters were generally of French nationality and regarded as inferior' (Westminster)

'The modern languages hold the lowest place in the estimation of masters' (Harrow)

'St Paul's boys do not look upon French as an important part of school-work.'

We find confirmation of this in the survey (mentioned above) by the Reverend R. H. Quick (1875). He instances, as a weakness of school language studies, that 'almost all' schools allowed only two hours per week, and quotes Mr Wilson of Rugby School in arguing for 'stratification' of studies, giving foreign languages more time (at least six hours per week) for beginners, with fewer periods later on. One hundred years later modern language teachers still vainly plead for such flexibility in time-tabling!

An added difficulty was that in their anxiety to show that their subject was a discipline in a respectable sense teachers were chary of listening to reformers like Marcel and Blackie. 'During the eighties, therefore,' says Gilbert, 'modern languages, although more generally accepted as a worthwhile discipline, were still taught very much by the grammar-translation method, oral French being despised as "nursery", "tea-party", "courier"[3] or "bagman" French.' Not until the teachers of the new discipline gained in confidence and established their own professional organisations could they welcome reforming ideas.

It was the immigrant French teachers of French who organised first. They formed the Société Nationale des Professeurs de Français en Angleterre and from 1882 held an annual conference. At their first conference they passed two resolutions: that French should be taught as a living language beginning with pronunciation and conversation, and that it should be taught by

Frenchmen. In 1883 they pressed for oral examinations and in 1887 (when Jowett addressed them) they recommended the direct method for all class teaching in French.

These Frenchmen clearly had an axe to grind, however, and, though their arguments could, with the help of Gouin and Sweet, convince the great Jowett, their classrooms were too often unruly for Heads of schools to be won over. The new development in the 1880s was the emergence of a generation of first-rate English-speaking teachers, of considerable scholarship, energetic and forward-looking, devoted to the 'newer methods'. They were slower to organise. Their first national conference was at Cheltenham in 1890, followed in 1892 by the formation of the Modern Language Association.

This generation of classroom teachers was inspired by the example of reformers in Germany, France and Scandinavia, whose papers they read avidly, and by a growing confidence, following the Great Exhibition of 1851, in the new technology.

Optimism and the new technology

The success of Viëtor's pamphlet in 1882 owed a lot to the climate of optimism in late Victorian times. It was a confident, adventurous climate, comparable to Harold Macmillan's England of the early 1960s, when we 'never had it so good'.

There are many parallels between the 1880s and the 1960s, two periods when the pendulum of language teaching swung towards reform. Both periods were preceded by technological advances in transport (the railway network in one age, jet aircraft and sputniks in the other) which dramatically shrank distances between speech communities. The invention by A. G. Bell of the electric telephone (1876) had a similar impact to the spread of television nearly a hundred years later. In 1878 Edison perfected the mechanical phonograph enabling linguists for the first time to store and reproduce *speech*, the raw stuff of their trade. The parallel with the widespread use of the tape-recorder in schools in the 1960s is striking. In the 1880s, also, the new linguistic discoveries of the *Junggrammatiker* and the phoneticians caused a revolution in thinking about language comparable only to the shock waves that followed Chomsky's *Syntactic Structures* (1957) and *Aspects of the Theory of Syntax* (1965). Both periods also saw the birth of new journals and institutions in which linguists and teachers challenged conventional ideas.

Viëtor's rallying call

Viëtor's eloquent but unoriginal message, therefore, found a willing audience. His desire to 'set children free' was based on the writings of Herbart while his teaching methods were influenced by the phoneticians, Sayce and Sweet. The sub-title of his pamphlet is *Ein Beitrag zur Überbürdungsfrage* (A contribution to the question of overloading) and the dedication is to F. W. Fricke, author of *Overloading the school pupil*. Language teaching, says Viëtor, accounts for nearly two-thirds of teaching time in the German Gymnasium (7,000 hours, not counting homework, over the five-year course) and so is a major part of the pupil's load. Viëtor begins by attacking the mother tongue teaching in German schools (ignorance of phonetics, inept grammar teaching) and then turns to foreign language teaching. He starts from the axiom 'Die Sprache besteht aus Lauten und nicht aus Buchstaben' (Language consists of sounds not letters), quoted from Sayce, 'How to learn a language' (1879). Furthermore, quoting Sayce again: 'Language does not consist of isolated words.' Failure to grasp this explains why, in Germany, 'school pronunciation of English and French is awful'. 'Our language teaching method is scarcely an advance on the Donatus system.' He cites Sweet, arguing that it is essential for teachers to have a firm grounding in phonetics for teaching both foreign languages and the mother tongue.

Turning to methodology, Viëtor attacks grammar-translation on the grounds that teaching grammar rules, instead of allowing pupils to discover the rules for themselves, takes the interest out of the work. He quotes Sayce further, stressing the difference between study of a living language and learning the rules of the classics. Translation into the mother tongue is permissible (to establish the meaning of a text) but translation into the foreign language 'is an art which has no place in school'. Even some classics teachers were joining in the cry: 'Tod den Regeln und Sätzen!' (Death to rules and sentences!)

Viëtor would make the mainthrust (*Schwerpunkt*) of teaching 'reading in context'. The final goal of reading is to enable the learner to 'think outside his mother tongue and in the foreign language'. It is interesting that in this connection Viëtor quotes Plötz with approval. For some historians, as Peter Hagboldt has remarked, Plötz is the embodiment of every linguistic malfeasance in linguistic pedagogy. His *Lese- und Übungsbuch*, however, is praised by Viëtor as a step forward (*jedenfalls ein*

Fortschritt). He returns finally to his 'overloading' theme: 'Come now! language teachers – show that half a field, well tended (*gepflegt*) and tilled (*bestellt*), bears more fruit than the whole field on which one repeatedly scatters handfuls of impure seed (*ungesäuberten Samen*). This will leave more time to get out on to the playground or into the woods!'

Felix Francke

Less oratorical than Viëtor's pamphlet but more closely argued was Felix Francke's little book, *Die praktische Spracherlernung* (1884). For Francke the essential fact about speech activity is that it is unconscious: 'All speech utterances flow out of the dark room of the unconscious, where all the speech material of the individual lies' (p. 11).

We can, he argues, proceed in two ways in studying a foreign language. First, we may try to make conscious the unconscious content of the mind. The language material becomes then a purpose in itself; this is what the grammatical method achieved. Second, we may wish to achieve the power of using the language by trying to construct in our minds an unconsciously working speech mechanism. These two ways of learning a language cannot be followed at the same time.[4] Francke states three principles:

1   The real word is the spoken word (hence the importance of phonetics)
2   Learn the foreign language in and through the foreign language so that expressions are acquired unconsciously
3   Try to associate the spoken word with the original idea, instead of linking the symbol of the foreign word through the eye to the word in the mother tongue. (Gilbert, 1953)

This became the credo of the direct methodists in all countries some of whom tried to avoid translation altogether. Francke himself did not go so far. Like Viëtor he would admit translation into the mother tongue while firmly forbidding translation into the foreign language.

The language teachers' response: the Cheltenham conference

Viëtor and Francke had their opponents, and the debate which ensued in the German journals and lecture halls was followed keenly in England where the reform movement was led by a group of practising schoolmasters of great energy. The German theorists helped to steer the English reform movement towards a

reliance on phonetics and 'direct method' rather than towards
the 'natural method' favoured by the French reformers, Lambert
Sauveur and François Gouin.

The focal point of the movement in England was the great
conference organised by schoolmasters[5] at Cheltenham in 1890.
All the giants were there: MacGowan, Widgery, Walter, Passy,
Viëtor etc. Viëtor read a paper in the debate on the motion
'phonetics should form the basis of all modern language
teaching'. He reviewed the German reform movement, acknowledging the help given it by Sayce, Sweet and Passy. (They had
earlier, in 1886, founded the International Phonetic Teachers'
Association.)

The conference passed resolutions supporting more oral work
and reading and calling for a more 'concrete' study of grammar,
while acknowledging that grammar must be learned systematically and could not be abolished without abolishing mental discipline. Two years later (1892) these energetic and practical teachers
founded the Modern Language Association.

Henry Sweet

The English schoolmasters, inspired by the debate in Germany, found few allies in their own universities. The shining
exception was the great Henry Sweet, Reader in Phonetics at
Oxford. His book *The Practical Study of Languages* (1899) is a
landmark in the literature of language teaching.

Sweet was a friend of Bernard Shaw whose brief preface to
Pygmalion is mostly about Sweet. The two men used to corres-
pond in shorthand. Shaw used the Pitman system which Sweet
called the 'pitfall system'. Shaw denies, in the preface to *Pygmalion*, that 'Professor Higgins' is Sweet but says 'he has touches of
Sweet', adding 'with Higgins' physique and temperament Sweet
might have set the Thames on fire. As it was he impressed
himself professionally on Europe to an extent that made the
failure of Oxford to do justice to his eminence a puzzle to foreign
specialists.'

Language *teaching* was not a respectable academic interest in
the universities. We must come back to this when we consider
the wider question of the universities' responsibility for the
shortage of teachers able to teach languages effectively.

Sweet's great book is full of insights into what he called 'our
present wretched system of studying foreign languages'. For

Sweet, as for his German contemporaries, the dragon to be slain was grammar-translation. Sweet carried the debate further with his analysis of what he called 'the arithmetical fallacy'. He argued that the company words keep with each other in a living language (we would now say 'collocation') is never quite predictable. It cannot be worked out by rules or arithmetical formulae. The learner must first meet the living language and experience the company words keep when used by native speakers or writers. Until he has met a particular usage the learner cannot be sure that it is one a native speaker would accept. This is what makes translation into the foreign language an excellent test, revealing whether or not the learner has in fact met the foreign idiom called for in the context, but it also makes such translation a dubious teaching device, since it invites the learner to guess at collocations that are arbitary and unpredictable and distracts him from what he ought to be spending his time on, namely meeting the foreign language in use and learning the company words keep in all its arbitrariness.

Sweet dismissed scathingly those reformers, inspired from France, who hankered after a natural method, imitating the acquisition of the mother tongue: 'The fundamental objection, then, to the Natural Method is that it puts the adult into the position of an infant, which he is no longer capable of utilising, and at the same time does not allow him to make use of his own special advantages' (p. 75).

Sweet's main theme was to stress the contribution of phonetics to the new science of language teaching. He called it the 'living philology'. Phonetics allowed the (otherwise ephemeral) spoken language to be made the subject of exact study, whereas formerly only written language could be observed and precisely analysed. This new science, armed with Edison's phonograph, enabled modern language teaching finally to come of age and to distance itself from the teaching methods associated with the classics.

French reformers: the natural method

Though the schoolmaster reformers in England were chiefly inspired by pleas for direct method and phonetics from Germany, French reformers favouring the natural method also had some influence, despite Sweet's scepticism. The ideas of Lambert Sauveur became known in England and the USA with the publication of his *Introduction to the Teaching of Living Languages* in

New York in 1874. He advocated emphasis on the living language through the use of natural conversation in class and the banishment from the classroom of the mother tongue. He would postpone literary criticism and grammatical analysis until the learner is able to understand the language.

A more famous French apologist for the natural method was François Gouin. His *L'Art d'enseigner*, published in 1880, in Paris, remained largely unknown in the UK until it was translated into English by V. Bétis and H. Swan in 1892. The book still makes compulsive reading. It is a strange amalgam of brilliant insights and egocentric commentary. The gist of his argument in favour of the natural method is based on his comparison, now one of the best known in the history of language teaching, between his own failure, as a post-graduate student of philosophy, in his desperate efforts to learn German,[6] in order to study under Hegel in Berlin, and the effortless acquisition of French as mother tongue by his nephew, aged two and a half, in the same period. The revelation came when Gouin accompanied the little boy on his famous visit to a water-powered flour mill and later overheard the child mimicking the miller's series of actions as he played by himself in the garden. Gouin extrapolated from mother tongue acquisition to (adult) foreign language learning without acknowledging that qualification was called for. His conclusions concerning the natural method are not supported by recent research in language acquisition. His teaching technique, however, based on his famous series of logically associated actions (the verb was for Gouin the key to language acquisition), had great success for a time.

Gouin was little known in France, says Hagboldt (1940), having his greatest success in Germany. Success in England was also late in coming. When Gouin was discovered by Bétis and Swan they founded the Central School of Foreign Tongues in London, using Gouin's methods which Howard Swan described in *The Systematic Teaching of Languages* (1894). Swan reports that 200 schools were already using Gouin's series method at that time, only two years after the appearance of the book in English. In 1895 the Technical Education Committee of Surrey County Council subsidised a course of Gouin French classes at Egham (Gilbert, 1953). D. T. Holmes reported in 1903 in his book *The Teaching of Modern Languages in Schools and Colleges*: 'The vogue of the method has been beyond question phenomenal.'

However, it was not the part of Gouin's method that claimed to be natural that was successful. To invite teachers to get their pupils to imitate the child acquiring his mother tongue when they were gardening in a gale in the classroom was unhelpful. Those ideas that Gouin shared with the German reformers, however, made the strongest impact: put speech before writing; subordinate formal grammar to use of the language; learn language while doing.

Among the many insights which enliven Gouin's own account of his method is a perceptive attack on translation into the foreign language, his now legendary analogy of the 'Emperor of China':

'Here is a hammer, a square, and a chisel and there lies a block of marble', the classical school says to its disciples. 'You have everything that is needed for carving any statue you please. You will now set to work and carve from this block the statue of the Emperor of China, *whom you do not know*, and it must be a good likeness.' (Gouin, 1880, p. 301)

Gouin here graphically makes the point that Sweet had made with his 'arithmetical fallacy': the company that words keep is arbitrary and cannot be predicted; the learner must meet collocation first by listening or reading.

Another original contribution from France was that of Inspector Hovelaque (quoted in Kelly, 1969) who postulated two kinds of pupil: those who learn primarily through their eyes (visuals) and those who learn through their ears (audials). 'It is tempting to surmise that control over language teaching as well as passing between the logician and the linguist has also been dominated by audials and visuals in turn' (Kelly, 1969, p. 322).

Language teaching theory has not followed up this insight though the possibility of 'setting' learners according to their preference for learning by eye or by ear is referred to, in passing, by Halliday, McIntosh and Strevens (1964) and the eye and ear are interestingly compared as channels for verbal learning in Kavanagh and Mattingley (1972).

Reform in the USA

The reform movement in the USA began with a strong bias towards the natural method. As early as 1818, N. G. Dufief had attacked the grammatical approach: 'How then is language to be acquired? I answer by adopting the mode by which nature teaches children their mother tongue.' Minds were not closed in the American universities. G. Ticknor, professor of Modern

Languages at Harvard, lectured in 1832 on *The Best Methods of Teaching the Living Languages*. He argued that the 'spoken and active methods were best: they should begin in early childhood and grammar should not be introduced until age 13'. He conceded, however, that for later learners a modified grammar-translation method was better than an oral method (Kelly, 1969, p. 320).

In 1867 Claude Marcel published in New York his *Study of Languages*. He advocated the abolition of translation-grammar rules. He wished to teach through comprehension tests and abundant listening: 'What is required for the exchange of thought is not so much the names of things as the power of affirming, denying and questioning about them.' Marcel's earlier ideas on reading were to be taken up in the Report of the Committee of 12 (1901) and the massive study by the Modern Language Association of America 1927–31 (Coleman, 1931).

Gottlieb Heness in 1866 set up a small private language school at New Haven. He is, after Dufief, the pioneer of the 'natural method' (anticipating Gouin) as a reaction against the grammar-translation tradition. Later in collaboration with Lambert Sauveur, who had independently discovered the natural method, Heness founded a school in Cambridge (Mass.) and ran summer schools for teachers. Among his students were some famous personalities including Eliot, Longfellow and Gilman (see Hagboldt, 1940).

The natural method also had its critics in the USA and some were not without wit: J. Lévy (1878) wrote an open letter to L. Sauveur: 'I have it from a very trustworthy authority that, in some New England town, a teacher of the "Natural Method" gambols round the room to express the idea of "run". If this be the general case, school committees will no longer be called upon to deliver certificates of proficiency to teachers of languages; this duty will devolve on P. T. Barnum [the great circus owner]!' (quoted in Kelly, 1969, p. 11).

It was in the USA nevertheless that the most thoroughgoing and longest-lasting experiment in 'immersion' methods of language acquisition was made, when in 1882 M. D. Berlitz and his brother founded their private school of languages for adults in Providence. The school was based on uncompromising direct method principles. Use of the learner's mother tongue was strictly forbidden. A lapse by the teacher into the learner's native language could lead to dismissal. The school had enormous success. Its branches soon spread round the globe and it still flourishes, with its strict direct method still observed. It must be remembered that Berlitz catered for motivated adults, who chose their target language and paid for the lessons, and were mature enought to put up with long, strenuous immersion sessions.

In the end, neither natural nor direct methods made headway in USA High Schools. The Modern Language Association study of 1901, and the massive study of American and Canadian Foreign Languages (17 volumes) 1927–31, reflected what were felt to be realistic views concerning the use that High School students were likely to make of European languages.

The direct method: Otto Jespersen

The Reform had many names in England. 'Natural method' was an early casualty. In 1899 Henry Sweet convincingly rejected the notion of natural method and ridiculed Gouin's claim that learning a language could be 'as natural as learning to fly is to a bird'. The Inspectorate spoke circumspectly of 'the newer methods'. When Otto Jespersen came to write his immensely popular *Sprogundervisning*, translated from the Danish in 1904 as *How to Teach a Foreign Language*, he was able to list 19 different names that had been given to the movement in the 1880s and 1890s. Most of the 19 names (see Appendix D) have now been forgotten and paradoxically it is by the name 'direct method' that the reform movement is now remembered. The principle of the direct method as Francke (1884) put it was: 'associate the spoken word directly with the original idea'. It had considerable success in Europe. In 1898 the International Congress of Modern Language Teachers in Vienna adopted the principle that the direct method should be used in all elementary teaching of foreign languages. Between 1900 and 1902 the Governments of Germany, France and Belgium declared direct method the only approved method for their state schools while in Germany Viëtor's phonetics won official recognition. Much of this success was owed to the powerful advocacy of Otto Jespersen.

Jespersen had launched the reform movement in Scandinavia in the 1890s by adapting Felix Francke's *Die praktische Spracherlernung*. His *Sprogundervisning* with its unpretentious style and obvious authority won many supporters for the newer methods. Where Jespersen was particularly influential was in encouraging teachers to select vocabulary on functional criteria and reading matter that had contemporary appeal. He quotes some hair-raising examples of unnatural dialogues from text-books used in school:

> 'Wo seid ihr?'
> 'Wir sind nicht hier!'

and disconnected sentences for translation of the type:

> 'Your horse had been old.'

He agrees with Sweet about the arithmetical fallacy and illustrates its idiocies with an example in Danish, taken from a tri-lingual shop sign in Copenhagen:

> Støvle- og skomager
> Boot- and shoemaker
> Botte- et cordonnier

Jespersen makes an aside on the impossibility of translation: 'English "bat" is "translated": (Fr.) chauvesouris, (Ger) Fledermaus, (Lat) vespertilio, (Danish) flagermus' but

The French, the German, and the Danish words call attention to the animal's resemblance to a mouse, the Danish word besides to its flapping movement (a suggestion which must be lost for the Germans, since 'flattern' has taken the place of 'fledern') but the French word to its bald appearance; the Latin word makes us think of the time of day when the animal is abroad, but the English word 'bat' is rather an abstract expression without any suggestiveness . . . traduttore traditore! (p. 54)

He suggests, as Comenius had done, that pupils should be encouraged to make their own drawings; for example, pupils should make simple pictures following instructions in the foreign language from their teacher or their partners.

He also advocates 'inventional grammar'. Although Sweet had 'poured scorn' on this idea, says Jespersen, Sweet himself proceeded to advocate something very similar (p. 133).

There is, however, full agreement with Sweet about phonetics. Jespersen calculates that an adequate phonetic alphabet for transcription of any of the main European languages can be compiled by the addition of five to eight new symbols to the conventional alphabet (p. 144).

For Jespersen the best name for the reform would have been 'living method' but he also commends 'direct' as a label and Jespersen probably more than any other reformer caused this label to stick. What did the method amount to when classroom teachers put into practice the theories advanced so eloquently by Jespersen?

The direct method in practice

What direct method meant to an open-minded schoolmaster of great distinction may be seen from the account by Dr von Glehn of the Perse School, printed as an appendix to the Board of Education Circular 797 (1912), 'A brief sketch of the theory and practice of what is generally called the Direct Method which it is attempted to carry out in this school':

The Direct Method rests on the following principle:

The essential condition for acquiring a real command of a language – both of the spoken and of the written idiom – is to establish in connection with that language the same Direct Association between experience and expression as exists in the use of the mother-tongue.

Since the best means of establishing this Direct Association is the constant hearing and speaking of the language, especially the rapid give-and-take of dialogue, the spoken idiom must be made the basis and, as far as possible, the medium of instruction.

Furthermore, now that psychological research has shown the important part played in the acquisition of language by auditory and motor associations (i.e. the memory of the physical experience in hearing and in articulation), it is obvious that language teachers must make full use of these factors in the building up of the foreign language in their pupils, instead of relying mainly on visual associations as has been done hitherto.

This means shifting the centre of gravity of language teaching from the aim of training one's pupils to *understand* the language and *know* its grammar, to the aim of giving one's pupils first and foremost *the command of the language as a means of self-expression*, to serve as a basis for the study of its literature and structure. It means that, especially in the elementary and intermediate stages, the inevitable gap between the 'active' and 'passive' knowledge of the language (i.e. between the power to use it and the power to understand it) should be kept as narrow as possible; in short, the keynote, the guiding principle of the Modern Language Course, must be *self-expression*, with all the forms of intellectual training that this word implies – composition in its widest sense, both oral and written.

It follows from the considerations here laid down that the intrusion of the mother-tongue into the modern language class room must be rigorously restricted, if not deliberately avoided, at every point.

Von Glehn goes on to distinguish between 'interpretation' (establishing the meaning of new material) and 'assimilation'. He allows that while 'most teachers agree' that in the 'interpretation' stage it may be inadvisable to make a fetish of explaining everything in the foreign language, the stage of assimilation should not be disturbed by the intrusion of the mother tongue. This important distinction was forgotten when the pendulum swung in the 1960s to audio-visual methods (so-called). Insecure teachers, anxious to be in the fashion, were to be seen going through every kind of contortion in front of their film-strip pictures, trying to get precise meanings across to their class without letting slip a word of English. But to the misconceptions of audio-visual methods we must return in the next chapter.

Von Glehn's distinction between 'interpretation' (understanding) and 'assimilation' (use) of new material was paralleled, he suggested, by 'recognition' of, and 'self-expression' in, old material.

These four processes alternate all the time . . . The Direct Method enables one, in each of them, to dispense with the mother-tongue more and more as the pupils advance, for it is based on a system of reproduction (leading to free composition) in which question and answer in the foreign tongue form the regular means of communication between teacher and taught, the new being linked to and explained by the old at every point.

This was both penetrating and practical. But how typical of his fellow teachers was von Glehn? We shall see that the changes brought into most classrooms by the Great Reform were in practice fairly limited. For a number of reasons which we must explore, the ferment of new theories left day-to-day teaching in classrooms little changed.

Progress of reform in the schools: Circular 797 (1912)

The clearest picture of how little the reform movement achieved even at its best in schools is given by Circular 797, in which von Glehn's account appeared. This was one of a series of Memoranda on the subjects in the curriculum which the new Board of Education began to issue soon after its creation by the Act of 1902. The Board delayed its report on the teaching of modern languages because of 'special difficulties' of the subject, particularly the 'insufficient supply of properly qualified teachers'.[7]

The circular acknowledges that what it calls the 'newer methods' during the past 20 years have 'vivified the whole study of French and German in the schools' and 'have been largely instrumental in raising modern languages to a position of dignity in the curriculum'. However, 'Reports received from the Board's

Inspectors show that, in many schools which claim to have adopted the newer methods, the staff is unequal to the task . . .' The Memorandum defined the newer methods in a footnote: 'In nearly every case the newer methods are, to a greater or less extent, influenced by the principles of . . . Direct Method . . . principles . . . which are not always understood.' To clarify what the schools understood by the newer methods the Board printed in an appendix detailed schemes of work in a sample of eight schools. The reports show some unanimity among the schools on one aspect of method only: the use of phonetic transcription by beginners in French (not in German).

The schools were selected 'from the large number known to be giving special attention to modern languages, so as to include schools of different types'. They were: Clifton College, Perse School (Boys), Leeds High School (Girls), Bolton Grammar School, Colchester Royal Grammar School, Sydenham County School, Holloway County School, Tottenham County School.

Use of phonetics

> In Grade I a book printed in IPA is used (IPA transcription is used in all 8 schools). The pupils *read* but are not required to *write* in IPA (Clifton)

> All the early reading is in phonetic transcription and with transition to t.o. [traditional orthography] in the second or towards the end of the first year. (Perse)

> In the Preparatory Department and Form I the work is entirely oral (with a native speaker); introduction to phonetics follows in Form II (sometimes in Form I). (Leeds)

> The first book used in French is in phonetic script. (In German phonetic script is only used by way of illustration.) (Bolton)

> Use is made of phonetics for teaching pronunciation but phonetic work is omitted entirely in the elementary stage and is begun later in the school. (Colchester)

> All beginners whatever their age are put through a course of French phonetics. Phonetic script is employed . . . for written work of all kinds including Free Composition. (Sydenham)

> In the elementary stage a phonetic transcription is used exclusively. Use is made of phonetics throughout the course for . . . correcting . . . pronunciation. (Holloway)

> Phonetic transcription is used exclusively at the beginning of the French course. (In German a phonetic chart is used to help pronunciation.) (Tottenham)

That seven of the eight schools were teaching beginners via phonetic script (at least for French) shows the impact made by the writing of Sweet, Sayce and Passy. It probably owes something also to the attractiveness of the reformed text-books using phonetic script such as those by Walter Ripman and Marc Ceppi. The unanimity with which most schools dropped phonetic transcription in one more swing of the pendulum in the 1920s and 1930s is a mystery to be examined in a later section.

Translation

This general (initial) agreement about the place of phonetics in teaching French contrasts with the lack of widespread enthusiasm in the schools for other innovations advocated by Sweet, Jespersen and others. Translation, for example, both from and into the foreign language,[8] was very much alive in classrooms other than von Glehn's at the Perse.

> Translation from French into English is done in all grades (as quickest means of ascertaining if French is understood and *as valuable mental training*).Translation *into* French begins from Grade IV onwards. (Clifton)

> A much modified direct method is used. . . . A good deal of time is given to *composition* (i.e. translation of English into French). [30 years after Viëtor and Gouin had set out to slay this dragon!] (Leeds)

> In the upper part of the school a course of English–French exercises based on the grammar is used. Some pieces of continuous prose are given for translation into the foreign language. A text-book of composition is used for German.

> No attempt is made to carry on the Modern Language class entirely in French or German. Translation is done at every stage. (Bolton)

Tottenham probably spoke for many well-meaning teachers:

> A little translation of French into English is begun at the end of the second year. But this practice is regarded by the school as a concession to the present requirements of external examinations. If the school had a perfectly free hand translation would be limited to the last two years at school.

This attitude to the demands of the public examinations contrasts with the magisterial statement of the great von Glehn:

> The Modern Language work of this school has been planned without special reference to the requirements of any external examination. This is felt to have been a great advantage. (Perse)

Grammar

It seems clear from the schools' reports that teachers were a
very long way from 'banishing the mother tongue from the
classroom'. Of the reformers' 'dragon to be slain' the translation
half was clearly alive and well in English schools in 1912. The
other half of the dragon was grammar. It, too, had resisted the
reforming St Georges except in von Glehn's classroom.

> sound mental training . . . should and can be derived from a
> judicious treatment of grammar and translation. (Clifton)

> Much attention is given to grammar and the formal side of
> grammar is begun early in the course. (Colchester)

> Careful attention is given to grammar throughout the course. A
> grammar book written entirely in French is introduced in Form
> Lower v (similarly in German). (Holloway)

> Grammar is not neglected at any stage but the more formal
> treatment of grammar is not attempted before the third year.
> (Tottenham)

Reading between the lines of Circular 797, it is not hard to see
that even the modest advances made in the eight schools reviewed were exceptional. The circular continually cautions
against the abandonment of old tried methods and against experiment unless teachers are sure that the old virtues are not lost.
Thus avoidance of the mother tongue often means 'a lamentable
waste of time'. 'Disappointing results of the modern language
work in many schools' follow from teachers 'doing too much' and
exacting too little 'strenuous work' from pupils. The circular
gives a 'serious warning against the use of a phonetic script by
teachers who have not a thorough mastery of the principles of
sound production'. Inductive grammar, says the circular, is possibly useful with young beginners, though 'even at this stage a
wisely chosen Grammar book may be found useful'. With 12-
year-old beginners 'it is necessary that grammar shall be systematically taught'. As for translation, 'something of great value will
be lost if the pupils are not trained in the difficult art of rendering
literary French and German into the best English that they can
command', and 'in the highest forms of all schools it may be
assumed that the curriculum will provide for the rendering of
continuous prose into French and German'.

It is clear from Circular 797 that Inspectors had been impressed
by the work of von Glehn[9] but chastened by what less perceptive
teachers were doing in the name of 'newer methods'. Many of the

Circular's criticisms were reiterated in the reports of 1916, 1918 and 1926, a clear indication of lack of progress in the schools.

In fact Circular 797 had little time to make any impact in schools or universities.[10] Within two years the country was at war. The circular of 1912 was in fact reissued unaltered by the Board of Education in 1925. By then, however, a number of things had happened to change the climate of opinion in the schools and to confirm the universities in their rejection of the new methods. It is significant that in 1923 Otto Tacke in Germany published a paper under the title Viëtor had used 40 years before: *Der Sprachunterricht muss umkehren!* Why had so little ground been won?

Whether, had it not been for the war, the example of men like von Glehn, and a continuing dialogue with reformers in Germany, might have brought about further big changes in language teaching in Britain, one can only guess. The report of 1868 (Taunton Commission) showed from what abysmally low standards the reforms had had to start and how entrenched were the prejudices opposing reform. There was real progress between 1868 and 1912 and it is a measure of the reformers' impact in some schools. Certainly language classrooms became more interesting and intellectually stimulating places; the whole business became more fun, thanks to Jespersen and Sweet. In most classrooms, however, the momentum of change, slight as it was, faltered after 1914. We can distinguish five factors contributing to this loss of momentum: the effect of the 1914–18 war; (paradoxically) Harold Palmer's highly original book, *The Scientific Study and Teaching of Languages*, published in 1917; the influence of the reports of 1916, 1918 and 1926; and the effect of the new national examinations set up in 1918. Underlying these last two was the failure of the Universities to take an interest in the *teaching* of languages or the problems facing the schools; there was for example almost no serious research in *method* between the wars and a similar neglect of in-service training for language teachers.

Counter-reform

World War 1914–18

The Board of Education *Inquiry into the Teaching of French in London Secondary Schools* (1916) leaves no doubt that modern language studies were hit hard by the outbreak of war in 1914.

'Many masters engaged in the teaching of French, including some who held highly responsible posts, have joined the Forces . . . their substitutes are . . . less qualified . . . serious disturbance of organisation.' Equally serious was the abrupt cutting of links with reformers in Germany; the international dialogue in which MacGowan and Widgery had been so active ceased overnight. Exchange of journals and learned papers was impossible. Worse still was the war-time prejudice against everything German. (Even von Glehn had to become de Glehn.) (In the USA[11] the German language, until 1915 overwhelmingly the most popular language studied in the High Schools, dropped virtually from sight, not to climb back until the 1930s). Plans had been laid in 1913 by the Board of Education in the UK to introduce a new national examinations system. The war caused the whole project to be put in the cupboard until it was over. The system of modern language tests finally set up in 1918 (School Certificate and Higher School Certificate) reflected a more cautious, university-dominated view than might have prevailed in the climate of 1913 when minds were more open to international dialogue about language teaching. In all these ways the war was a disaster for the hopes of the reformers.

Harold Palmer

It may seem strange to include Palmer's forward-looking book *The Scientific Study and Teaching of Languages* (1917), in the story of counter-reform. Palmer was no mere conservative. In his dedicatory preface to Edouard Mathieu he recalls how with his companions

At the Société Polyglotte . . . we would preach reform and carry glad tidings of phonetics, of ergonics or of semantics . . . So free from prejudice were we, and so open were our minds, that we would accept and reject the doctrine of the Direct Method at least once a year. You will remember our search for the one true standard and universal method, the goal that ever seemed so near and yet which ever proved just beyond our grasp. (preface: omitted from 1968 edition)

He recalls their conclusion: 'Ce n'est pas la méthode qui nous manque, c'est la base même de la méthode.' It is this foundation that he sets out in his book. Palmer seeks not one universal method but a set of principles from which can be derived different methods adapted to particular ends.

In order to clear the ground, Palmer corrects some misconceptions of the reformers about the place of translation in language learning: direct method, avoidance of translation, banishing the mother tongue altogether, is time wasting. 'You, a teacher of English, are giving lessons to a Norwegian. Your pupil asks you the meaning, or the meanings, of the English verb *to realize*. Do not waste twenty precious minutes in forging definitions which will be imperfectly understood; refer your pupil to a good English–Norwegian dictionary, of which there is no lack' (p. 61).

But reference to the mother tongue is not simply a regrettable necessity. It is to be welcomed if second (and third) languages are to be learnt because 'semanticising' takes too long if we do not take over into the new language much that we have learnt in the mother tongue.

We have learnt, let us say, mathematics, chemistry, or geology in our own language; we wish to read up or refer to works on these subjects written in some foreign, non-cognate language. Are we, then, to study these sciences anew *ab ovo* in order to avoid the pernicious act of consulting the bilingual dictionary? *Poser la question, c'est la résoudre.* Let there be no illusion on this point; the most fervent partisan of the Direct Method translates, whatever his impressions to the contrary may be . . . He is reading a technical book dealing with chemistry; the word *Wasserstoff* occurs repeatedly. Our reader does not refer to a bilingual dictionary, it is true, but in the end he says to himself: '*Ach so, das Wort Wasserstoff bedeutet sicher Hydrogen.*' (p. 57)

(One might object that an English reader speaking to himself would be more likely to say in English: 'Oh, *Wasserstoff* must mean hydrogen!' Palmer's substantive point, however, is unaffected.)

The idea that banishing the mother tongue from the classroom dialogue was not the same thing as banishing it from the pupils' heads had been made by Otto Jesperson, *en passant*.[12] Palmer goes further. He argues that whatever advantages there may be in 'direct semanticizing' (i.e. in avoiding *translation* which is 'indirect semanticizing') the overriding principle to observe is 'direct programming'. By this he means taking the 'shortest and easiest route to practical mastery' of the language. The two, he argues, are mutually exclusive. 'The claims of the Direct Programme [i.e. frequency and ergonic combination] must be given priority over any claims whatever.'

There can be little doubt that the long section IV, The Principles of Linguistic Pedagogy, in which Palmer exposed the fallacy of direct method, marks a decisive point in the debate. As Circular 797 had shown in 1912, very few schools had tried to banish the mother tongue completely. The conditions of 'gardening in a gale' made it impracticable. Nevertheless, the theoretical arguments for direct method were plausible and confused many teachers. The distinction drawn by Palmer between 'direct semanticizing' (establishing meaning) and 'direct programming' (finding the shortest route to mastering the language) pointed to a flaw in the direct method argument which was to trip up some well-intentioned reformers in the 1960s. It is the error of confusing the two stages of initial presentation of new language (grasp of meaning), and acquisition of fluency in using new language. In the first stage, use of the mother tongue can obviously save time, while in the second stage, intervention of the mother tongue can only waste time.

Palmer's other interesting ideas made less impact. His distinction between 'primary' and 'secondary' matter, the first memorised, the second constructed from primary matter, is worked out with a wealth of practical examples. His 'ergonic' chart of French, a kind of gigantic substitution table for the whole language with 'ergons'[13] as replaceable units, is a *tour de force* though, as Palmer admits, it is in too unfinished a state to be more than an illustration of a possible way forward.

Curiously the most provocative element in the complex design mapped out in Palmer's *Scientific Study* has had least attention. This is his insistence on the importance of subconscious comprehension: the spontaneous and automatic assimilation of the language 'without conscious effort, analysis or translation'. As we have seen, this was an idea originally suggested by F. Francke. The need to develop the pupil's 'subconscious assimilation' by progressive, listening activities throughout the course is a part of Palmer's programme that well repays study seventy years later (p. 90).

Palmer did not so much oppose the 'newer methods' of the reformers as leave them behind, while revealing how muddled and unsatisfactory many of their ideas had been. On one point he is in agreement with Sweet, Jespersen and von Glehn: he gives an important place to phonetics, though he counsels against an 'overdose' of phonetics (as of any other 'lack of proportion' in the teaching programme).

The young men who returned from the war in 1918, the year after Palmer's book was published, to train as language teachers, must have found it stimulating reading, filled as it is with practical suggestions and examples for classroom exploitation. Unfortunately teacher training in the universities failed to exploit its insights. Nothing of comparable verve and clear-headedness was waiting to inspire the generation who returned to their language classrooms in 1946. The message of the book is: forward to a scientific, meticulously programmed method, based on a new concept of 'ergonic' analysis, not back to what he saw as the muddled concepts of 'direct method'.

The reports of 1916, 1918 and 1926

The main points made by Circular 797 (1912) all reappear, sometimes with wording unchanged, in three further reports[14] which complete the picture of the counter-reform in modern language teaching.

Circular 797 itself made little immediate impact on classrooms. There is a rather sad paragraph at the end of the Board of Education report of 1916 regretting that Circular 797 was 'not known to teachers' and reminding the profession: 'It may not be sufficiently known that [it] represents not only the accumulated experience of the Board's Inspectorate but also a large body of other expert professional opinion.'

This cautious attempt to share responsibility with 'other expert professional opinion' reflects the unease of a well-meaning, but relatively powerless Inspectorate, caught in a dilemma. On the one hand it is clear that the arguments of the reformers and the example of teachers like von Glehn had made a deep impression on some HMI. On the other hand the lack of suitably qualified teachers in schools, the pressure of entrenched university opinion and the requirements of written examinations seem to have inhibited HMI from throwing their full weight behind reform.

There are slight differences of emphasis between the successive reports, but they all agree on the inadequacy of teachers to cope with the newer methods: 'The reports of the earliest inspections [1900–5] show that the supply of properly qualified teachers of French was lamentably inadequate . . . no other main subject . . . was so ill provided . . . in one case a French master was advised to visit his Latin colleague in order to learn how a living language might be effectively taught . . .' (Board of Education, 1926, p. 6).

By 1926 output at least was much increased. Between 1908 and 1914 the annual output of honours language graduates from

British universities rose from 60 to 200. By 1923 it was well over 300 and the supply of women language teachers was even exceeding demand. (About half of those teaching French in 1926 were graduates.) But if greater numbers of teachers were now arriving in classrooms, their education and training were still woefully inadequate. It is true that standards in the worst schools had risen. 'The days when it was actually possible to hear a master give to "dites-moi" the vowel sounds of "bright boy" are not likely to return.' (1926) Nevertheless concern about teacher preparation runs through all the reports:

The course of work required for a degree in modern languages is far from adequate to qualify these graduates for skilled professional service (Board of Education, 1912)

Not less urgent is the need of systematised provision for professional training (Board of Education, 1916)

For a qualitative and quantitative improvement in the supply and training of teachers for schools we must look first of all to the improvement of Modern Studies in the Universities (Leathes, 1918)

The most striking defect is not so much ignorance of the language as lack of skill in the art of teaching . . . the student of French is rarely brought face to face with the real problems he will encounter as a teacher . . . [The new teacher arriving in his classroom] feels that his training has nothing to do with the actual problem he has to face (Board of Education, 1926)

Teacher training was clearly in need of reform but the mischief lay deeper, in the degree courses themselves. If direct method failed it was at least partly because teachers did not acquire at university the necessary fluency and confidence in the spoken language to sustain an active dialogue in the classroom. The teaching of language was not given high priority in degree studies. Typical of the universities' attitude to language study was their neglect of phonetics.

Phonetics and the 'living philology'

The one plank in the reformers' platform about which there was general agreement among the schools featured in the 1912 circular was the value of phonetics. Subsequent Inspectorate reports all endorse this, while warning against the use of phonetics by teachers without adequate training. The failure of modern language courses at universities to provide a thorough grounding in phonetics was symptomatic of the general failure of universities to meet their obligations towards the schools.

The Cambridge Modern and Mediaeval Languages Tripos, reconstructed in 1917, is singled out for praise in the 1918 report.[15] The Tripos has become in our own day possibly the most flexible language degree in the English-speaking world and is deservedly greatly respected, but in the 1930s the Tripos was heavily biased towards literary study and philology and away from mastery of the spoken language. There was no possibility of study abroad; the oral was derisory; phonetics had no place. It is true that teachers who had read for the Tripos in the 1930s would, if fortunate in their supervisor, have been encouraged to read a considerable amount of the history and thought of their chosen speech community and could have taken special Part II questions on architecture or painting, as well as on important contemporary developments in, for example, education. To this extent, Cambridge in the 1930s had reacted imaginatively to the strictures of the 1918 report: 'None of the courses give any adequate place to the history of the life, the thought, the institutions of the foreign countries.' Nevertheless even the most enlightened of degree courses gave quite inadequate preparation for teachers who aspired to conduct a dialogue in the classroom using the foreign language in a register that would interest their pupils. The fact is that degree courses were aimed (probably unconsciously) at the selection and preparation of future university researchers in literature or philology. It was as if the university teachers were concerned only with a selection procedure which would produce a few graduates in their own image each year. The needs of the 90% of language graduates who would not stay on at the university to research but would go out into secondary schools or into commerce, industry, journalism or administration, were scarcely considered. Generations of potentially useful language graduates were sent into schools armed only with second-hand opinions on a narrow range of literature, knowing very little about phonetics and still less about the geography, economy, politics, institutions, school system and so on, of France or Germany, quite unable to perform orally in the kind of language needed in the classroom and ill prepared to answer the kinds of questions that school pupils ask about life in the foreign speech community.

The teachers prepared in this way naturally went on to teach their sixth formers in their own image, and acquiesced in a Higher School Certificate apparatus of prose translation and set-books which was a junior version of the degree course that they knew.

It is now a commonplace of curriculum planning that the test question to ask of a course of study at each stage is: what is in it for those who will *not* proceed beyond this stage? In the 1930s the foreign language curriculum both at sixth form and at university level conspicuously failed this test. The teachers prepared in these courses were ill fitted to take up the torch that MacGowan and Widgery had lit before the first world war.

The Leathes Report 1918: Modern Studies (the report of the Committee on the Position of Modern Languages in the Educational System of Great Britain) deserves close study. It is the only national inquiry into modern language teaching that has ever been conducted.

The background was an initiative by central government in curriculum planning which has never been repeated (though as the 1970s closed there were welcome signs of a recovery of nerve led by Her Majesty's Inspectorate). The Board of Education had published in Circular 826 (1913) an outline of the advanced courses in classics, science and modern studies which central government would be prepared to grant-aid. In 1916 two national committees were recruited to advise on the details of these proposed advanced courses in science and modern studies (classics was already well established). The newly approved advanced course in modern studies would consist of two languages other than English (of which Latin could be one) together with modern history. In addition 'systematic instruction in the mother tongue' was to be a common element in all three advanced courses.

The chairman of the Modern Languages Committee, Stanley Leathes, CB, was a former Cambridge history don, one of the editors of the *Cambridge Modern History*, and author of *What is Education?* (1913). He also had some experience of directing public examinations.

The Leathes Report reflects the chairman's vision as a historian in its farsighted recommendations for a new sixth form curriculum. Its weakest section is on teaching method, where the chairman had less direct experience, and where the Report failed to give a lead which might have maintained the momentum of reform after the war.

The committee recognised that the universities held the key to the future of modern studies in schools: 'in none of our universities and in no branch of Modern Studies can the staff be considered even approximately sufficient'. It recommended the creation, over a ten-year period, of 55 first-class professorships (15 for French and 10 each for the other four main European languages) and 110 lectureships. But first sufficient good candidates must be attracted to modern language studies.

The size of the problem was indicated by the numbers of sixth formers awarded Oxbridge scholarships. In 1911–12 entrance scholarships were awarded by Oxford and Cambridge Colleges as follows (out of a total of 440):

classics	205
history	56
modern languages	8

Leathes called for the immediate establishment of 200 State Scholarships annually for modern languages to be awarded by a national advisory committee (*not* by the universities). The training ground for the future scholars would be the new sixth form. This would be divided into three 'Advanced Courses' (classics, science and modern studies) linked by the study, common to all three, of the mother tongue. Students in the classics and science streams '*should not abandon languages altogether* [our italics], but should have systematic practice in the reading of foreign books' (para. 97). Seventy years have elapsed since these enlightened, but modest, recommendations – *circumspice!*

Motivation for the systematic reading of foreign books by classics and science sixth formers was provided by the creation of a 'subsidiary' paper alongside the 'principal paper' in the new Higher School Certificate set up in 1918.[16]

Subsidiary papers in modern languages were taken by science and classics specialists in increasing numbers up to 1950 when the subsidiary papers were abolished by ministerial decree, despite the fact that every year about twice as many candidates took subsidiary, as took the principal HSC papers, in French. One wonders whether those responsible for the disastrous hatchet work of 1950 had ever studied the 1918 report. There is a case, perhaps, for requiring that those who take the axe to well-tried traditions in education should first be required to show some acquaintance with the arguments and evidence of their predecessors who created the institutions that they wantonly destroy.

The committee went on to look at the degree studies to which sixth formers on the modern studies side would proceed: 'While the University course is not primarily intended for the training of teachers it should incidentally provide most of what teachers require.' How ironically that recommendation reads after 70 years of waiting for the universities to provide, even incidentally, in their language degrees 'most of what teachers require'. A letter to the committee from 31 university professors and readers is printed as an appendix to the report. Included in the letter's proposals are two that might, if implemented, have greatly altered the pattern of university language teaching between the wars:

i   that each university language department should include a 'lecturer in linguistic pedagogy' (proposed by some signatories only)

ii a phonetics laboratory should be available common to all language departments modelled on Daniel Jones' laboratory at University College, London.

We still await action in most university language departments along these lines!

After teacher education came initial training for the classroom. Here the committee drew attention (para. 181) to an existing Board of Education regulation which was little known and seldom implemented, allowing training by attachment to schools approved by HMI: apprenticeship to master craftsmen in the classroom. 'The teachers selected to carry out the work of training should receive extra allowances. . .' and their schools should be frequently inspected to see that the training was systematically carried out.

It is close to the system now adopted in France.[17] It would have had the great merit, compared with the proliferation of postgraduate certificate courses in university departments of education, colleges and polytechnics, that 'master teachers' would have *remained in their classrooms* and not been drawn out into tertiary institutions, and thus been lost to the secondary schools. Prestige and career advancement might have remained where they should be, closely linked with classroom excellence.

Another farsighted recommendation concerned in-service training: 'Government machinery' should

certify the proficiency of teachers of modern subjects. The normal Certificate should guarantee adequate training in and mastery of phonetics as well, of course, as a thorough knowledge of the written and the spoken language with a satisfactory standard of pronunciation and enunciation. . . . Moreover, however good the profiency originally possessed by a teacher, it is necessary that he should have opportunities to return from time to time to the foreign country to renew his intimacy and revive his knowledge. (para. 187)

There followed a most perceptive recommendation, never implemented, that there should also be a Higher Certificate for teachers of modern subjects to be acquired after, say, five years' experience in teaching (para. 188). This should be an honour hard to win and therefore worth the winning. 'Real practical skill should be an essential requirement . . . there should be evidence, oral and written, of further progress in the language . . . It would be most advantageous that teachers after starting work should have some object to work for with a view to improving themselves and their prospects.' The committee also made the proposal that 'the status and standard of the scholastic profession would be greatly raised if it were understood that schoolmasters and schoolmistresses might be worthy candidates for professorships at the Universities. In other countries there is free circulation between the schools and the Universities, but not in Britain.'

Merely re-reading these paragraphs of the report reminds us how far universities still are in the 1980s from facing up to any of these challenges thrown down by the Leathes Committee 70 years ago. This part of the report is radical, fresh and convincing. When, however, the committee turned to teaching methods, on which the rest of the edifice would depend, classroom realities compelled caution. Here the historian chairman and his non-linguist colleagues[18] reflect the views of their witnesses. Most of the evidence they were given recommended the old tried methods:

Direct Method has certain inevitable dangers . . . if attention is concentrated too exclusively upon the spoken language, too much is apt to fall upon the teacher; the contribution of the pupil is apt to be slight . . . students are not so well grounded, knowledge is superficial and inaccurate . . . after all the effort that has been made during the last two decades this verdict is very disappointing . . . the falling off was attributed by our informants to misuse of the Direct Method. . . . If the study of modern languages is to earn its due estimation, the highest possible accuracy and scholarship must be systematically cultivated. (para. 198)

Admitting that the dangers of misuse of direct method were 'no less great than the travesty of classical methods which they superseded', Leathes advises (with tongue in cheek perhaps): if teachers in a given school disagreed, 'concentrate the believers in Direct Method at the lower part of the school and the disbelievers in the higher part'.

On translation into the foreign language: 'universities were unanimous that it is a most valuable test of scholarship . . . more exacting then free composition . . . the committee was not prepared to go against the weight of the evidence . . . though it suspected that the university view was influenced by tradition'.

On grammar:

whatever method is used, grammatical accuracy must be required at every stage . . . even a Frenchman has to learn the rules for the concord of the past participle when used with an auxiliary verb . . . the learning of a language is and must be a difficult task; it cannot be made easy. In conclusion . . . the importance of mere fluency of speech should not be overrated. Grammatical accuracy and scholarship should be demanded. (para. 196)

Too forward-looking for the universities in so many ways, this great report was realistic about classroom methods. Its perceptive authors looked critically at what the Great Reform had achieved in schools and found little fundamentally changed. What was more, they saw no prospect of change. 'If only six periods a week can be given to it, it is illusory to hope that children can be got to "think in French".' This was to acknowledge that in conditions resembling gardening in a gale, fluency in speaking was an unrealistic aim for average pupils. This argument in effect is the starting-point for the 'way ahead' to IL proposed in Part III of this book. The Leathes Committee did not pursue its implications, however. Instead the committee settled for a different objective: concentration on reading and writing (as the classics teachers had had to do). This was less unrealistic if 'immersion' was impossible. Essentially it meant giving written translation pride of place. Viëtor, Gouin, Sweet and Jerspersen might denounce translation as the dragon to be slain, but it was one exercise that lent itself to the conditions of the short, occasional FL lesson buffeted by the gale of English.

Providentially there was created at that moment a national system of written language examinations monitored by the Secondary Schools Examinations Council (SSEC) dominated by university teachers. In these examinations translation into the foreign language was entrenched as the central, most prestigious test. It remained so entrenched until 1964 when the one examining board that had not been set up under university auspices managed to break the log-jam.

The effect of the written examination after 1918

The Taunton Commission of 1868 had drawn attention to the proliferation of examinations taken by pupils in secondary schools.

By 1911 the situation had got worse. To the existing examinations (Oxbridge College Scholarships, Civil Service entrance, Army and Navy examinations, exemption from university intermediate examination, London Matriculation, and the various professional bodies' entrance papers) were added several varieties of 'junior' and 'local' certificates taken at 14 and 15. The Consultative Committee to the Board of Education, created by the 1902 Education Act, recommended (1911) the setting up of an Examinations Council representing the Board of Education, the local education authorities and the university examining bodies to supervise all external examinations.

In 1917 the Board of Education acted on this recommendation. The universities were recognised as responsible bodies for the conduct of new School Certificate and Higher School Certificate examinations, and the SSEC was set up to advise the President of the Board.[19] School Certificate papers in French were set from 1918 onwards; by 1928 ten university examining boards were setting papers and in that year the Board of Education published a *Report on the Position of French in the First School Certificate Examinations* (Educational Pamphlet No. 70).

The small committee chaired by Professor R. L. G. Ritchie found 'widespread' and 'in the main justified' criticism of the School Certificate papers among teachers. Witnesses were unanimous that the examination had 'come to be considered as a goal'. It 'reacts very strongly on the teaching of French in the schools'. The various boards differed in the time allowed for written papers but were alike in one thing: 'The Oral Examination cannot be considered to be anywhere treated satisfactorily.' Not only was the oral test optional but 'candidates who take the conversational test have generally to pay an extra fee'!

The main recommendation made in the report is that the oral test should be compulsory and that out of a total of 200 marks for the Certificate, 50 should be awarded on the oral (including dictation and a reading test).

The suggestion that the oral should account for 25% of the total mark was a bold one. It was not implemented. Ten years later, in 1938, the percentages awarded for the oral by two leading boards were as follows:

Joint Matriculation Board: oral including dictation   16%
Oxford and Cambridge Joint Board: dictation only (no
compulsory reading and speaking test until 1950)   9.5%

The report's proposals about the oral remained a dead letter but the recommendation that the next highest mark should be given for *translation into French*[20] was more successful. The 'prose' translation in fact became the central (because 'rigorous') part of the School Certificate (and later GCE) examinations and repeated attempts to set a paper without 'prose' (e.g. by the Associated Examining Board in the early 1960s) were vetoed by the university members of the Secondary Schools Examinations Council until 1964. It was only the powerful lobbying behind the scenes of the Annan Committee (1962) that prepared the way for a change of heart in the Ministry of Education. Schools until the mid-1960s willingly or unwillingly gave priority to work at 'prose' translation since it earned higher marks than any other test.

The 1928 report expressed no opinion on 'the relative merits of the various teaching methods' used in the schools. In the event the shape of the examination determined teachers' priorities. The examining boards' failure to implement the radical proposal of the Ritchie Committee for a 25% mark for the oral component meant that the examination became almost exclusively a written test. The oral, sometimes optional, carried few marks; the written language was the main concern and translation into the foreign language was the main skill rewarded. This influenced classroom objectives more decisively than any theory discussed in training courses or in the professional journals. The 'counter-reform' was complete.

It is impossible to reflect on this outcome of the movement launched by the generation of MacGowan and Widgery without a feeling of sadness that so much generous endeavour should be disappointed. Of course much was gained. Language classes, at least for a select minority of able grammar school pupils, were challenging, exciting and enjoyable places in the 1930s, 1940s and 1950s. The methods used, however, owed little to Sweet and

Jespersen. Phonetics and direct method were mere echoes from an old song, except in a very few schools.

Moreover the majority of the able pupils leaving grammar schools after five years of French, though they may have had a more interesting time than the pupils observed by the Clarendon Committee in 1864, in fact had not learned to use their French. They could make little or nothing of their language skills in their adult lives. The adult population of Britain, including its most highly educated element, was, and still is, incapable of joining in a spoken dialogue in a foreign language. Curiously, throughout the 100 years of controversy, the essence of the problem had only been glimpsed intermittently. It was that unless the learner is exceptionally gifted, spoken mastery of a foreign language must be learned by a mixture of teaching and immersion (IL), as the Tudor grammar school charters had insisted and as private tutors like John Locke had realised. A reading knowledge is another matter but oral mastery cannot be acquired under FL conditions, gardening in a gale. Yet at no time through all the years of controversy did anyone follow up the glimpses of the real problem; nobody suggested substituting an IL for an FL approach. It was going to take a second world war and imminent national disaster to produce the first experiment in IL on a national scale.

NOTES

1 Viëtor's pamphlet was originally issued under the pen-name of *Quousque Tandem*, the opening phrase of Cicero's first oration against the Cataline conspiracies. It was the name later adopted by a group of reformers at the Philosophical Congress in Stockholm (1886) and translated by Otto Jespersen as *Cannot we soon put an end to all this?* It expressed both anxiety for change and impatience with the obstacles holding back reform. In 1923 Otto Tacke published a paper in Leipzig with the same title as Viëtor's famous pamphlet, thus by implication commenting on the lack of effect after forty years of the Great Reform (see page 212).

2 In the USA there was less support for the spoken language. In 1901 the Report of the Committee of 12 of the Modern Language Association stated: 'the ability to converse should not be regarded as a thing of primary importance but as an auxiliary to the higher ends of linguistic scholarship and literary culture' (quoted in Mackey, 1965). The four-year study, 1927–31, by the American and Canadian Committees on modern languages showed the persistence of the traditional interest in reading methods (Coleman, 1931; 1934).

3 The phrase 'couriers' Tripos' was used by the opponents of the
Modern and Mediaeval Languages Tripos at Cambridge, established
in 1886. Though the Tripos has developed into a splendidly flexible
language degree responsive to a very wide spectrum of students'
interests, its early emphasis was on 'rigour' (prose translation, philology and literary criticism) partly as a reaction against the 'couriers'
Tripos' jibe. In 1894 an optional 'pronunciation' test was introduced;
in 1909 this became an optional 'conversation' test. In 1917 the Tripos
was reconstituted with an oral test for which, however, very little
credit was given.
4 Subconscious learning was also given an important place by H. E.
Palmer (1917). Francke and Palmer come close to the argument developed in the 1970s by Stephen Krashen of the University of Southern California; his *Monitor Model* is referred to in Chapter 6. This in
turn recalls the distinction made by Carl Dodson (1978) between
'medium-orientated' and 'message-orientated' classroom exchanges,
to which we refer in Chapter 6.
5 Such as W. S. MacGowan of Cheltenham College, a regular contribu-
tor to the German periodical *Die neueren Sprachen*, and W. H. Widgery
of University College School, who reviewed German books on
method and 'worked himself ill', helping MacGowan organise the
Cheltenham conference. The conference is reviewed in *Journal of
Education*, vol. XII (1890), pp. 335ff.
6 These involved, among other trials, the committing to memory, in
one month of unremitting work, of the entire German dictionary –
resulting in damage to his eye-sight and a nervous breakdown!
7 'Again and again Inspectors reported cases where the work of one
able and energetic Master was largely wasted because his pupils
passed from him to others who were unable to continue the work on
similar lines. These difficulties were . . . intensified by the (new) aims
and methods' which made greater demands than the formal study of
grammar and translation.
8 Circular 797 uses the expressions 'composition' and 'translation' to
distinguish translation *into* the foreign language from translation
into English; the expressions were familiar in Latin and Greek
teaching.
9 By 1925 the great von Glehn of the Perse School, now Dr de Glehn,
was taking French prose translation classes in King's College, Cambridge, with students reading Part I of the Tripos. The present author
can testify that this erstwhile authority on direct method was still in
the 1930s the most lively (and awe-inspiring) teacher of French 'composition' one could imagine. With his great Edwardian beard, commanding voice and completely bi-lingual mastery of French and
English he mounted a truly terrifying assault each week on those – all
too many – students in his enormous class whose 'proses' suffered
from the ultimate sin of 'négligence, monsieur!'. There was no be-
trayal of principle in this; von Glehn had always argued that 'prose'
was only for advanced students. One had the impression, nevertheless, that he would have preferred a Tripos without 'prose'.
10 The Board of Education *Inquiry into the Teaching of French in London*

Secondary Schools in 1916 found that 'few language teachers had ever heard of Circular 797'.

11 W. R. Parker (1966) noted that in 1915 about 24.4% of all secondary school students (in USA) were studying German (compared with 8.8% studying French and 2.7% Spanish). Almost overnight Americans developed a hysterical distrust of all things German. By 1922 the percentages were: German 0.6%; French 15.5%; Spanish 11.3% and in 1944: German 2.6%; French 10.8%; Spanish 12.3%.

12 'If we think it is possible entirely to prevent English words from turning up in the children's consciousness we certainly deceive ourselves' (Jespersen, 1904, p. 62).

13 Palmer contrasts 'ergons', i.e. bits of the language that 'work' (Gk *ergon*: work), with 'etymons', i.e. entries in the dictionary. A typical category of ergons might be 'ergons which answer the question *when?*' (e.g. yesterday; on Sunday; last month; a long time ago; at Christmas; during the holidays, etc.).

14 1916 Board of Education: Report of an Inquiry into the teaching of French in London Secondary Schools;
1918 Leathes Report on the Committee appointed by the Prime Minister to enquire into the position of modern languages in the educational system of Great Britain (Cd. 9036);
1925 Circular 797 (1912) reissued;
1926 Board of Education (Educational Pamphlet No. 47) Memorandum on the position of French in Grant Aided Secondary Schools in England.

15 The report regrets that, even in 1918, the oral test was not indispensable for Honours in the Tripos and language was not given enough recognition in Part ii. Nevertheless, it was 'a promising and courageous effort to initiate a new era in modern language study'.

16 The subsidiary paper came to count as one half of a principal paper, towards the total of three passes required for university entrance. There was thus a real inducement to take one (or two) 'subsidiaries' as an insurance against failure or partial failure in one of the three principal subjects.

17 It is significant that the concluding recommendation of the whole report is that the Board of Education and Civil Service Commissioners should jointly undertake an enquiry into the methods employed in French state and university examinations, such as the *Agrégation* and *Licence*.

18 The historian H. A. L. Fisher was also a member of the committee until he resigned to become President of the Board of Education and architect of the 1918 Education Act.

19 It was a sub-committee of the SSEC (the Beloe Committee) which in 1958 laid the foundation of the CSE (Certificate of Secondary Education) for pupils then in the secondary modern schools which developed after the second world war.

20 Professor Ritchie was (with Moore) author of a manual of passages for prose translation into French very widely used in the thirties, forties and fifties in sixth forms and universities. His proposal regarding the oral was all the more enlightened.

6　The search for solutions

Language behaviour is largely a matter of habit
Nelson Brooks, 1960

Language is not a habit structure
Noam Chomsky, 1966

My guinea-pig died with its legs crossed
Quoted by Julian Dakin (1973) from tape-recording of
eight-year-old

In contrast to the check to reform of the outbreak of war in 1914, the second world war can be seen as a watershed, 'a Massif Central giving rise to a number of streams' (Dr D. C. Riddy in Hoy, 1977). One of these streams undoubtedly was intensive, immersion learning. In both the UK and the USA the realities of global war revealed a critical lack of linguists (or rather of 'languists', the term preferred by Nelson Brooks to denote one who masters a foreign language as distinct from a student of linguistics).

In the USA, after Pearl Harbor, the need was for speakers of Japanese and Chinese and in the post-war years of Vietnamese. In the UK the most pressing need was for languages not studied in the school system, notably Russian. There was no reservoir of graduates. Teaching had to start from scratch.

The solution found in both countries was a combination of formal with 'immersion' teaching. In the UK this was provided through intensive courses for translators and interpreters run by the Joint Services school. The courses begun in war-time continued for selected national servicemen until the ending of national service in 1958. They proved highly effective. One of their valuable side-effects was to send into schools and universities a stream of excellent teachers of Russian who were also ambassadors for new methods challenging conventional thinking about language teaching.

The instructors on these war-time courses enjoyed many

advantages that the less fortunate language teacher might envy: the students were carefully selected; they were also motivated strongly to succeed because failure meant 'return to duty' of a more unpleasant kind. The rejection rate was high; regular tests were held and the principle of the survival of the fittest was firmly applied. The ratio of instructors to learners, moreover, was more favourable than in conventional classrooms and the teaching was highly intensive. The students were immersed in the foreign language, as in the Middle Ages students of Latin had been. The 'gale of English', which ever since the seventeenth century had whistled round the doors of foreign language classrooms, was stilled.

The significance of the Joint Services intensive courses was not grasped in schools at first. Ealing Technical College was the first civilian institution to experiment with intensive methods when, in the late 1950s, Mabel Sculthorp promoted crash courses for commercial purposes, using the first language laboratory to be installed in the UK. It was not until the 1960s that immersion experiments began in the universities. In the 1970s a number of enterprising schools developed intensive courses. Before we review these developments we must look at a succession of panaceas which attracted the enthusiasm of the most enterprising teachers in the post-war years.

Reducing the learner's load

After the failure of the Great Reform of the turn of the century it was natural for the question to be asked: could the solution lie not with reform of teaching methods but through simplifying what has to be learnt? The search for ways of reducing the learning load had therefore begun well before the war (and it continues actively still). We can distinguish a number of different approaches to reduction of the load:

i   construction, by hunch, of an 'island vocabulary' intended to suffice for non-specialist purposes (the sole example: Ogden's *Basic*, a list of 850 words in English)
ii reduction by statistical methods of the total lexicon to a beginner's vocabulary conceived not as a self-sufficient list but as a jumping-off platform for further learning (examples are numerous: the best known is *Le français fondamental*, a *vocabulaire de base* of 3,000 words)
iii reduction of the vocabulary to the words most likely to be needed by a particular specialist user (example: German for chemists)

iv   reduction of the grammar to the rules needed for a defined purpose (example: a German grammar for reading only)

v   reduction of the learning load to a syllabus selected on 'functional/notional' criteria, the language needs of the prospective learner having first been analysed (example: the syllabus proposed by Wilkins, 1972)

vi   reduction of the load by offering a staged series of limited, defined objectives, with tangible reward at the completion of each stage (examples: the Council of Europe Unit/Credit scheme and the 80 'graded test' schemes now operating in some 60 LEAs in England, Scotland and Wales).

Each of these proposals has interesting lessons for the language teacher.

i. Basic

Basic was the invention of C. K. Ogden, a self-taught genius who in the 1930s edited the journal *Psyche*, an annual review of applied psychology, and his friend I. A. Richards, dean of King's College, Cambridge. The name is an acronym, standing for British American Scientific International Commercial, though Ogden himself commonly referred to his word list as '*Basic English*'. Ogden makes this claim for his list, published in 1932:

It is possible to say almost everything we normally desire to say with . . . 850 words which can be written on an ordinary sheet of notepaper. The words [of the *Basic* list] have been scientifically selected to form an International Auxiliary Language ie. a second language (in science, commerce and travel) for all who do not already speak English . . . By the addition of 100 words required for general science, and 50 for any particular science, a total of 1,000 enables any scientific congress or periodical to achieve internationalism . . . The number of necessary nouns is 400, of adjectives 100, of verb forms (operators) 100. To avoid awkward periphrases a supplementary list of 200 names of picturable objects (common things such as the auctioneer exhibits daily, parts of the body etc.) and 50 adjectival opposites etc. brings the general total here exhibited to 850. (Ogden, 1932a, p. 9)

Ogden makes a number of other claims for his list. One of these is particularly forward-looking:

The *Basic* vocabulary dispenses with practically all phonetic ambiguities; and when a machine for typing from dictation is invented *Basic* will prove an ideal language for the purpose.

Fifty years later, in the 1980s, such machines for typing from dictation have begun to reach us from Japan! It was in Japan, in fact, and in India, that *Basic* had most success in the 1930s. This success had already begun to wane, however, when during the war Winston Churchill was fired with enthusiasm for *Basic* which he saw as a way of extending the use of English as the main world vehicle language, redressing at least linguistically the contraction of British imperial power. Ogden was invited to prepare plans for a massive post-war exploitation of his invention. Alas, Churchill's enthusiasm cooled rapidly and the plan was shelved. After the war Ogden was awarded £8,000 compensation for the failure to keep the promises made. Soon afterwards he died, his hopes disappointed. The following extract and its 'translation' into *Basic* may illustrate some of the possibilities and limitations of the 'island vocabulary':

From Abraham Lincoln's Gettysburg address:

It is rather for us to be here dedicated to the great task remaining before us – that from these honoured dead we take increased devotion to that cause for which they gave the last full measure of devotion – that we here highly resolve that these dead shall not have died in vain – that this nation under God shall have a new birth of freedom – and that government of the people, for the people, by the people shall not perish from the earth.

And a *Basic* version by C. K. Ogden:

It is for us to give ourselves here to the great work which is still before us, so that from these dead who are in our hearts we may take an increased love of the cause for which they gave the last full measure of their love; so that we may here come to the high decision that these dead will not have given themselves to no purpose; so that this nation, under the Father of All, may have a new birth in the hope to be free; and so that government of all, by all and for all may not come to an end on the earth. (Wynburne, 1960, p. 67)

The foreign language teacher may ask, since *Basic* is the sole example of such an 'island vocabulary', what is its relevance for him? It is included in our survey of panaceas because, had *Basic* succeeded as Ogden and Richards hoped, it might have become the sole international auxiliary language. This would have made it less necessary for most English speakers to master a foreign language and the post-war history of our discipline would have been very different. It failed, however, despite the brilliance with which the idea was worked out. Linguists have raised the obvious objections. The first is that English does not stand still. The *Basic* list therefore can have no permanence. Whose responsibility would it be to up-date it? Its usefulness depends on willingness to translate from the languages of the world into *Basic* on a massive scale. Who would do the translating? Could a translation be made from (say) Japanese into *Basic* by a translator who did not command English itself? Then the *Basic* words had been chosen to render (with the necessary periphrases) normal English. Was it certain that idioms in other languages could be rendered within the narrow compass of the *Basic* words?

Though *Basic* never recovered the initial success it enjoyed in the 1930s there was an interesting post-script. This had been foreseen by I. A. Richards. Writing in 1935 in *Basic in Teaching* he claims for *Basic*: 'Its chief power is to develop our grasp and discrimination in handling expository logical statement, in taking adequate account of the ideas and their order in arguments . . . this is the point at which current methods of teaching English are least adequate. Sir Philip Hartog some time ago, in his study *The Writing of English* ably summarised the wide and overwhelming evidence for this conclusion.'

What is needed is a persistent automatic direction of the pupil's attention in reading upon the differences between what is being said and the other things – often so similar superficially – which he may so easily suppose are being said . . . the peculiarity of Basic is that, as an analytic instrument, it forces us to consider contexts and connections so insistently. (p. 101)

Thirty years later in a provocative book, *Vertical Translation and the Teaching of English* (1960), S. B. Wynburne returned to this suggestion. He proposed that instead of teaching foreign languages in school we should spend the time on the exercise of 'vertical translation', i.e. translation from English into *Basic* and vice versa.

Wynburne gives this example of a translation set to senior pupils (from Gerard Manley Hopkins' *The Habit of Perfection*):

> Elected silence, sing to me
> And beat upon my whorlèd ear,
> Pipe me to pastures still and be
> The music that I long to hear . . .

The *Basic* translation of these lovely but difficult lines is as follows:

The Dress of Religion: The Best Way of Living
I have made my selection: quiet is what I am looking for. Waves of quiet, come to the curved inner part of my ear and with your pipe, be my guide to quiet fields; quiet is the only sound for me . . .

Richards' and Wynburne's proposal has not been taken up by English teachers. Meanwhile the *Basic* approach to reduction of vocabulary has been overtaken by more recent attempts to lighten the learner's load.

ii. Statistical reduction: le français fondamental

The idea of a *vocabulaire de base* is as old as Comenius. From the 1930s onwards, the use of statistics was invoked in the selection of vocabulary lists based on counts of frequency. Such statistically based vocabularies have been produced in all the major European languages, the best known being perhaps *Le français fondamental* (Gougenheim et al., 1965). This was a list of some 3,000 words in French based on a statistical count of frequency in use. Its elaboration was entrusted to a team based at the Centre de Recherche pour la Diffusion du Français (Crédif) at Saint-Cloud. The list is in two parts. The first part or *série* is based on a count of spoken French. This presented problems to the Crédif team because their first frequency counts based on recordings of the language used in spoken dialogues proved to be unsuitable in several ways for pedagogic purposes. Strict adherence to frequency counts would have omitted from the list words considered essential in language teaching such as those associated with cleanliness and godliness. There were other gaps: for instance only five of the seven days of the week proved to be frequent enough in the counts made to deserve a place in the list on frequency alone. Pedagogic arguments and frequency conflicted.

Equally serious was the problem of words known to be frequently in the minds of French speakers, though not often spoken (the *disponible* or 'available' words). The research team therefore supplemented the 'frequently spoken' words by an equal number of additional words chosen on pedagogic grounds. This gave a total of some 1,400 words in the first *série*. To these were added some 1,600 words in a second *série* chosen almost entirely on a frequency count of written French. Both *séries* were given a grammatical supplement indicating rules of grammar that the Crédif team suggested might be taught in the first years of study of French.

Despite its imperfections this was an important pioneering effort. The account of the work by Professor Gougenheim and his colleagues is a valuable contribution to the study of the role of word counts in language teaching and of their limitations. In addition to clarifying the notion of *disponibilité* or 'availability' (the extent to which a word, though not often used, may be present in the mind of the speaker/hearer), it gives some precision to the notions of 'range' (the number of different texts in which a given word occurs) and 'stability' (the regularity with which a word recurs in different texts and contexts). The basic notion of 'frequency' itself proved to be an elusive one. Ostensibly it is the number of times a given word occurs in a 'corpus' subjected to statistical analysis. When word counting begins, however, difficulties arise: the first is that there is no satisfactory definition of the items that are to be counted. Rebecca M. Valette (1967) contrasts 'words' with 'lexical units'. One word may represent many different lexical units as in her example:

> Joe belongs to the human *race*
> Joe went to the dog *race*
> Joe and Sam *race* each other
> Joe and Sam *race* across the room
> Joe and Sam *race* turtles (p. 151)

For the teacher, looking for guidance to a statistically based word list, should each of these occurrences of 'race' be given its own frequency?

There are many other difficulties about the definition of what is to be counted. One relates to the problem already mentioned of the word that may be present in the mind but seldom spoken (the word that the Crédif team called *disponible*). Gougenheim and his team tried to get at such words by asking teams of schoolchildren to write lists of the 20 words that first came into their minds when specific topics were suggested (for example, clothing, food and drink)

Perhaps the fundamental weakness of any statistical rank order of frequency is that it can only be true of the 'corpus' of texts that is analysed. No matter how wide the net is thrown, the frequency of a given word will vary with the subject matter of any particular text studied, except in the case of a small number of words of grammatical meaning which carry little lexical meaning. In fact statistically the words that carry most meaning in any text are the least frequent.

Recent work on reduction of the vocabulary load has abandoned statistical techniques in favour of criteria which owe more to the tradition of Ogden and Richards.

iii. Languages for specific purposes

Here foreign language teaching has followed far behind the teaching of English as a second language. The catalogues of the publishing houses competing in the field of English teaching materials, one of England's fastest growing industries, now offer a bewildering range of such books as *English for Nurses, English for Geology, English for Commercial Purposes*, etc. Foreign language materials used in schools are less vocationally specialised, partly because schools are concerned with comparative beginners. However *French and German for the Office* or *German for Chemists* courses have begun to close the gap at the 16–19 year level between the imaginative English materials for defined purposes and the generally less innovative foreign language materials.

In the field of examining foreign languages, definition of vocabulary has made more progress. It has been a concern of foreign language teachers that whereas in other subjects, such as geography, biology, and mathematics, the syllabus for the 16+ examination was defined in great detail in the examining board's prospectus, the content of the syllabus in the foreign language (especially the vocabulary to be learnt) was largely unprescribed. The candidate could only guess in what areas of vocabulary he/she would be tested. The test was in 'French'; it did not specify French in what context, or for what purpose.

The Nuffield/Schools Council project at Micklegate, York (1967–75), as part of its work on new language courses (*En Avant, Vorwärts*, and others), discussed with the GCE and CSE Examining Boards new optional papers to be taken by schools using the project materials. In framing their papers the boards agreed to take the vocabulary of the Nuffield/Schools Council materials as the syllabus (at least as to 75% of the test). Although the new GCE alternative papers lapsed with the ending of the Nuffield/Schools Council Modern Language Project, work on defining the content of the GCE 'O' level examination continued. Draft syllabuses were produced in French, German and Russian, which have contributed to a clearer consensus among examiners as to what is an appropriate vocabulary content for the examination.

This work has been carried further by the CSE boards and there has been a welcome growth of Mode III syllabuses, in which the content of the examination syllabus is defined in detail by the school course of study on which it is based.

Mention should be made, also, of the examinations of the

Institute of Linguists, which effectively define the syllabus by prescribing the subject areas in which passages for translation will be set. Some schools are beginning to show interest in entering pupils for the Institute's examinations in preference to those of the GCE boards, especially in view of the increasing irrelevance of GCE 'A' level language papers to the expectations of the vast majority of students in sixth forms and further education courses. The development of a content-defined ancillary or subsidiary paper for sixth formers, with optional sections such as 'French for Social Studies', 'French for Scientists', 'French for Tourists', has been mooted, building upon existing 'O' level papers such as 'French for the office'. An alternative approach suggested in Schools Council Working Paper 28 (1970) would be to encourage sixth formers to select their own menu of reading (with guidance) following their own individual tastes and interests.

In the field of languages for specific purposes for adults much the most important work has been done by the Council of Europe team directed by John Trim. To this we return in a later section.

iv. Reduction of the grammar: comprehension v. production
Could the grammar to be learnt, like the vocabulary, be limited to that which is needed for special purposes? Does a nurse or a chemist, in addition to making use of a specialist vocabulary to label the concepts that are needed in his/her work, also use *grammatical* structures that are peculiar to nursing or chemistry? Research has so far not suggested that this happens frequently. It may be that there are certain structures or patterns of speech which are more or less frequent in discussions of chemistry than (say) in literary criticism but if so, these same patterns will probably be met in discussion of the other natural sciences. Another possibility is that grammatical structures may be specific to certain functions or notions transacted in specified situations rather than in specific vocations. We return to this question in our discussion of the 'functional/notional syllabus' in section v.

Another possible approach to simplifying the grammar that the learner has to master might be to concentrate on the grammar required for listening or reading only and omit the rules which only operate in speaking or writing. This notion is attractive. It fits the common experience that it is easier to understand what we hear or read in a foreign language than to operate the complex system of rules needed to *produce* correct utterances. Why not therefore spare the learner who only wishes to read or listen the effort of learning rules for production?

The notion, attractive as it is, conflicts with what some linguists (notably N. Chomsky) have maintained. They have described 'competence' as one internalised grammar, not two separate ones, to which the (idealised) speaker/hearer makes reference both in comprehending and in generating sentences. Chomsky's 'competence' is of course 'mother tongue competence'. He has, however, on occasion argued that second language competence must be subject to the same linguistic constraints.

The pragmatic language teacher facing his (not too highly motivated) classes every day may find this hypothesis hard to accept. Surely, he will protest, production (encoding) of even a simple utterance in, for example, German is a largely grammatical process requiring recall of a complex of rules, while comprehension (decoding) seems to depend largely on recognition of word meanings.

To take a simple example, in order to answer the question: How did you come to the office this morning? the student of German produces: *Nicht mit dem Wagen, mit der Strassenbahn.* In order to generate or encode this answer (even when the verb is taken as understood, thus simplifying the grammar) the student has to recall from memory a considerable amount of knowledge and to operate complex rules:

Recall
1 How does the German say   not?   (*nicht*)
                                 by?   (*mit*)
                                 car?   (*Wagen*)
                                 tramcar?   (*Strassenbahn*)

Rules
2 Is *mit* followed by accusative or dative?
                (dative)
3 To which of three gender classes do the nouns belong?
                         Wagen   (masculine)
                         Strassenbahn   (feminine)
4 What is the form of the definite article (dative)?
                         masculine   (*dem*)
                         feminine   (*der*)

Apart from the effort of recall of the vocabulary items, our teacher could argue, there are at least six grammatical choices to make before this phrase can be correctly generated or encoded (discounting the possibility of spelling errors). Contrast this with the student's task when *decoding* the phrase: *Nicht mit dem Wagen, mit der Strassenbahn*. Here the problems are scarcely grammatical. It is not necessary to remember that *mit* takes the dative case (unlike, say *auf*) nor to recall the genders of the two nouns nor how to decline the definite article, masculine and feminine. All that is necessary is to attach meanings to the words, five out of seven of which are among the commonest in the language. Superficially, therefore, it might seem that a German grammar solely for decoding must be much simpler than a grammar for encoding, since most of the rules included in the latter could be omitted from the former.

This argument, however, cuts a number of corners. To begin with, the listener does not hear:

Nicht mit dem Wagen, mit der Strassenbahn

What he hears is more like:

nichtmitdemwagenmitderstrassenbahn

A great deal of grammatical processing must be done before this string of sounds can be divided at the appropriate *constituent*[1] boundaries.

The written form is certainly easier (for practised readers) in two ways: the constituent boundaries between words and clauses are marked by the printer's spaces and punctuation; it can be held before the eyes and scanned repeatedly unlike the spoken form which must be retained in the ephemeral short-term memory while it is 'processed'. Even with the written form, however, the reader must be able to identify parts of speech and know word-order rules in order to understand how words and clauses relate in the sentence.

Dan Slobin (1979) has analysed the grammar rules of a restricted language: Russonorsk. This was a trade language used in the Arctic Ocean during the brief summer thaw periods when Norwegian fishermen traded fish for Russian agricultural products in the centuries before the 1917 revolution: 'a language with a minimal grammar and vocabulary, used for a limited range of functions. The simple grammar which developed in this language clearly reveals the minimum core of devices a language must have in order to be processable.' These are 'word-order rules, one general verb marker, one general preposition, some question words, and some means of indicating yes/no questions, information questions and statements'.

Slobin has suggested that we can learn about the grammar of comprehension from studying young children understanding quite complex grammatical meanings long before they show in their own speech that they can operate the grammar. He cites work by Huttenlocher (1974) suggesting that it would be a mistake to underestimate the understanding of grammatical structure of which 18-month-old children are capable.

Recent research by psycholinguists has moved from focus on the notion of a 'reference grammar', internalised by the speaker/hearer, to interest in 'processing strategies' which involve much more than grammatical rules.[1] To quote Slobin again.

What cues does the listener use to construct constituents and determine their meanings? Grammars do not describe ongoing processing, although it is clear that grammatical units, such as clause, sentence, and others, are involved in such processing . . . The listener . . . is constantly trying to build an internal representation for the sentences he receives, relying on all available information: grammatical structure, meaning, knowledge of the world, knowledge of the speaker, knowledge of conversational rules and so forth. No one of these aspects of structured knowledge is sufficient to account for the processes of comprehension. (p. 43)

We might add that, as in all learning, expectation may be the most important element in this mix of factors which determine comprehension.

It seems, then, that rather than thinking of two different grammars, of production and comprehension, we ought to consider two different kinds of processing in each of which grammar plays a part as one element only in a complex of resources.

This is an active area of research among psycholinguists and there is much yet to be made clear. Meanwhile language teachers cannot afford the luxury of awaiting the researchers' final word. Their students are waiting to be taught.

Perhaps for the language teacher, approaching the problem pragmatically, the most important difference between production and comprehension has little to do with grammar, but concerns the memory. The average learner can *recognise* about five times as much as he can *recall*. In comprehension the features of the message are given, on the page or on the work-table of the short-term memory, there to be recognised and processed. In production, the processing makes great demands on recall memory, with all the difficulties that entails.

The 1980s are likely to see an increasing interest in 'reading only' courses among academics and others who need to keep abreast of foreign publications. Even more interesting may be the growth of bilingual dialogue in which each speaker (or writer) uses his own language. Not the least benefit of bilingual dialogue is that the speaker (writer) is able to say precisely what he means in his mother tongue without approximations or infelicities. For businessmen concerned with possible legal complications arising from correspondence, this may be much the best way to conduct business. As such bilingual communication becomes widely accepted and practised (for example, in commercial correspondence and conferences, academic colloquia, telephone dialogues, radio and television interviews, etc.) it will be necessary for the major language communities to adapt their language learning objectives (for all but specialists) to the requirements of decoding from, rather than of encoding into, foreign languages. This suggests obvious possibilities for making the school course more interesting and rewarding for the non-specialist linguist and we shall return to it in Part III when the future place of the foreign language in the curriculum is discussed.

v. The functional/notional syllabus

The traditional syllabus for language teaching was constructed of 'units of learning' defined in grammatical terms. This produced the grammatically structured syllabus, based on the view that since all learners have to learn the same grammar, the order of learning should be the same for all.

In the early 1970s considerable interest was aroused by a proposal to take a different starting point, asking the questions: Who is the prospective learner? What are his/her needs? Can we structure the syllabus according to the functions that he/she can be predicted to want to perform in the language?

This led to the further question: In order to perform the predicted functions, what notions (general or specific) must the learner be able to communicate? If these could be known, in very general terms, not necessarily specific to any one language, then an inventory of exponents of the functions/notions in a given language could be worked out which would comprise a functional/notional learning syllabus for that language. The theory of the functional/notional syllabus was set out by Wilkins (1972, 1976). It has been elaborated by the Council of Europe team led by John

Trim (1973, 1980) and in papers by R. Richterich (1977, 1980) and van Ek (1972, 1980).

To the early concepts of functions (for example, greeting, approval, seeking information) and notions (for example, quantity, time) have been added the concept of situation in which notions are communicated. Four components of situation have been distinguished:

1 the social roles that the learner will play
2 the psychological roles that the learner will play
3 the settings in which the language will be used
4 the topics that will be dealt with.

Within these situations the learner will engage in certain language activities (for example, conversation or writing a letter).

The germ of the 'functional syllabus' can be found (like so much in language teaching) in Henry Sweet's classic *The Practical Study of Languages* (1899). Sweet suggested that in place of the traditional grammar whose content is arranged under formal grammatical categories (the verb, the adverb, the preposition, etc.) there was need for a grammar which grouped items by functional categories. Such a grammar would stand in relation to the traditional grammar as the thesaurus stands to the (alphabetically ordered) dictionary.

H. E. Palmer (1917) carried the idea further. His 'ergons' were linguistic items that 'did work' or functioned, as opposed to 'etymons', the inert dictionary (or grammar book) items, listed alphabetically (or by formal categories). Palmer's massive 'ergonic chart' of French is a precursor of the 'functional syllabus'.

Ogden and Richards' *Basic*, as we have seen, was also compiled, intuitively, on notional criteria. It offered the learner the means to express, within the limits of the *Basic* words, all the notions likely to be needed for everyday purposes, given a certain dexterity in finding circumlocutions and equivalents in *Basic*.

The originality of Wilkins' proposal in the 1970s was that it proposed a taxonomy of functions/notions based not on hunch or intuition, as in Palmer's ergonic chart or in *Basic*, but on a study of the linguistic needs of particular learners.

It is precisely on this ground that the concept of a functional syllabus has been criticised, for example by O'Neill (1979). He quotes the late Julian Dakin: 'Communication is essentially personal, the expression of personal needs . . . in situations that are never quite the same.' O'Neill adds: 'We cannot teach people to communicate in a foreign language if we become obsessed in everything we do with specific, clearly defined functions and purposes. . . . We cannot be certain exactly what use the learner will make of the language we teach.' He quotes Dakin in asking how the teacher could possibly have predicted the language 'needs' of the eight-year-old who volunteered in a tape-recorded interview the unexpected information: 'My guinea-pig died with its legs crossed.'

The same point is made by Stevick (1976):

The surrealistic story which on paper looks asinine may, in the hands of a teacher who understands its use and evidently believes in what he or she is doing, become an instrument for producing astonishing degrees of retention both lexical and structural. . . . On the other hand talking about real objects or events that have nothing to do with long-term needs, either intellectual or practical, aesthetic or social, is notoriously unproductive. (p. 44)

Other critics have pointed out that there may be good *pedagogic* reasons for the selection of learning units – or for introducing them in a certain order. The functional syllabus may give an inventory of material to be mastered eventually by the learner but it does not in itself determine the order in which the items are best learned. O'Neill states categorically that teachers do not help their students unless they try to introduce the grammar in some kind of flexible but orderly fashion: 'If you simply march your troops into the loudest bits of gunfire, the "communicative situations" you can be pretty sure they will have to deal with, you are more likely to give them a bad case of shell shock than help them to survive' (O'Neill, 1979).

Some applied linguists (such as Reibel, 1969; Newmark and Reibel, 1968) pointed to the way in which the child is, in fact, exposed to the 'indiscriminate gunfire' of the mother tongue, without grammatical structuring, and yet manages to find its way into the grammar needed for its own purposes. They asked could this not apply to foreign language learning? This raised the familiar, recurring question: is foreign language learning a different process from learning the mother tongue, permitting, even requiring, economy of effort? Many teachers would maintain, with O'Neill, that this is so. Coulthard asks,

in a syllabus that is structured communicatively, where the students learn to produce communicative acts in a relevant sequence and acquire

at any one time only those aspects of grammar necessary for the realisation of a particular act . . . how can the student be assisted to relate
a particular structure to the overall framework of the language?
(Coulthard, 1977, p. 139)

Perhaps the most important qualification to make about the
functional syllabus is that any inventory of linguistic items can be
potentially functional only. It is not truly functional unless the
items listed are used in authentic communication, with true
'intention to mean'. It would be perfectly possible for the linguistic patterns of utterances in Wilkins' inventory to be used in a
series of mechanical, language laboratory pattern drills, in which
case they would be no more functional than the traditional
grammar-book exercises.

It should be said that this is appreciated by the Council of
Europe team. They have recognised that a functional inventory
and a functional learning method are not at all the same thing. In
the 1980s the search is on for functional language learning *activities* and this theme is developed in Part III of this book. The
work done on the functional/notional syllabus has been useful
preparation, clarifying many of the problems involved.

vi. Unit/credit and graded tests

The Council of Europe work on the functional/notional syllabus discussed above forms part of a wider project (Trim et al.,
1973) aiming at developing a 'unit/credit' system for adult
language learning in Europe.

The overall aim of the project is to break down the global
learning task into portions or units each of which corresponds to
a component of a learner's needs, and is systematically related to
all the other portions. Each learner can be advised which units to
take and in what order. After each unit, official recognition or
credit is given. The most direct way of describing a given unit is
by a statement of what the learner will be able to do after successfully completing the unit. This is called the 'learning objective' of
the unit.

The first practical outcome of this work has been the unit
described as the threshold level. 'Exponents' or inventories of the
linguistic items required to be learned to communicate at this
level have been worked out for English, French, German and
Spanish.

The English threshold level inventory consists of some 1,050 words for productive and receptive use and a further 450 for receptive use only. To this must be added numerous compounds and derivatives that can easily be guessed. This represents the lowest level of general language ability to be recognised. Lower levels of ability may suffice for certain, restricted needs, but they would not constitute *general* ability.

Early estimates of the threshold level assumed that it might represent one year's learning (or 100–150 hours). Since the threshold level, when worked out by its authors, seemed more demanding than they had first imagined a 'lowest general level' would prove to be, they have proposed a 'half-way stage' (which might be thought of as a 'survival level'), a short-term, mainly oral, objective requiring no more than an average learning period of eight to nine months. They have called this the 'waystage' (van Ek, Alexander, Fitzpatrick, 1980).

The unit/credit concept supposes that the learner, once past the threshold level, would proceed to further specialist language units of his choice, determined by the kind of analysis of need discussed in the previous section. These specialist units have not yet been elaborated (see Appendix A: New Examinations).

While the Council of Europe work on the threshold level was going on, a parallel movement had begun in comprehensive schools in the UK. In a number of areas working parties of teachers began to devise systems of 'graded tests', offering short-term objectives for secondary school beginners, aimed at motivating pupils for whom the distant goal of CSE or GCE seemed impossibly remote or unreal.

Such grades were well established in another difficult skill area, that of learning musical instruments. The eight grades in pianoforte, violin etc. had proved their worth in motivating young players. One great advantage was that each grade could be taken when the young learner was ready, so that each individual could go up the steps of Parnassus at his own best speed. The learning was individualised, each 'grade' had its clearly defined syllabus and each stage was publicly rewarded by a certificate. The 'grade' model, as we saw in Chapter 2, had also proved successful in the field of English as a foreign language.

The first proposals to apply a graded test model to foreign language learning were made in the early 1970s by David Rowlands, then Director of the Schools Council Modern Language Project, York, and Brian Page of Leeds University (Page 1974,

Harding and Page 1974). Since 1977 the graded test movement has gathered great momentum in comprehensive schools as teachers have searched for ways of improving motivation among young learners, especially in the difficult third year (age 13+). The alarming figures for drop-out from French classes published in the HMI survey (1977) showed the urgency of the problem.

There are now some 80 'graded test' experiments in England, Scotland and Wales. In most of these schemes a certificate is awarded to the successful candidates who pass the test at each grade. Sometimes the certificate is signed by the chief education officer. In one scheme (York) the certificate is awarded by the university. The certificate generally contains an account of the language performance tested. Most of these schemes are the work of teams of teachers who have given a great deal of their leisure time to it. Sometimes the graded objectives are linked to a specific course book. In other cases the elaboration of the graded tests has led publishers to produce materials matched to the teaching objectives.

Already many positive advantages can be claimed for graded tests. The not-too-distant objective is clearly motivating. Less able pupils can achieve success. Teachers' perception of objectives has been sharpened as has their understanding of the different ways in which children of varied abilities can achieve success. This has led teachers to give credit for skills such as listening comprehension which are often undervalued (Salter, 1980; DES 1983).

A carefully controlled monitoring project conducted by M. Buckby and B. Page and a working party of teachers funded by the Schools Council has shown that comprehensive school pupils (and their parents) respond most positively to the challenge of the graded test, compared with control groups of pupils taught French without such immediately realisable objectives. (Buckby *et al.* 1981)

There are, at the same time, cautions to be expressed about a performance-orientated syllabus. Does concentration on a short-term performance goal squeeze out aspects of language study which are not measured by performance tests, such as understanding (which is more than knowledge) of the foreign country, its history, geography, institutions and the values of its way of life or insight into the way the language works and how it contrasts with English? These are important aspects of a school education in modern languages which aims to be more than mere instruction in performance skills.

Another limitation of the schemes so far tried is that individual pupils do not take the graded tests when they are ready, as young musicians do their instrumental grades. Whole forms are entered for each test, as for CSE. Thus one of the main advantages claimed for the graded objective is lost.

There seems also to be a danger of the graded test limiting what is done by the abler pupils. An equally unwelcome possibility is that tests, once produced (and the working parties disbanded), might become static and discourage initiative (Salter, 1980). Already there are signs that teachers of other subjects are demanding similar graded objectives. Might this lead to a proliferation of tests, leaving pupils too little time for learning which is stimulated by curiosity rather than by a wish to collect 'badges'? These are important qualifications to the welcome that must rightly be given to so much imaginative and cooperative development work by teachers on their own initiative.

However, many of those working on the graded test projects are aware of these qualifications and will seek to meet them. What is certain is that a good attack on the language and a sense of achievement are indispensable foundations for a useful apprenticeship. For this reason the unit/credit and graded test movement must be seen, among some disappointments encountered by language teachers in the 1970s, as a promising approach to reducing and defining the learning load, while motivating the learner, especially the young and less able learner.

Audio-visual: method or myth?

Two new technological aids came into general use in classrooms in the late fifties and early sixties: these were the portable and not too expensive tape-recorder, using plastic tape in place of the steel wire of the earlier experimental models, and the equally portable film-strip projector. It is impossible to exaggerate the potential offered by the tape-recorder to language teaching. Previously it had been possible to bring native-speaking voices into the classroom only on records, with no facility for rapid play-back or pin-pointing of particular passages. Now the new machine made not only editing but self-recording possible. Sophisticated 'twin track' recorders enabled the student to listen to a model utterance while recording his own responses on the same tape, for later comparison. The new technology caught publishers and text-book writers unprepared.

The only materials immediately available were those produced in France and in the USA. Experiments soon began in a few schools using French audio-visual courses. The first course to arrive was Teachers' Audio-Visual Oral course (TAVOR). This had been produced in 1952–5 by V. Y. Kamenev at the Headquarters of the NATO forces near Paris for use in teaching French to the fifteen different nationalities represented among SHAPE (Supreme Headquarters Allied Powers in Europe) personnel. (At that time NATO had the use of the first 'language laboratory' in Europe.) Kamenev's *Cours audio-visuel préliminaire de français* was tried out in the UK for the first time in 1956–7, in a girls' school at Beeston, near Nottingham. Two years later S. R. Ingram used the course in East Ham. This experiment became well known and soon some 2,000 pupils in a number of English-speaking countries were learning from the TAVOR Aids materials.

In the early 1960s a second French audio-visual course, *Voix et Images de France*, produced for the French Government at Crédif under the direction of P. Guberina and P. Rivenc, reached some classrooms. This was intended for adult beginners and was based on the vocabulary of *Le français fondamental*. It was soon followed by an audio-visual course for junior pupils *Bonjour Line* (also a Crédif production), which was used successfully (throughout the East Riding of Yorkshire, for example) by schools offering 'French from Eight' in association with the Pilot Scheme.

It is easy to understand the attractiveness of these courses for British teachers, who were gaining access to tape-recorders but were starved of recorded material to play on them. The British classroom, however, was a very different place from the multi-national classroom of SHAPE or the multi-ethnic classrooms in Francophone Africa towards which much of the Crédif research was orientated. There, the mother tongues of the pupils could not be known in advance to the course writers or to the teacher. Meanings, in the presentation stage of new language learning, could be conveyed only by action or by pictures. There was no alternative to an audio-visual approach.

In the British classroom, however, the mother tongue of all the pupils *was* known to the teacher. Meanings could be conveyed much more easily by using English. The range of meanings that can be conveyed visually is severely limited. A picture of a pale-faced girl in bed may represent unambiguously: 'Elle est malade'; but how does the artist or photographer convey by pictures: 'Elle a la grippe' or, still more difficult, 'L'an dernier elle a eu la grippe'?

This is not the chief reason, however, why enthusiasm for audio-visual courses cooled in the 1970s. It became clearer to teachers after some years' experience that the expression 'audio-visual *method*' (of language teaching) is a misnomer. All that the audio-visual technique could accomplish was to *present* new language and (within severe limits) show its meaning graphically and entertainingly.

Even as an aid in the presentation stage, however, the picture is less effective than handling solid objects. In the course of normal cognitive development children pass through three learning stages. J. S. Bruner has called these successive kinds of learning:

1 the 'enactive' stage (manipulating the world of objects in the pre-school stage)
2 the 'iconic' stage (learning through pictures which represent the real world)
3 the 'symbolic' stage (learning through symbols, notably the highly sophisticated symbols of the written language).

The three stages overlap and learning 'enactively' and 'iconically' never stops, so that, for example, the best apprenticeship courses for adolescents exploit all three ways of learning:

1 handling materials and tools (enactive)
2 reading diagrams, blueprints, circuits (iconic)
3 reading explanations, lectures, etc. (symbolic).

This is a three-stage pathway to learning which all pupils will have travelled in the mother tongue. Experience shows that younger learners especially gain in confidence if the same sequence is followed in foreign language learning also. This means beginning with an enactive stage. To start straightaway by projecting an image on the screen was to begin in the middle!

Presentation in any case, even the best enactive presentation, is only the first step in language teaching and much the easiest. After the initial presentation and recapitulation (prompted usefully by actions, objects and pictures) there remain at least two further stages before a new structure in the language can be said to be learned: *assimilation* and *emancipation* of the new item from its original context. These two crucial steps, which demand more subtle classroom skills on the teachers' part than the straight-forward presentation stage, are the nub of language teaching. The initial presentation (with explanation of meaning) is by comparison a trivial step. Harold Palmer, as we saw in Chapter 5, had made this distinction clear as long ago as 1917.

Early enthusiasm for audio-visual materials probably owed something to teachers' folk-memory of direct-method injunctions to 'banish the mother tongue'. The visual seemed to offer a way to do this. In practice it was soon apparent, as Harold Palmer had seen, that there is no way of banishing the mother tongue from the pupil's head. On the contrary in the presentation stage it is essential not to do so, but to capitalise on the vast amount of semanticising that the pupil has accumulated already via the mother tongue. The pupil simply has not got time to reconceptualise his whole 'world view' in the new language. Thousands of concepts, both simple ('sweet'/'sour') and complex ('true'/'untrue') already learned must be carried over into the new language, with any necessary cultural adjustment or refinement. At the later stages of learning (assimilating, emancipating what has been presented) the mother tongue is rightly avoided, but in the presentation stage to banish the mother tongue is to tie the teacher's hands wastefully. Had the early materials been described merely as an aid in the presentation of language a great deal of confusion might have been avoided.

That the audio-visual panacea had not answered teachers' prayers became clear in the 1970s when at conferences and in-service courses, teachers trying to use audio-visual techniques constantly asked their tutors: But what do I do in the third year, when I have presented the film-strip *ad nauseam* and my pupils can repeat the cue phrases by heart?

It was this question that the Nuffield Foundation/Schools Council team tried to answer by giving special attention to the transition from 'presentation' to the reading/writing stage. The French course *En Avant* was produced by a team which began work in 1963 at Leeds University under A. J. Spicer. It was intended for eight-year-old beginners in the Ministry's Pilot Scheme. The early stages made extensive use of visuals, especially of the flannelgraph and the film-strip.

Work was begun at the same time on Nuffield audio-visual materials in Spanish (*Adelante*), Russian (*Vperyod!*) and German (*Vorwärts*), all intended for 11+ beginners.

176   *The search for solutions*

These Nuffield courses broke new ground in many ways, not least by the teamwork of their production. The units of material, as they were drafted, were circulated to some 50 schools which were testing the material and returning monthly reports. In the light of schools' comments the writing team revised the materials. The revised versions were in their turn scrutinised by a consultative committee, including experienced teachers, university researchers and HMI.

The 'transition to reading' stages of these courses, and especially the imaginative use of magazine-type readers and the innovation of the treatment of grammar in the later stages, for example the French *A Votre Avis* materials (produced under the auspices of the Schools Council at York), pointed the way forward to a variety of imaginative classroom activities, and new examining techniques.

The 'language laboratory'

Voyage dans la lune

A l'ouverture de la boîte, je trouvai dedans un je ne sais quoi de métal presque semblable à nos horloges, pleins de je ne sais quelques petits ressorts et de machines imperceptibles. C'est un livre à la vérité, mais c'est un livre miraculeux qui n'a ni feuillets ni caractères; enfin c'est un livre où pour apprendre, les yeux sont inutiles; on n'a besoin que des oreilles. Quand quelqu'un donc souhaite lire, il bande avec grande quantité de toutes sortes de petits nerfs cette machine, puis il tourne l'aiguille sur le chapitre qu'il désire écouter, et au même temps il en sort comme de la bouche d'un homme, ou d'un instrument de musique, tous les sons distincts et différents qui servent, entre les grands lunaires, à l'expression du langage. (Cyrano de Bergerac, *Histoire comique des estats et empires de la lune*, 1657)

It took almost exactly 300 years for Cyrano's amazingly prophetic vision to become reality. When in the 1950s the tape-recorder came into classrooms language teachers at first did not know what to do with it. Instead of experimenting open-mindedly with the marvellous new aid, teachers, encouraged by administrators, were mesmerised for a decade by the false promise of yet another panacea: the 'language laboratory'. This took different forms, all variants of the basic pattern of a number of tape-recorders, wired to a control console, enabling the teacher to listen to and speak to students as they worked at pre-recorded exercises. It was in no sense a 'laboratory', but the misnomer has stuck.

In the USA, as part of the reaction to the first Russian sputnik (National Defense Education Act of 1958), an abundance of federal dollars financed a vast expansion in the use of language laboratories. 'In 1957 64 institutions of higher education [in the USA] used language laboratories. . . . By 1961 the number had risen to 2,500 secondary schools and 700 colleges and universities' (Turner, 1965). The explosion in the UK came later and was more modest but still represented a very considerable investment. In November 1962, there were 20 laboratories in Britain, including one in a school. By 1963 there were 116; by January 1970, 1,500, half of these in schools. By 1973 about one-third of all secondary schools teaching modern languages had a language laboratory of some kind. In both countries disenchantment quickly followed. Already by the mid-1970s most of the American installations were gathering dust. In the UK, though experimentation continued and particularly enterprising use was made of tape cassettes in the 1970s, the initial enthusiasm for language laboratories cooled considerably.

The audio-lingual method

The early enthusiasm for the language laboratory had co-incided with the vogue of the audio-lingual method, which sought to adapt to language learning the behaviourist theories of learning of B.F. Skinner. Two influential writers, Nelson Brooks (1960) and Edward Stack (1960), applied to language teaching the theory that language learning required the formation of a hierarchy of speech habits. These could be learned by practice in responding to cues in progressively complex (and rapid) pattern drills. The 'habit theory' had proved strikingly successful in Skinner's experiments in teaching animals to perform complex skills (for example, teaching pigeons to play ping-pong using their beaks as bats). Skinner himself applied his life-time's experience of animal learning to human verbal learning in his *Verbal Behavior* (Skinner, 1957). Despite Noam Chomsky's excoriating review (Chomsky, 1959) this remains a most important statement and a *tour de force* of intellectual achievement. Its inadequacy as an account of language acquisition, however, has been argued by Chomsky in a number of astringent papers with which any theory of language must now come to terms.

In 1966, addressing American language teachers at their Northeast Conference, Chomsky derided audio-lingual methods, language laboratories and 'habit formation' theories:

Linguists have had their share in perpetuating the myth that linguistic behavior is 'habitual' and that a fixed stock of 'patterns' is acquired through practice and used as the basis for 'analogy'. . . . Language is not a 'habit structure'. Ordinary linguistic behavior characteristically involves innovation, formation of new sentences and new patterns in accordance with rules of great abstraction and intricacy. . . . It is important to bear in mind that the creation of linguistic expressions that are novel but appropriate is the normal mode of language use. (1966, p. 154)

Chomsky's view of mother-tongue acquisition postulates a 'language acquisition device' (LAD), an innate hypothesis-forming mechanism which the child applies to the language environment to which it is exposed and which enables it to internalise a set of grammar rules. These rules characterise the structure of the language and underlie both production and reception. The LAD is highly specific to language acquisition with no necessary resemblance to other learning processes.

This account conflicts with behaviourist accounts at almost every point but especially in its rejection of the idea that learning is a process of habit formation acquired via a process of stimulus response as in a language laboratory (see discussion pp. 212–15).

Yet a different account is given by Piaget, though he is closer to Chomsky than to Skinner. For Piaget language learning is not *sui generis*, as for Chomsky, but is one aspect of, and dependent upon, general cognitive development. Piaget also differs from Chomsky in his view of what is inherited. He does not see the child as inheriting an LAD, a complex 'blueprint' of the linguistic 'universals' likely to be met in whatever language is encountered, but rather as inheriting a limited number of learning functions, of which the most prominent are 'assimilation' and 'accommodation'. The child tries to apply these innate functions to every new experience: 'assimilating' new experiences into 'schemas' or structures of activity/thought already learned; 'accommodating' to new experiences by changing the detail of the existing schemas. For Piaget it is not 'stimulus-response' that accounts for learning but the progressive enriching of structured patterns of thought through the exercise upon the environment of innate learning functions (Sinclair, 1969).

But how much of Chomskyan or Piagetian theory can the foreign language teacher adapt to his classroom practice? There seems little doubt that, as when acquiring the mother tongue, the learner of a foreign language *who is immersed in the foreign language environment* does proceed by 'trial and error' and does indeed constantly create novel forms (many incorrect) which are shaped by feedback from the language community and by Piaget's 'assimilation' and 'accommodation' into conformity with the rules of the grammar. But in the traditional classroom, limited to a few hours each week, gardening in a gale of English, can the teacher trust to Chomskyan or Piagetian processes of acquisition, or is he able – indeed compelled – to try to accelerate the process, by using different methods? Piaget and Chomsky are less helpful in answering this question. Neither has made any special study of foreign language learning. Chomsky flatly pronounces: 'I am frankly rather sceptical about the significance for the teaching of languages of such insights and understanding as have been attained in linguistics and psychology' (Chomsky, 1966, p. 152). To the central question how do L1 and L2 differ? we attempt an answer in Part III of this book.

Under Chomsky's influence the pendulum in language learning theory and in linguistics swung away from behaviourism. The arguments against 'stimulus-response' theory and habit formation as a sufficient explanation of verbal learning were succinctly summarised by Wilga Rivers in a book that was widely read, *The Psychologist and the Foreign Language Teacher* (1964). She examined critically the basic tenet of the 'audio-lingual' method, that 'Foreign language learning is basically a mechanical process of habit formation' with its corollaries:

1 Habits are strengthened by reinforcement
2 Foreign language habits are formed most effectively by giving the right response not by making mistakes
3 Language is 'behaviour' and behaviour can be learned only by inducing the student to 'behave'.

While not rejecting 'pattern drills' as 'suitable techniques for making foreign language responses automatic at the manipulative level' Wilga Rivers stressed the dangers and limitations of mimicry–memorisation, and the role of motivation, of insight into pattern, of the learner's interests, of humour and of meaning, in learning. She questioned particularly one tenet of the audio-lingual method: the insistence on withholding the written word in the early stages of learning. Since 'interference' from native language habits is inevitable, 'it might as well be faced in the early stages so that the student can have a longer period of association of correct sound with written symbol'. Wilga Rivers also stressed the emotional element in learning language. The student is more dependent on the teacher for learning in the foreign language class than in other subjects and this makes teacher–pupil relationships peculiarly important. 'The teacher . . . must be conscious of the invidious, frustrating and insecure position in which the student finds himself in the early stages . . .' (p. 162).

This was a most influential book, firmly grounded in theory and in experience of the classroom. It effectively widened the discussion of teaching method and revealed the insufficiency of habit-formation theory as exemplified in the early audio-lingual courses.

Meanwhile a series of classroom studies, nearly all conducted in the United States, threw doubt on the claims made for the language laboratory in practice. The most relevant research for UK schools was the carefully controlled York study (Green, 1975). This showed that, *exploited in the most typical way*, the costly language laboratory did not improve the performance in German of 11+ beginners, when compared over three years with use of the same materials played on a single tape-recorder in the classroom. The York study was unique in holding all the variables, including teacher effectiveness, constant for three years. A more limited experiment in an Essex comprehensive school (Winter, 1977) produced the same result.

As Green makes clear, many possible ways of exploiting the great potential of the tape-recorder were not measured by the York study. Nevertheless by the mid-1970s there were few teachers or administrators who still believed that the language laboratory was the panacea that it had been thought to be in the early 1960s. Once more great expectations seemed to have been disappointed.

The early teaching of modern languages (ETML)

The next panacea to excite teachers' hopes in the 1960s was lowering the starting-age for foreign language learning.

The Pilot Scheme (*French from Eight*), launched in England and Wales in 1963, caught the imagination of the public and the attention of educational administrators both at home and abroad as no other development in the curriculum had done. Interest in lowering the traditional starting-age was worldwide in the 1960s. UNESCO organised two conferences on the subject (1962 and

1966). *Foreign Languages in Primary Education* (Stern, 1963) stressed the social, political, economic and educational arguments for an early start. In the USA FLES (Foreign Languages in the Elementary School) represented a radical change in the curriculum since the commonest starting-age for the foreign language hitherto had been 15+. In the wake of the National Defense Education Act (1958) a number of experimental FLES schemes were begun amid high hopes, which were on the whole disappointed: ' . . . psycholinguistic research provides little support for an early start in FL study. Adolescents and adults practically always do better than very young children in everything but pronunciation . . . only moderate support for FLES programs has been provided by a number of research projects' (Oller and Nagato, 1974).

In Japan there was great interest in starting English in the elementary school but there, too, Oller and Nagato found that even when FLES students had the advantage of six years of EFL study on entering junior high school, non-FLES students caught them up by the eleventh grade. 'The FLES program did not have a lasting positive effect as measured by our tests . . . the major obstacle being . . . lack of coordination between the elementary and secondary programs . . . FLES and non FLES students integrated in the same classes from the eighth grade on . . . FLES students must mark time'.

In Europe interest in ETML was greatly stimulated by the work of the Council of Europe, 'the only inter-governmental organisation to have pursued a coherent policy for the improvement of modern language teaching' (Hoy, 1977). Resolution (69) 2 of the Committee of Ministers of the 22 member states urged 'that in all schools at least one widely spoken European language should be taught from the age of about 10 . . . with a view to extending such teaching as soon as possible to all boys and girls from about this age' and called for experiments into the feasibility of introducing one widely spoken language 'for *all* . . . at the earliest stage before the age of 10'. Three Council of Europe working parties (Reading 1967, Wiesbaden 1973 and Copenhagen 1976) consistently supported ETML.

ETML in the UK: the French Pilot Scheme

The French Pilot Scheme was probably the most radical intervention in the curriculum by central government that has ever been attempted. The scheme was announced in Parliament on 13 March 1963 by Sir Edward Boyle, then Minister of Education. He said that £1,000,000 had been set aside by the Nuffield Foundation for the development of modern language materials and that the Nuffield programme and the Ministry's Pilot Scheme would go forward side by side with the general expansion of modern language teaching to children at the junior stage which had already begun in many parts of the country. Already 200 schools in England and 80 in Scotland were teaching a foreign language, nearly always French, in 58 LEAs. In 40 of these LEAs the initiative had come from the schools themselves.

Though it was stressed that the scheme was a cooperative one, involving partnership between the central government, LEAs, the Inspectorate and the Nuffield Foundation, it is fair to see behind its inception several powerful 'éminences grises' without whom so radical an intervention in the curriculum would surely have been defeated by what historians of another bureaucracy (that of Spain in the nineteenth century) have called the 'traditional obstacles'.

The Annan Committee, reporting in the spring of 1962, had stressed the potential benefits 'if the regular teaching of a first modern language were started in good conditions and by the right methods in primary schools'. In the same year a working party of the Federation of British Industries called for a feasibility study of such a proposal. This lead won the support of a remarkable civil servant, Derek Morrell, a man cast in the mould of the great Robert Morant, architect of the Education Acts of 1902 and 1904. Morrell, educated in a French *lycée*, a sinologue capable of seeing beyond the parochial bureaucratic horizons, made light of the 'traditional obstacles', of which there has been no lack since his untimely death. Opinion in the early 1960s was running strongly in favour of experimentation with early teaching.

The theory of the critical age

Interest in ETML had been stimulated by the final chapter, later issued and widely read as a pamphlet, in a book by the Canadian brain surgeons W. Penfield and L. Roberts, *Speech and Brain Mechanisms* (1959). The authors, arguing from evidence of brain damage and its effect on speech and from Penfield's experiments with his own children, argued that 'the time to begin what might be called a general schooling in secondary languages, in accordance with the demands of brain physiology, is between the ages of four and ten'. This seemed to many readers to be reinforced by their own observations. It was a commonplace in America for instance, a 'nation of immigrants' in Kennedy's phrase, that where an immigrant family settles in a new speech community the children learn the new language effortlessly within a few months and speak it with an accent indistinguishable from that of their new neighbours, while the adult immigrants retain the accents of their homeland over many years no matter how hard they try and no matter how much they learn of phonetics or grammar.

The most powerful theoretical support for the notion of a 'critical age' for language acquisition came from the Harvard biologist Eric Lenneberg, in his *Biological Foundations of Language* (1967). The theory was seductive. It depicted the brain as growing rapidly in the early years, the rate of growth being fastest in the period from a few months before birth to about the age of two, when the curve begins to flatten, with nil growth after puberty. Brain growth is not, as with growth of the rest of the body, an increase in the number of cells. The number of cells of the central nervous system cannot increase, after the first few weeks after birth. Whereas physical damage elsewhere in the body is remedied by the generation of new cells to replace those lost, with new cells constantly replacing cells removed from the surface of the body, in the outer skin layer, nails, hair, etc., the brain cells can only decay and disappear in the blood stream, never to be replaced. Loss of cells from puberty onwards is a steady flow, and from middle age becomes a torrent.

Brain growth is an expansion in the space *between* the cells and in the network of nerve connections which link the cells (neuropil). The growing complexity of this network, especially rapid in the very early years, coincides with the child's acquisition of the mother tongue and with other formative learning experiences. The learning pathways of electrical impulses followed by chemical deposits, facilitating subsequent use of the nerve cell connections made during the earliest years, were thus seen to be highly important since they set up routines and expectations that the child would bring to all subsequent learning.

Between birth and puberty, as it grows in size, the brain changes in two ways. It becomes less 'plastic'; damage to one area of the cortex or outer layer can, in the young, lead to another area taking over the function associated with the damaged area but after puberty this is rare. Also, as puberty approaches, 'laterality' of function, that is the association of one or other of the two hemispheres of the brain with particular functions, becomes increasingly specific. The dominant hemisphere, nearly always the left, becomes closely associated with speech. Lenneberg supported his neurological account with evidence from 'feral' children, brought up in the wild, who, it was claimed, could not acquire language outside the critical age. Some parts of this account have since been challenged.

Psychologists now believe that lateralisation may be complete before the age of two (Kinsbourne and Smith, 1974). The interpretation of the data from feral children is also now much more cautious. It is now suggested that if there is a critical age it may not be for language but for 'propositional, analytic and serial processing' (Clark and Clark, 1977). The evidence now suggests that children's ways of learning language may change quite radically as they grow up, with different learning strategies appearing about the age of seven and with a further change about puberty.

There can be little doubt, however, that when the Pilot Scheme was launched the idea of the critical age was widely accepted. The fact that most of the evidence referred to mother-tongue acquisition was disregarded.

There was, it is true, some anecdotal evidence that an early start on a foreign language could work wonders. In the private sector of schooling, languages had for years been taught very successfully to selected, motivated pupils, the best of whom took common entrance examinations at the age of 13+, reaching a standard comparable with GCE 'O' level which is commonly taken at 16+. Some brilliant teachers of French in LEA schools had also achieved remarkable results with young children, including even children in infant schools.

The enthusiastic response of LEAs to the Ministry's initiative in launching the Pilot Scheme reflected the national mood. Of the 146 LEAs in England and Wales about 80 volunteered to fulfil the Ministry's conditions of organisation and in-service training and from these 13 pilot areas were chosen to begin French in September 1964. Each pilot area (part of an LEA) contained an annual age-group of about 480 pupils. The conditions agreed were that all pupils in the 8+ age-group in the area should begin French and continue to at least the age of 13+ and that the L E A would guarantee effective continuity for all pupils into the secondary school. The remaining L E As were not to be denied and some 90 'associate areas' were recognised which kept closely to the Ministry's conditions without taking part in the evaluation of the scheme by the National Foundation for Educational Research.

By 1965 some 21% of all junior schools included some French in their curriculum. By 1970 the figure was estimated to be 35% (Hoy, 1977).

Meanwhile, it was planned to make three appraisals of the scheme. 'First the statistical evaluation of the pupils' attainments in the language is being carried out by the National Foundation for Educational Research . . . At the same time members of H M Inspectorate are making a general appraisal of the scheme . . . (to be) analysed by the National Foundation in a supplement to its own report. Finally, everyone . . . will be making his own informal assessment – children – teachers – parents '(Schools Council, 1966). In fact, the three appraisals were never published. An HMI appraisal was included in the NFER *interim* report (Burstall, 1970) but no HMI appraisal appeared in the NFER's final report, published in December 1974.

The NFER evaluation of the Pilot Scheme

Most observers saw the Pilot Scheme as primarily a massive longitudinal experiment designed to answer the question: 'Is any substantial gain in mastery achieved by beginning to learn French at the age of eight?' This was the first of the 'main issues' listed as requiring an answer by Schools Council Working Paper No. 8 (Schools Council, 1966). In order to try to answer the question the NFER team selected three experimental cohorts of children (between 5,000 and 6,000 in each cohort) beginning French in the years 1964, 1965 and 1968. Cohort I ran into difficulties and the final evaluation was based on the 1965 and 1968 cohorts.

Control groups of pupils starting French at 11+ were given the same tests as the experimental cohorts. The tests were:

A test of listening comprehension, towards the end of year 1.
Battery 1 Tests of listening, reading, writing, speaking towards end of
    year 3 in primary school
Battery 2 Tests of listening, reading, writing, speaking towards end of
    year 2 in secondary school

Battery 3 Tests of listening, reading, writing and speaking given only to
   Cohort 2 and to a control group starting at 11+ towards the end of year
   5 in secondary school
   (Some of the tests were given only to samples [1 in 5, or 1 in 10] of the
   cohorts.)

Though the most interesting part of the NFER evaluation is
the analysis of the reactions of pupils, teachers and Heads to the
early start, it was by the results of the performance tests that the
main issue was decided. As we saw in Chapter 1 the verdict was a
categorical negative. 'Pupils taught French from the age of eight
do not subsequently reveal any substantial gains in achievement.' Burstall conceded that there was consistent superiority in
listening comprehension by the pupils who began early and that
they had a more favourable attitude to the subject than the
11-year-old beginners, when they had been successful. This was
not reflected in any higher achievement, however.

Several of Burstall's other findings are of the greatest interest.
To summarise:

Girls scored significantly higher than boys at both primary and secondary stages;
There was a linear correlation between the status of a child's father's
occupation and his or her performance in French;
Children in small rural primary schools scored higher than pupils in
large urban schools and they continued to score higher even after two
years in secondary school;
Both girls and boys in single-sex schools did better than pupils of either
sex in co-educational schools;
Pupils in the south of England took a much more favourable view of
learning French than pupils in the north;
Many young children soon became bewildered when French was used
indiscriminately in class to give instructions without ascertaining that
they were clearly understood;
Many young learners expressed 'detestation' of the tape-recorder.

Two positive factors influencing achievement were early experience of success and the opportunity to go to France and meet
French people. Positive expectations from the Head of the school
also influenced pupils' achievement.

The impact of this wealth of valuable data was masked, however, by the publicity given to the main finding that there was no
'critical age' for French and no magic in an early start.

It was a measure of the wide interest that the Pilot Scheme had
aroused among parents and educationists as well as language

teachers that the result of the NFER evaluation came like a bombshell. When the report *Primary French in the Balance* (Burstall et al., 1974) was published, it received wide publicity and it was generally interpreted as a verdict of no confidence in primary French. In support of this interpretation the final paragraph was quoted, with its last sentence (emphasised in heavy black type in the original) given prominence and the more tentative nature of the previous sentence overlooked:

Such then, in summary form, are the answers to the questions originally posed ten years ago. Their brevity must, of course, be balanced by careful reference to the detailed evidence in the body of this report. *Now that the results of the evaluation are finally available, however, it is hard to resist the conclusion that the weight of the evidence has combined with the balance of opinion to tip the scales against a possible expansion of the teaching of French in primary schools.* (p. 246)

The NFER evaluation did not escape trenchant criticism in the journals. Criticism was mainly directed not at the thoroughness of the NFER evaluation, which was widely recognised, but at the team's interpretation of some of its data. H. H. Stern, editor of a UNESCO study of young learners and a world authority on the early teaching of modern languages, found some of the reasoning in the NFER report inconsistent: 'A maturational explanation in favour of older learners is reasonable only if environmental factors cannot account for the relatively disappointing results of the experimental group. Such environmental factors can certainly be found.'

It is not difficult to suggest environmental, as opposed to maturational factors which might have made children's learning in primary school less effective than learning at secondary level:

1 Primary teachers' lack of knowledge of French: 'rather more than 50% [of the pilot area teachers] had only an 'O' level qualification in French, and about one quarter an 'A' level qualification' (Schools Council, 1966). At secondary level most of the teachers were graduates, many with a year's study in France as part of a four-year university course.
2 The primary teachers lacked language teacher training. The 75% of teachers referred to in point 1 above, with at most an 'A' level qualification, had had little or no initial training as language teachers though many short courses were offered by HMI and LEAs. Most secondary school language teachers had taken a year's PGCE course in teaching method after a four-year degree course.

3   The primary teachers were using new materials (80% used *En Avant*) of which they had had little previous experience. They had no way of judging pace, or foreseeing the difficulties the materials would give to pupils. At the same time they were learning how to use new aids such as the tape-recorder, the film-strip projector and the flannelgraph. At secondary level with the 11+ beginners the teachers were using well-known materials, with whose pace and difficulties they were familiar, and methods tried over many years.

4   It was seen from the outset that an important challenge of the Pilot Scheme was the attempt to teach French to a much wider range of ability in the (comprehensive) primary school. 'It is the first large-scale attempt in this country to teach a modern language to pupils of all abilities' (D. C. Riddy, Staff Inspector, quoted in Schools Council, 1966). Nevertheless primary teachers had to use the same materials with the same objectives, for *all* pupils regardless of wide differences in the pupils' own mastery of English, in motivation, home background and language learning aptitude. It is fair to add that the NFER report was particularly valuable in drawing attention to this as one of the most difficult problems revealed by the Pilot Scheme.

5   Time allowed for French in the various schools was an important variable that the NFER evaluation did not control. Some schools took time from English; others found time in other ways. The research design did not differentiate. The fact that at secondary level many teachers set homework each week in French obviously had an important bearing on children's learning, yet no account was taken of the time spent on French at different levels.

If the NFER evaluation did not claim to control such contextual variables in the two learning processes (at primary and secondary levels) that it compared, it did, on the other hand, break new ground in its discussion of some maturational variables, notably the verbal precocity of girls compared with boys. So marked was this difference shown to be that, as one observer remarked, it could well be taken to justify the continuation of primary French for girls but not for boys!

On attitude, as a maturational factor, the evaluation was equally interesting. The big maturational difference between primary school children and adolescent pupils is in their capacity for empathy. Here the NFER report did a valuable service by showing how this capacity, the ability to see the world from someone else's point of view, is at its height at the age of about eight or nine but declines rapidly with the onset of adolescence.

The decline is associated with insecurity and it is especially marked among boys from low status homes for whom adolescence is often traumatic, as they see approaching the need to take on roles which our society arbitrarily identifies as 'masculine' and for which they do not feel competent, i.e. most of the decision-making roles at both family and job level.

Learning a foreign language, like learning to be outgoing to other cultures in a multi-racial society, makes heavy demands on empathy. The learner is required not only to show interest in the foreigner and his way of life, as in a geography or history lesson, but to *behave* like the foreigner, making the foreigner's ridiculous noises out loud for his mates to hear!

The NFER team, of course, did not measure attitudes to other difficult areas of the curriculum. Had they done so, other subjects might have been declared to be 'in the balance'!

Some commentators drew attention to the sharp decline in the numbers of pupils tested as they moved up the school. The point was made by C. J. Gamble and A. Smalley (1975): 'The findings are therefore based on observation of Cohorts 2 and 3, comprising some 11,300 pupils at the beginning of the project and a mere 1,227 pupils in 1973'.

There were other criticisms of details of the evaluation (Buckby, 1976; Bennett, 1975; Nicholson, 1975). It would not be profitable to review the (often acrimonious) debate that followed its publication. As we saw in Chapter 1, the fate of ETML in the UK had already been decided before the completion of the Pilot Scheme. It had been decided as soon as it was apparent that the will was lacking to overcome the shortage of qualified staff and resources.

ETML in several other countries ran into the same difficulties (Oller and Nagato, 1974). In France the Ministry of Education halted proliferation of experiments in ETML in 1973. (But not all 'early start' schemes failed.[2]) The commonest difficulties were:

1 lack of suitably qualified teachers at primary level, able to act as class teachers and at the same time able to teach the foreign language
2 inability of teachers in primary and secondary schools to cooperate closely enough to ensure a smooth transition from primary to secondary level in the foreign language, avoiding holding back the ablest pupils while continuing to encourage slower learners.

The growing research evidence that older pupils progressed faster than younger ones (except in pronunciation) obviously weighed with wavering LEAs. But the staffing problem tipped the scale. Though as Hoy (1977) showed, some French teaching below the age of 11 continued in about 20% of schools, interest and encouragement from the Department of Education and from HMI ceased.

It seemed to many observers that one more panacea had failed. By contrast the innovation described in our next section, 'intensive teaching', had a happier outcome.[3]

Immersion courses: IL *v.* FL

The effectiveness of 'immersion' had been demonstrated by the wartime Joint Services courses which had been continued in peacetime until the ending of national service in 1958. Civilian experiments in intensive courses were slow to catch on. The first experiments were begun at Ealing Technical College in the late 1950s under Miss Mabel Sculthorpe, using the first language laboratory to be installed in the UK. Following the Annan Report (1962) ten-month intensive courses in Russian for teachers of other languages were instituted in polytechnics at Liverpool, Birmingham and London. A dramatic demonstration of the effectiveness of intensive 'immersion' with motivated, able adults was given by the work of Dr Trudie Berger at the Language Teaching Centre, York. Beginning in 1968 she conducted an annual intensive beginners' course in Italian. She showed that it was possible for her (very able) graduate students to reach GCE 'O' level, Grade 1, starting from scratch, in some 80 hours of intensive work (little more than two weeks) compared with the five years taken in school when 'gardening in a gale of English'. She later repeated the demonstration in German, with similar striking results.

All these variations on the theme of 'intensive' learning had been conducted with adults. The exciting development in the 1970s was the successful extension of this technique to schools, where the problems of timetabling and organisation were so much greater and where levels of aptitude, and motivation and pupil : staff ratios were much less favourable than in universities and polytechnics.

Experiments in schools took many forms, some of which are described in the symposium *Intensive Language Teaching in Schools* (Hawkins and Perren, 1978).

i. Within the school timetable

Two kinds of intensive teaching have been found possible within school hours:

(a) 'sections bilingues': These are variations on the model, most fully developed in the nine European Schools which serve EEC personnel, in which the foreign language is the medium in which part of the curriculum (commonly geography and history) is taught, ideally by native-speaking teachers. Pioneered in 1972 in Mill Hill, an independent school, *sections bilingues* have been developed also in LEA schools (Goff's School, Hertfordshire; Haygrove School, Somerset, and elsewhere) with most encouraging results.

A notable feature of the Somerset experiment is that when in 1975 it was opened to the whole ability range,

the slow learners coped well . . . they were able to speak the target language confidently and coped with the written work at least as competently as they did with written work in English. There were a few pupils . . . who would have liked to have given up the study of the French language while continuing to study geography in French. Perhaps there is a future for the project, though not the only one, as a foreign language course for the lower ability pupils, for whom reasonable targets might be a high level of comprehension and the ability to converse freely, although not necessarily with accuracy, in the target language. (King, 1978, p. 52)

(b) 'bain (douche) de langue': Here the model has been the weekly 'blocking' of the language lessons to provide an 'immersion' in the language enriched by use of tape and film and the presence of a number of adults (including students in training) able to speak the foreign language and to promote an active dialogue. The difficulties of timetabling and staffing are formidable, however. Occasionally teachers of great verve and energy such as David Cross at Archbishop Michael Ramsey School, ILEA, have launched experiments which have overcome the logistical obstacles. This model makes demands on school administrators that hitherto have proved insuperable in most schools. We return to this aspect of the problem in Part III

ii. Out-of-school intensive courses

(a) residential courses: In 1968 the Hertfordshire LEA adviser, Miss V. Howe, began a series of residential French weekends for

primary school pupils. She engaged the pupils in non-stop, active use of French by a carefully planned sequence of games alternating with films; and by bringing together a large number of adult French speakers to converse with the children. By the 1970s a great many variants on this theme for older pupils have been worked out by the more enterprising L E A advisers and teachers. Notable among these have been one-day, weekend and vacation courses (such as those organised by Somerset County and by the Inner London Education Authority) at which no English is spoken, and where the serious work of the course is enlivened by meals with appropriate menu, films in the foreign language, play-reading, reading competitions, singing etc.

(b) study abroad: A different model for older pupils is the study visit abroad. Calday Grange Grammar School, Cheshire, pioneered in the early 1960s an arrangement whereby 'A' level candidates spent a whole term as members of a German *Gymnasium* or a French *lycée* during their lower sixth year (some pupils going to both countries, thus being abroad from January to August of the lower sixth year). Shorter stays, residential weeks, etc., are now commonplace and Leicestershire County has given the lead by renting hostel accommodation abroad, with warden and library facilities, where whole families can spend a week studying the foreign language. The adult learner has not been forgotten. The B B C now organises residential weeks (at Rennes, Brittany) for its adult beginners studying with the multi-media course *Ensemble* and *Sur le Vif.*

iii. Remedial courses

A typical example of an intensive remedial course is the one-week 'catching-up' course for fifth formers in need of help in facing CSE/GCE, held annually by the Language Teaching Centre, York University. Here the tutors are graduate volunteers, following the PGCE course at York. They tutor the fifth formers (also volunteers) in groups of two or three for a week, having first employed 'diagnostic' tests to reveal precisely where the pupils' French is weak. (Howson, 1978).

iv. Beginners' courses

Intensive courses have been used to give a flying start into the language. The sixth-form Russian course described by David Rix

(1978) begins with an intensive 'immersion' of four or five days early in September. This technique had been tried in 'service' courses for undergraduates at several universities and polytechnics. A common practice is to offer intensive weekends during which tutors find that they can make exciting progress into the language, covering as much of the syllabus as used to be covered in a whole term when students attended classes for only two sessions per week.

v. Reciprocal courses

A different kind of intensive learning is offered by the 'reciprocal' course. This concept was developed in a series of experiments at the Language Teaching Centre, York. In 1968 a Spanish/English reciprocal course for serving teachers was held. Since 1974 annual French/English reciprocal summer courses for teachers have been held. These courses are now included in the Department of Education and Science, Teachers' Short Course Programme, and organised and staffed by HMI.

The reciprocal course is based on the idea of a return to IL (immersion learning). It seemed self-evident that use of the foreign language would become most natural (and learning most rapid) if the learner could engage in one-to-one dialogue with a native speaker. Securing a tutor: student ratio of one to one is usually prohibitively expensive for most organisers of courses. The solution offered by the 'reciprocal' technique is to bring together equally matched groups of learners from two different countries, who wish to learn, or perfect, each other's language. The students are grouped in pairs (or fours or eights, the two languages always equally matched) and they work on alternate days or alternate sessions in the two languages, each individual alternating in the roles of tutor (in his native language) and student (of the foreign language). The success of the reciprocal course turns on three factors:

1 The motivation and willingness to work of the participants. The constant change of role and unrelenting pressure are far more tiring than the conventional rhythms of the taught course. Even at meal-times the intensive learning/tutoring activity goes on

2 The provision of well-chosen language material on tape, film or text with carefully designed exploitation to provoke dialogue in the mixed language groups

3   The skill of the group tutors (one tutor from each language for each mixed group of students) in promoting a rhythmic inter-play between work in pairs and dialogue in mixed groups.

A typical exercise exploited in the reciprocal course goes like this. In the morning session a difficult dialogue on tape is listened to in the mixed group and a question paper is distributed, testing comprehension as well as appreciation of linguistic points, and of references in the text (political, historical, social, geographical, literary, etc.). The students then split up to work in pairs, the non-native speaker seeking from his/her native-speaking partner answers to the problems posed by the exercise. The native-speaking student who is tutor for the day in effect 'coaches' his partner in generating answers in the foreign language. When the mixed group later reassembles for the afternoon sessions, the less linguistically confident members of the group are encouraged to take the initiative in discussing the text, utilising the prompts given them by their native-speaking partners. On the following day, of course, the process is repeated in the other language, with the roles reversed.

A series of courses for sixth formers organised by Mary Dal-wood at York has shown that with motivated 17-year-olds the reciprocal technique can be equally effective.

In mastery of the spoken language, and especially in 'feeling for the language' – the instinctive sense of what is appropriate – the progress made on intensive reciprocal courses has been strik-ing. There are other notable gains. The daily one-to-one dialogue in pairs proves to be an invaluable means of bringing up to date conceptions of the foreign country, its institutions, education system etc. which can so quickly become out of date. As a re-fresher course in knowledge of the way of life of the foreign country the reciprocal course proves more useful than the conventional lecture series.

Even more important for teachers (and sixth formers) is the opportunity to form close links with a school or family in the other country. The annual reciprocal courses now organised by HMI have led each year to a growing number of firm school links, or partnerships between individuals, which have in turn encouraged exchanges and study visits of great variety.

The success of reciprocal courses in the 1970s may point the way forward to a pattern of language learning for adults to be developed in the future, especially for those who wish to acquire specialist language skills. Imagine an English lawyer wishing to acquire the French which will equip him to practise in France. A generalist teacher of French who has read only French literature can scarcely help him; he needs to learn not only the French language but French law. The concepts conveyed by the language can only be understood by a French lawyer. The same must be true for doctors, accountants, engineers etc. It is not difficult to envisage language courses for English professional groups in which, after an intensive stage bringing them all to the 'threshold level' in (say) French, they come together in a reciprocal course with an equally matched group of French specialists wishing to acquire English, to work in pairs in alternating sessions on materials dealing with the specialist concepts shared by both sides. In the model of modern languages in the school curriculum that we describe in Part III, in which intensive teaching builds upon the apprenticeship in language learning of the secondary stage, the reciprocal technique will have an important place.

Use of radio and television in foreign language teaching

Broadcast programmes for the foreign language learner go back a long way. As early as 1924 simple radio talks in French and Spanish were offered by the BBC, accompanied by a printed text in the *Radio Times*. In the past fifteen years the services offered by the BBC and to a lesser extent by ITV have expanded. It is not easy to say with certainty how many schools regularly include use of radio and/or TV in their foreign language teaching but the Autumn 1985 *Survey of Listening and Viewing* (carried out by the BBC's Educational Broadcasting Services Research Unit on behalf of the Educational Broadcasting Council of the BBC and the Educational Advisory Council of the IBA) indicates that the figure is around 55%.

Two developments have greatly encouraged schools' use of broadcast material. The first has been the relaxation of copyright regulations, allowing schools and colleges to copy broadcast programmes and keep them for three years for educational purposes thus building up valuable 'listening libraries'. Secondly the availability of the cassette recorder and more recently of the videorecorder has set free teachers from the restraints of timetabling lessons to coincide with broadcasts.

One great advantage of the videorecording, shared by the

'radiovision' programme (radio broadcast accompanied by filmstrip) which it has largely superseded, is that it can be exploited in class in several ways. For example the class may be asked to listen to and watch the programme and after some discussion of linguistic points (vocabulary, points of grammatical interest, of pronunciation etc.) the programme may be replayed with the sound turned off, and a member of the group may be asked to try to reproduce, or approximate to, the original commentary. After class discussion of omissions etc. and praise for good effort, the programme may be heard again. Attention to the finer points of the commentary is nicely concentrated when members of the class do not know which of their number will next be asked to 'volunteer' to attempt the role-play commentary. Interesting experiments in the use of interactive video have been carried out by Brian Hill at Brighton Polytechnic, who has found a great increase in motivation through its use, by Anny King at Hatfield Polytechnic, and by a team from the Ealing and Buckinghamshire Colleges of Higher Education.

So much material is now available that the teacher's main problem may be one of choice. There are four main sources of material. The first is the programmes aimed specifically at schools by BBC radio and TV and by the much smaller (but excellent) output of Thames Television. (Addresses are given below.)

In addition to the schools programmes there are programmes aimed mainly at adult learners (BBC Continuing Education) which many teachers have found useful in schools also. These make extensive use of on-the-spot recordings, unscripted film and sound recordings.

The third source is the BBC External Service (broadcasts by radio in French, German, Spanish, Italian and Russian) which many sixth formers listen to with profit.

Finally there are the increasing numbers of news items (interviews), films, and documentaries in foreign languages broadcast by BBC and ITV. Pressure from many quarters has encouraged both BBC and ITV not to fade out the foreign language, substituting voice-over translation in English, as was their common practice, but to show the English version on the screen in sub-titles, enabling the interested language learner to hear the foreign speaker while referring to the sub-titled 'prompt' where necessary. A word of caution, however, should be added concerning this valuable learning aid. The permission to copy material aimed at schools does not apply to such material, and copying even for use in class could infringe copyright.

Some idea of the menu on offer in the four languages most commonly studied in schools in the UK can be seen from this summary of the programmes for schools in one year (1986/7) from BBC alone:

BBC radio:
FRENCH: *Voix de France* (10 programmes; 'A' level); *Horizons de France* (5 programmes; GCSE level); *Business and Practical French* (4 programmes; 16–19 age); *A Propos* (3 programmes; 4th/5th year); *La Parole aux Jeunes* (2 programmes; Graded Obj. levels 3/4); *Encore une Etape* (5 programmes; Graded Obj. levels 3/4); *Branchez-vous!* (3 programmes; 2nd or 3rd year of French)
GERMAN: *Deutsch für die Oberstufe* (8 programmes; 'A' level); *Deutscher Club* (6 programmes; 'A' level); *Authentic German for GCSE* (5 programmes; levels 2/3); *Deutsches Magazin* (4 programmes; 4th/5th year level)
SPANISH: *Advanced Level* (3 programmes; 16–19 age); *Help Yourself: Business and Practical Spanish* (8 programmes 16–19 mixed ability)

BBC Television:
FRENCH: *France Français* (10 programmes; GCSE level); *La Marée et ses Secrets* (5 programmes; Graded Obj. levels 2/3); *Dès le Début* (5 programmes; lower secondary)
GERMAN: *Advanced Level* (3 programmes; 'A' level); *Mach's gut!* (5 programmes; Graded Obj. levels 3/4); *Encounter Austria* (5 programmes; 2nd/3rd year level); *Treffpunkt Osterreich* (5 programmes GCSE level)
SPANISH: *Encounter Spain* (5 programmes; 2nd/3rd year level); *Descubra España* (5 programmes; GCSE level); *Dicho y Hecho* (5 programmes; 2nd/3rd year level)
ITALIAN: *The Italians* (5 programmes; Upper Secondary); *Gli Italiani* (5 programmes; Upper Secondary)

Two of the above series (*Horizons de France* and *Deutsch für die Oberstufe*) include a radiovision programme, with film strip.

Reference should also be made to a format pioneered by BBC Continuing Education under the dynamic leadership of Sheila Innes. This is the 'multimedia' programme, combining radio with TV, illustrated text-book, LP records/cassettes, grammar notes, notes on the life of the country, tutor's notes including text of comprehension passages, word lists etc. This was the formula used in the courses for beginners, *Ensemble* and *Kontakte* More recent Continuing Education materials that could prove useful in schools in the 1986/7 session are:

A Vous la France! (the successsor to *Ensemble*; multimedia); *Télé-Journal* (authentic television newscasts in French, German, Spanish and Italian suitably edited to help the learner); *Excuse my French* (for absolute beginners); *France Actuelle* (follow-up to *A Vous la France!* in form of documentaries to improve comprehension); *Buongiorno Italia* (multimedia); *Deutsch Express* (2nd stage); *Franc Parler* (3rd stage).

Though the BBC leads the field with this rich array of programmes there are excellent ITV programmes. Thames Television offers the *Action-Télé* series in collaboration with a well-known textbook of that name. In the session 1986/7 a new series of 10 Thames programmes for 13–15-year-olds is promised based on recordings in a French town. This will offer schools a library of authentic dialogues corresponding to the situations identified in GCSE syllabuses. In German the three series of *Partner* (15 programmes) have been welcomed by schools, and Thames Television has arranged in-service discussions for teachers, on ways of exploiting TV, in conjunction with Hatfield Polytechnic.

Teachers who wish to obtain further information may find the following addresses useful:

– Educational Broadcasting Councils for the United Kingdom: Villiers House, The Broadway, Ealing, London W5 2PA
– BBC Educational Broadcasting Information: address as above
– BBC publications: PO BOX 234 London SE1 3TH
(but most publications linked to schools radio programmes in foreign languages are published by:
  Brighton Polytechnic: The Language Centre, Polytechnic, Falmer, Brighton BN1 9PH,
while publications connected with schools TV are obtainable from:
  CILT: Regent's College, Inner Circle, Regent's Park, London NW1 4NS)
– BBC Education Officer with responsibility for foreign language work is Anthony Barley, Broadcasting Centre, Woodhouse Lane, Leeds LS2 9PX
– Thames Television Education Office: Thames TV, 149 Tottenham Court Rd., London W1P 9LL
– BBC Enterprises, Education and Training at Woodlands, 80 Wood Lane, London W1 0TT, offer a library of videocassettes in French, German, Spanish, Italian, Russian, Greek and Gaelic.

Teachers interested in enriching their teaching by use of the programmes broadcast or by exploiting the growing library of available videotapes will find the following publications helpful:

Video in Language Teaching by Jack Lonergan. Cambridge University Press, 1984
Video in the Language Classroom edited by Marion Geddes and Gill Sturtridge. Heinemann, 1982.

Computers and language learning

The microcomputer is now widely accepted as an item of school equipment not only in the secondary school but also in the primary school. The explosive increase in numbers entering for 'computer studies' (GCE 'O' level) and 'computer science' (GCE 'A' level) reflects this development:

			Boys	Girls
computer studies	1980	entries at O level	10,036	4,149
	1985	entries at O level	43,947	18,538
computer science	1980	entries at A level	2,051	576
	1985	entries at A level	7,670	1,652

It is safe to assume that there are few schools which do not have access to a micro, especially since such provision has been given some priority by the government at a time when capitation funds for textbooks have been severely restricted.

It is less easy to estimate how many schools are using micros *for foreign language learning*. An educated guess, based on sales of the software programs at present available, suggests that the number may be more than 1,000, out of a total of 7,860 state secondary schools.

The micro has many obvious attractions for the language teacher. Pupils welcome the challenge of solving problems with it and playing games on it. There is a natural feeling, reinforced in many homes, that the micro is part of the future. Pupils cannot fail to observe how the micro has entered almost every walk of life: shops, offices, banks, hospitals etc.

Technically the micro marks a qualitative leap foward in information storage and retrieval. Use of the disc drive allows almost instantaneous access to data. The contrast with the frustrating minutes that it takes to locate language items recorded on tape/cassette is striking. As with tape-recorders, computers can be linked together and pre-programmed by teacher or technician. This enables pupils (probably working in pairs) to progress at their own speed while the teacher can monitor the screens in turn. Material can be saved from one lesson to the next. Printout from the screen can easily be obtained, on paper or on transparency (for use with the overhead projector in class later).

With all these advantages it is natural to ask what is the potential of this marvellous new aid in the foreign language classroom? An excellent introduction for the teacher is the joint MLA/BALT publication *CALL for the Computer: Computer*

Assisted Language Learning for the Modern Language Teacher (MLA/ BALT, 1986). This handbook by teams of teachers from the two Associations was funded by MEP (Microelectronics Education Programme) now superseded by the Microelectronics Support Unit based on the Department of Education and Science, London. It describes available programs designed to assist teaching the skills of listening, speaking, reading and writing, dividing the software into such categories as: 'authoring packages' (enabling teachers to create their own software); word-processing (where pupils work on their own texts); simulations/ role-play based on real-life situations; database; adventure stories and games; programs with sound; and miscellaneous packages (i.e. programs directed to a particular grammar point or to reinforce some area of vocabulary). This practical guide contains, in addition to an inventory of software available, helpful case studies of the use of the micro in classrooms, a list of useful addresses and suggestions for further reading.

Another valuable introduction for the language teacher is *Using Computers in Language Learning: a Teacher's Guide* by Graham Davies of Ealing College of Higher Education. The book includes a section on English Language Teaching by John Higgins of the British Council (Davies and Higgins, 1985). This contains a summary of the ways in which the micro has been exploited so far by the software available: traditional gap-filling; multiple-choice tests; free format question–answer dialogues; input validation; generative programs; simulations; word games; cloze; text reconstruction; translation; free composition; and by linking the micro with a tape recorder or video recorder, for dictation or listening comprehension. (Cf. the developments referred to above, p. 196, in this field of interactive video.)

Of course an obvious limitation at present must be that the pupil's interaction with the micro is restricted to typing in responses on the keyboard. Machines that will respond to oral messages are just beginning to appear, but their general use must be some years away. Even with this limitation, however, imaginative and often amusing interaction is possible at quite elementary levels. Good examples are the programs produced by the team of Barry Jones, Fred Daly and Wac Brodzki at Homerton College, Cambridge (Jones et al. 1986).

In *Quelle Tête!* (and its German counterpart *Kopfjäger*) the learner has to select features to build up, on the screen, a 'photo-fit' face in response to the instructions received.

In *Jeu des ménages* (German equivalent *Umziehen*) the user arranges furniture in a house, practising spellings, genders, use of prepositions etc.

A parallel development which has lessons for the foreign language teacher is the use of the micro in the *English language classroom*. Here an interesting introduction is *Primary Language Learning with Computers* by George R. Keith and Malcolm Glover (1987). Of particular interest are the programmes described in this book for teaching the 'language arts' and raising pupils' 'awareness of language'.

Though enthusiasts for the micro, the authors show balance in their approach and quote the cautions that have been expressed by, for example, F. Smith (1983): 'If teachers and children are able to make use of the creative and interactive potential, then I think we are on the threshold of a world of learning scarcely imaginable. The alternative is the employment of computers in ways that will destroy literacy. And teachers alone must decide and assert the way computers will be used in education.' A computer program for *foreign language teaching* which does not 'threaten literacy' but rather points the way forward to creative interaction, using the foreign language to solve real problems of the kind likely to be met by the user ('authentic' use of the foreign language), is the work of the Cambridge team referred to above (Jones, Daly, Brodzki). *Granville – the Prize Holiday Package* puts the learner (or pair working together) in the position of having five days' holiday in the seaside resort of Granville (modelled on a real town with a wealth of detail). The user is required to take a series of decisions: what to do; where to go and how (train? bike?); what to eat/drink; how much to spend etc. Pocket money is specified and the computer keeps a daily, nagging account of disbursements, reminding the user if too much (or too little!) is being spent on meals etc. The user's responses, via the keyboard, call both for understanding of the language and the diagrams, and for accurate spelling and use of currency, stamps etc. in a realistic setting such as pupils will encounter on a visit to France, and in 'authentic' language. Details of this imaginative program may be had from the publishers, Cambridge University Press.

If computer programs for the foreign language classroom develop further along these lines the future for the new technological teaching aid looks bright.

Looking further into the future, there are clear signs that the micro will have increasingly attractive uses, both for those learning foreign languages, and for foreign language users. Could the interests of these two possibly conflict? Machine translation makes rapid strides. Already we have generally available programs which enable the user to search a given text and *correct* all spelling errors. But the machine correction may not *teach* the user to avoid the error in future. Correction of errors of other kinds (genders, misuse of cases after prepositions, order of pronouns etc.) 'correction without learning' cannot be far away. It is possible to see, in these developments, cause to reflect on the warnings of Davies and others that 'literacy' may be at risk. These speculations may perhaps remind the foreign language teacher of the fears expressed by some of their maths and science colleagues, that the pocket calculator has undermined pupils' competence in the basic skills of multiplication and division.

The answer must lie with teachers. They must be aware of the possible implications of the methods they use and be resolute that the long-term interests of giving their pupils a sound base of *understanding* on which to build should guide their decisions when exploiting the new technology. We are reminded, once again, that in the foreign language classroom there can be no substitute for grasp of the structure of the new idiom; no short cuts, therefore, to avoid 'grammar'! The foreign language teacher's true professionalism may well be tested by the challenge to use the new technology to make the exploration of the new structures an interesting adventure, rather than a device to by-pass the painful necessity of understanding them.

Panaceas from abroad

To conclude our review of panaceas of the 1960s and 70s we should mention two 'methods' echoes of which reach us from abroad but which have not so far been tried in British schools.

The Silent Way

The Silent Way comes, like audio-lingualism and the language laboratory, from the USA. It is the invention of C. Gattegno, a famous pioneer in the use of 'enactive' ways of teaching mathematics and mother tongue. In *Teaching Foreign Languages in Schools – The Silent Way* (1972) he turns his long experience in the use of the 'Gattegno Rods' (ten rods of various lengths and colours developed for teaching 'number' to young children) to foreign language teaching. The rods are combined with a phonic chart, drawings and worksheets. The emphasis is on making maximum use of a small vocabulary, with the learners doing almost all the speaking, the teacher remaining silent, except for the single modelling of each new input. All speech is accompanied by action (mainly using the rods). The most original aspect of the method, however, is its emphasis on developing the learners' confidence in their developing use of the new language and their ability to help one other to use to the maximum the language they can control – while the teacher remains silent. The stress is on interaction between students, rather than on constant prodding by the teacher, on the absence of competition between students and on tolerance of error.

Suggestology

This panacea is of Bulgarian origin, its chief exponent being Georgi Lozanov, director of the Institute of Suggestology in Sofia, sponsored by the Bulgarian Ministry of Education. The technique of 'suggestology' is described in detail by Lozanov in his book *Suggestology and Outlines of Suggestopedy* (1978). Lozanov stresses that his method is not to be confused with either *hypnopedy* (hypnopoedia): learning during sleep (a technique chiefly experimented with in the USSR) or *hypno-hypnosopedy*: learning under hypnosis.

Lozanov's method relies on relaxation and passivity in the learner, not on sleep or hypnotic trance. He claims that suggestology 'combines the techniques of yoga, the psychology of suggestion, psycho-drama and sub-vocalisation'. It is 'the science of the art of liberating and stimulating the personality both under guidance and alone'. In this book Lozanov describes how experiments began in 1964 in the Department of Psychiatry in the Post-Graduate Medical School in Sofia. The following year a Suggestopedy Research Group was set up by the Ministry of National Education ('suggestopedy' is defined as 'suggestology applied in the process of instruction'). Experimental courses in French and English were begun in November 1965, with control groups against which to compare progress. The results, as described in great detail by Lozanov, were dramatic.

Lozanov prefaces his account of the results with a warning that they ought not to surprise us. The human memory, he points out, is greatly under-used. Only 4% of its potential is normally exploited. This has been shown by memory training among the Yogis in India. Some of the Yogis' disciples, called Stotrayas, have as their sole occupation the memorising of Brahman scriptures, the four Vedas. One alone of these, the Rig-Veda, the oldest work in Indo European literature, consists of 1,107 hymns (10,550 verses, 153,826 words). An Indian in Bombay, Audhani, is reported as having learned all four Vedas by heart. He could also recite a poem in any language from memory after a single hearing! Lozanov quotes other feats of memory: the Maori chief Kaumatana who recited for three days on end the history of his tribes over 43 generations, without a single note; and the case of K. M. at the Suggestology Research Institute, who learned to calculate mentally faster than an electronic calculator. Lozanov's argument is that the memorising of his students, though remarkable, is modest compared with the potential of the human memory when aided by relaxation techniques.

In Lozanov's language teaching a suggestopedic session is in two parts: active and passive. In the active part the teacher reads the new (French or English) words and phrases three times with a Bulgarian translation. A 'special intonation' is used (this is not explained) while students listen and follow on a printed programme. In the passive part of the session the students put aside the printed programme, and relax – without concentrating on anything in particular – while the new words and phrases are read again by the teacher 'with special intonation'. Lozanov stresses that though the students relax they must not sleep ('the teacher wakes up sleepers with a light touch').

An average of 80 new words a day are memorised, including grammar, spelling and pronunciation. Students' progress in the experiments described was certainly 'miraculous'. Moreover they reported side benefits from the relaxation therapy such as loss of nervous symptoms (headache, tiredness, nausea).

In 20 days the whole of C. E. Eckersley's Book 1 and (in the French group) the whole of Mauger Vol. 1 were learned on a programme of two normal academic hours per day (after students' normal work) plus one hour for a suggestopedia session, which meant that they worked until 11.00 pm each night. The work is still going on in the T. Samodumov Pedagogy Institute in Sofia.

How are we to interpret these reported experiments? Lozanov makes confident claims, for example, that suggestology refutes

Freud, and that 'Jung and Adler did not understand the social facts. It was the error of existentialism that it considered the individual as independent of the objective world. Feedback in learning is all important.' He quotes D. N. Uznadze to the effect that the response to a stimulus depends on the 'set up' of the individual, which depends on the individual's past experience. All this Lozanov sees as supporting his assertion of the enormous influence of suggestion on the individual.

Suggestibility varies across individuals, in degree and in time. H. J. Eysenck (1947) has suggested a classification for human suggestibility. Are we to see in the 1980s a development of language learning by suggestology, perhaps even a 'psycho-epidemic'? It is possible and Lozanov's experiments merit careful study.

Nevertheless the reports from Sofia do raise a more immediately engaging question. Does the success of deliberately switching off effort and concentration lend confirmation to the theory, which we have traced through Francke and Palmer up to Krashen in our own day, that language acquisition is mostly unconscious and benefits from distraction of the attention away from the *medium*? The theory is seductive. It seems, at least, compatible with the suggestion that learning is most effective when the pupil's attention is taken away from the surface forms of language and concentrated on the *personal meaning* that he or she intends to convey. This concentration on personal meaning is the essence of the immersion learning (IL) which will have an important role in the way ahead, to which we turn in Part III.

A Universal Auxiliary Language?

We should not conclude our review of the search for solutions without some reference to the dream that has haunted language teachers and learners down the ages, of constructing a language that would be universal and free from the irregularities that make existing languages difficult to learn.

Until the seventeenth century Europe had, in Latin, a *lingua franca* which fulfilled at least the first condition. But though a marvellous vehicle for philosophical discussion Latin lent itself less easily to dissemination of the new scientific ideas. In 1629 the French philosopher René Descartes (who wrote a treatise on optics in Latin) took up, in his *Lettre à Mersenne*, an idea suggested by Francis Bacon, that science needed a new language. (Father

Marin Mersenne was the eminent scientist who was, in 1636, to measure the speed of sound.)

The idea attracted the open-minded members of the new Royal Society in London. One of them, Bishop John Wilkins (brother-in-law to Oliver Cromwell), gave it practical shape in 1668 in his *Essay Towards a Real Character*. He was aided, incidentally, by another member of the Royal Society, Samuel Pepys, who provided lists of nautical terminology. Wilkins' aim was to create a linguistic vehicle for the propagation of the new discoveries in which the Royal Society was interested. Some scholars have suggested that he had a baser motive and that, prompted by Comenius, he hoped to provide a means of removing ambiguity from *theological* debate and thus advance the cause of protestantism. Comenius, in fact, published his own appeal for such an international language, in *Via Lucis*, in the same year, 1668.

Wilkins' approach to his problem, like other seventeenth-century proposals, was logical, 'a priori'. He categorised the universe of objects and concepts into 40 generic groups and invented written symbols (the 'real character') to refer to them, rather as musical symbols relate to the sounds of the instruments or as mathematical symbols relate to the logical steps in algebra. It was what the seventeenth century called a *pasigraphy* (Greek 'pas' = 'all' and 'graphě' = 'writing'; i.e. a system of signs intelligible to all men).

This approach reflected the seventeenth-century's passionate interest in two related inventions: shorthand writing and secret codes. Samuel Pepys was only one of many inventors of systems of shorthand. Interest in codes and cyphers (on which Comenius commented on his short visit to London in 1641) was fostered by the Civil War and the need for security at a time when families and townships were cruelly divided and espionage was rife.

A third strand in seventeenth-century approaches to 'universal language' was music. Another bishop, Francis Godwin, in his *The Man in the Moone* (1620, published posthumously 1633) proposed a 'musical language', each letter of the alphabet being allotted a note on the musical scale.

Interest in the logical or 'a priori' approach persisted into the nineteenth century. Francis Godwin's plan has an interesting echo in the proposal (1859) of the Frenchman Jean Sudre for a musical language 'Solresol' based on a musical score.

Towards the end of the century, however, the search changed direction. The proposal made in 1879 by Johann Martin Schleyer, a German Monsignor reputed to be able to speak 70 languages, was based on an 'a posteriori' approach, building on available elements from existing languages. Shleyer's new language *Volapük* ('Vola' = genitive 'of the world'; 'pük' = 'speech') used symbols drawn from common roots in the European languages. To these symbols Schleyer ascribed 'meanings' in terms of dictionary definitions. The languages from which his roots were taken were German, English and Romance, with German predominating. The following is the opening part of The Lord's Prayer in Volapük:

O Fat Obas, kal binol in süls, paisaludomöz nem ola!
Kömomöd monargän ola! Jenomöz vil olik, as in sül i su tal!

Between 1879 and 1889 Volapük was the rage of Europe. Some Parisian stores even gave their staffs special lessons in Volapük. However the grammar proved unnecessarily difficult and the sound system included *umlauts*, familiar in German but less so in English. The Volapük craze collapsed in 1889 at an international conference amid acrimony and confusion.

Already, however, in 1887 Dr Ludwig Zamenhof had published his auxiliary language *Esperanto* ('he who hopes') which was to have a different fortune. It is generally regarded as the most successful attempt so far (with one exception to be discussed later) to fulfil the ancient dream. Zamenhof saw his proposal as a contribution to peace. He was a Polish doctor in Bialystok where Poles, Lithuanians, Ukrainians, Russians and Jews lived in uneasy hostility. This extract from a poem written by Zamenhof shows something of the idealism which inspired his invention:

L'Espero	*Hope*
En la mondon venis nova sento.	A new sentiment has come into the world.
Tra la mondo iras forta voko;	A mighty call is passing through the land;
Per fhigiloj de facila vento	On wings of a light breeze
Nun de loko fluga gî al loko	From place to place now let it fly.
Ne al glavo sangon soifanta	Not to the sword thirsting for blood
Gî la homan tiras familion.	Does it draw the family of mankind.
Al la mond eterne militanta	To the ever warring world
Gî promesas sanktan harmonion	It promises holy harmony
. . .	. . .

(Extract and literal translation from The International Auxiliary Language Esperanto by G. Cox. British Esperanto Association, 1906)

The roots employed by Zamenhof were taken from English, German and Romance but unlike Volapük the Romance roots predominate. Zamenhof, profiting from the experience of Schleyer, made a simple grammar of sixteen rules and a sound system that is easy for Europeans (less easy for Orientals).

It is now claimed that several million people speak Esperanto, 150 periodicals are published in it and a score of radio stations broadcast in it. English pupils can now offer Esperanto in CSE examinations at 16+ and there is a part-time lectureship in it at Liverpool University, privately funded. In Norway the railways use Esperanto in timetables; the Swiss use it to promote tourism; Dutch telephone kosks have notices in Esperanto and some commercial firms (Philips, SAS) advertise in it. Over 200 members of the British House of Commons are declared supporters of Esperanto, in 1987, its anniversary year.

There have been innumerable attempts to launch universal languages since Volapük and Esperanto. The best known have been: *Idiom Neutral* (1902) a development of Volapük; *Ido* (1907) a splinter off-shoot from Esperanto; *Novial*, created in 1928 by Otto Jespersen; *Interglossa*, invented in 1943 by the English mathematician Launcelot Hogben. Perhaps the only serious challenge to Esperanto as the front-runner, however, comes from *Interlingua* (1951) the invention of an American Dr Alexander Gode and the International Auxiliary Language Association and financed by the ample fortune of Mrs Vanderbilt Morris. Interlingua is an *extracted*, rather than a *derived*, language; that is, it employs words taken whole from existing languages without modification, the languages used being French, Italian, Spanish and English (to a lesser extent German and Russian). Words are only used if they appear in at least *three* of these languages and it is claimed that Interlingua can be read by anyone who knows at least *one* of the languages concerned.

The following is an example of this *extracted* language:

Professor H Oberth, un del pioneros in el campo del rochetteria scientific in Germania e plus recentemente un associato de Dr. W. von Braun in su recercas de rochetteria al arsenal Redstone in Alabama, ha elabore un vehicula adoptate al exploration de luna.

There has been little attempt to promote Interlingua as a spoken language but many scholarly journals summarise their papers in Interlingua, including over 30 medical journals.

What does the future hold for international auxiliary languages? Linguists have raised two questions for the long term. The first concerns the relationship between language and thought. It has been put succinctly by Professor R. B. le Page, a former president of the Linguistics Association of Great Britain:

Language only works as a means of communication to the extent that the experiences, including the linguistic experiences, of a group of people, overlap. . . . Were it possible to envisage concepts as having an independent existence of their own it would be possible to conceive of a universal language through which these concepts could be manipulated, independent of any language community, and unchanging throughout the ages. The language of symbolic logic and the language of mathematics are the nearest we are likely to get to such a universal language. . . . Artificial languages such as Esperanto are neither universal in their patterns or conceptual analysis nor organic. (le Page, 1964, p. 8)

But does not the linguist's theoretical objection conflict with the evidence that Interligua and Esperanto do, in fact, work for some users and can succeed in transacting concepts between members of different speech communities? Perhaps the confiict may be more apparent than real. Members of different speech communities may, after all, share some concepts. For example, a well-known politician, Lord Wilson of Rievaulx, has put it on record that when he was a Boy Scout he corresponded with scouts in other countries in Esperanto. This would, presumably, confirm Professor le Page's axiom. Boy Scouts world-wide from whatever country do share certain concepts because of their common training and experience. There must be other groups who share concepts for similar reasons. Doctors would be a good example; hence the usefulness for them of Interlingua transcripts of medical articles. This nevertheless places clear restrictions on the claims that should be made for the auxiliary language.

A second caution was expressed by the 'father' of modern linguistics, Ferdinand de Saussure, in lectures he gave in 1914:

Artificial languages cease to be controlled by their creators the moment they are put into circulation. From that moment the creator is powerless to preserve their original form, the meanings attached to their words etc. Esperanto is an attempt of this kind. If it succeeds [in being widely circulated] can it escape the inevitable rule? (Saussure, 1983, p. 76)

And if Esperanto is doomed to imitate natural languages and become as irregular as they are, what becomes of its main appeal? This would leave the possibility of an existing, widely used language being adopted internationally (as English is now for some purposes e.g. air-traffic control). Some claims have been made that Mandarin Chinese in Latin transcription could be even more suitable than English as the world vehicle. Sadly the difficulties of any existing national language being accepted internationally are only too obvious.

The age-old dream, then, may be a mirage. And the language teacher or learner who has tasted the excitement and satisfaction of mastering a foreign language with all that it entails in growing understanding of the way of life of a living speech community, and of its culture, history, government, industry, as well as its song, its legends, its sense of humour, will not shed too many tears if the dream of by-passing such an adventure proves illusory.

NOTE

1 A lucid account of 'processing' of messages, starting with the identification of 'constituents', is given in Clark and Clark (1977). The constituent is the 'unit of speech perception' (Fodor and Bever, 1965). The Clarks suggest that language teachers can help learners by marking the constituents (e.g. with pauses). Grammatical gender also helps to identify members of a constituent segment.

2 Professor Michael Clyne has described (Clyne, 1986) an interesting series of 'early start' programmes in schools in the state of Victoria, Australia, culminating in a model pilot bilingual programme at Bayswater High School, to cater for children who had begun their German in primary school. In his book, *An Early Start: Second Language at Primary School*, he not only gives a lucid account of the pioneering Australian work but sets the early teaching of second languages in the UK and other countries against a scholarly account of recent work in psycholinguistics. Clyne's evaluation of the Australian work is a model of balance and of careful analysis of the factors that must be weighed when judging the effect of 'early start' programmes.

3 A magisterial account of many of the issues discussed in this section can be found in H. H. Stern's *Fundamental Concepts of Language Teaching* (Stern, 1983). Professor Stern's work is informed not only by a deep knowledge of the history of language teaching in the UK but by his wider perspective as a leading figure in language teaching in Canada and North America. His thorough and perceptive study appeared too late for our discussion to benefit from it but the reader who wishes to pursue the 'fundamental concepts' raised here is referred to Stern, especially his magnificent bibliography, as essential reading.

Part III

The way ahead

7   How are foreign languages learned?

I contrast 'serious' utterances with . . . teaching a language.
J. Searle, *Speech Acts*, 1969

The first step is . . . conceptualising language – becoming aware of it as a separate structure, freeing it from its embeddedness in events.
M. Donaldson, *Children's Minds*, 1978

'Whereas up to half of the world's children may be fluent in two or more languages without any formal instruction, only a handful of those taught a foreign language in the classroom ever seem to reach a very high level of proficiency in that language, regardless of the method of instruction used' (Kennedy, 1969).

Kennedy's observation suggests that it is not learning a foreign language that is difficult but learning it in the classroom and during adolescence.

How is this to be explained? Teachers have been searching for the answer for three centuries. We have reviewed some contributions to the debate, from the abandonment of immersion learning as supplement to class teaching in the seventeenth century despite the philosophers' arguments for the new inductive learning, through the four decades of great debate on the 'newer methods' unleashed by Viëtor in 1882, to the explosion of innovation that followed the Nuffield Foundation initiatives of the 1960s.

If we tried to draw a balance sheet of lessons learned from so much debate, how much could we enter on the positive side? The two most promising recent developments have been graded, defined objectives (unit/credit) and intensive immersion courses. What other advances could we claim? We have made some progress in classroom techniques. The role of visual aids, after much confusion, is better understood, though the advance on Comenius' pioneering use of pictures is only slight. It is at least an advance that we no longer talk of an 'audio-visual method'. There has been some progress, too, in the selective presentation of vocabulary though here too, since Comenius took the first step, progress has been modest. As to the presentation of grammar, inductive learning of grammar has won the argument over deductive ('construe') methods. It is now generally agreed that translation into the foreign language, though probably the most exacting and precise testing device for registering the presence in, or absence from, the learner's experience, and memory of the required foreign language 'collocations', is not an effective teaching device. We have learned to encourage our pupils to go to meet the foreign language, in reading and in dialogue with native speakers, and to 'quarry' their own working capital of the language, on which to work inductively.

Other big steps forward have been first, the spectacular improvement in materials for our quarrying, helped by the priceless new aid, the tape-recorder; and second, the preparation of teachers. Our young teachers now enter classrooms with much greater mastery of the spoken language and experience of residence in the foreign country than the products of pre-1960s degree courses, while expanded in-service provision has raised professional standards.

On the negative side of the balance sheet stands Graeme Kennedy's stark estimate: 'only a handful of those taught a foreign language in the classroom ever seem to reach a very high level of proficiency'. The vast majority of British pupils in comprehensive schools revolt against the foreign language and drop it at the earliest opportunity. An adult in the UK who can use a foreign language effectively for pleasure or business is a rarity. Yet outside the classroom half the world's children effortlessly master two or more languages. This is the paradox from which we must start our search for the way ahead.

Acquiring the mother tongue and learning a foreign language

When we compare the process of getting the mother tongue (L1) and learning a foreign language (L2) *in school*, some of the differences point obviously in favour of L1:

1. Time devoted to language practice.

mother tongue (L1)	*foreign language* (L2)
'The oral production of words by children is prodigious . . . It is not unusual to find a five-year-old using ten to fifteen thousand	In a class of 30, with 4 × 40-minute lessons per week, each pupil can expect to speak (in question and answer with the teacher) for ½

mother tongue (L1)	*foreign language* (L2)
words per day' (N. Brooks, 1960).	minute each lesson or an average of 2 minutes a week, not counting chorus work or work in the language laboratory. C. J. Dodson (1967) worked out that one year's contact with the foreign language in school corresponded roughly with *one* week of contact in the natural first language environment.

2. Ratio of 'learners' (L) to 'models' (M), as index of amount of attention given to learners' individual language needs.

Learner surrounded by models in family, playgroup, etc.	A single model (the teacher) surrounded by (30?) learners.

(Note also that the L1 model, the parent, is loved, prestigious, all-powerful, synonymous (temporarily) with truth. And the L2 model?)

3. Language and concept formation.

Learning language is part of the process of 'categorising the universe' e.g. learning names for parts of the body is also *discovering that they exist* and what they are like. The excitement of discovering concepts – and naming them – motivates the language learning.

Much (not all) L2 learning is *re-naming* already known concepts (e.g. what is the French for the sun and the moon etc.). The excitement (motivation) of discovering a new concept is missing – the learner already knows the concept exists. The excitement of *learning a new name* for it is less compelling. Compare 'telling the time' in L1 and L2: the first experience is an exciting discovery about the parcelling out of time into hours and minutes; the second a mere recoding of familiar concepts. (But see paragraph 10)

mother tongue (L1)	*foreign language* (L2)

4. Immaturity of conceptual development matching immaturity of language – and tolerance of error.

At L1 stage the concepts are simple, matching simple repetitive language and small vocabulary. Error is endearing and even encouraged.

Concepts are complex – inability to express them frustrating. Error is hard to tolerate – insecurity and embarrassment ensue.

5. Decline of 'empathy'; of mimicry; growth of self-consciousness in adolescence.

Although the debate on (Lenneberg's) 'critical' age is unresolved there is agreement that 'empathy' declines as adolescent insecurity approaches; young learners (below age 11+) show more readiness to mimic (unconsciously) and have fewer inhibitions (e.g. acting, singing, playing with opposite sex, with pupils of different colour, culture, etc.).

Adolescent insecurity, embarrassment, make foreign language behaviour less easy. Physical changes (e.g. voice breaking) make some classroom activities less welcome, the unfamiliar (in language, dress, colour of skin) less readily accepted. Racial prejudice is most virulent in adolescent and post-adolescent years. Acceptance of racial differences and willingness to behave in the foreign language probably both depend on a common characteristic: *capacity for 'empathy'* – the ability to see reality as someone else sees it – which in turn depends on confidence and security.

Other differences, however, seem to work in favour of L2:

6. Memory. Both short-term memory (STM) and long-term memory steadily improve with maturity up to the age of approximately 18.

Acquired when STM and longer-term storage are immature.

Memory comparatively mature and retrieval techniques well established by practice.

7. Concentration, studial habits.

Concentration short-lived and vulnerable.

Concentration comparatively controlled.

8. Intervention of parent/teacher to facilitate learning.

Although there is evidence that (some) parents do unconsciously select and direct items to help babies acquire language, the baby

The teacher's intervention and the careful selection of teaching materials *can* (though do not always) greatly economise learners' effort

mother tongue (L1)	foreign language (L2)
is generally exposed to a random linguistic bombardment from which to extract or create the rules of L1 grammar.	and time taken to induce the grammar of L2.

9. Expectations.

Much is still obscure in the debate about innate disposition to get L1 but there is no evidence that concepts (e.g. the calendar, telling the time, food and drink) are innate. They all have to be learned. Semantic networks are slowly built up and matched to language. This continues into adult life. Higher education (e.g. in law) involves learning many new, subtly discriminated, concepts and precisely matching these concepts with language.

The L2 learner comes to the task with clear expectations of many of the conceptual networks to be met. This should make for economy of learning, since a great accumulated capital of concepts, especially abstract concepts (e.g. justice, religion, loyalty) or the concepts of measurement (month, century, kilometre, volume, mass, etc.) must simply be transferred to the new code. The 'semanticising' does not all have to be done again (cf. Palmer, 1917).

10. Handling of abstractions.

Babies learn 'enactively' in their first years and their language is limited to the universe that is present to the senses of sight, hearing, touch etc.

From about age 12 the learner becomes increasingly able to handle explicit abstractions and to go from the particular to the general: this should greatly speed up analogising and induction of regularities from language met.

So far our comparison of mother tongue and foreign language learning seems evenly balanced. There is nothing to explain wholesale failure in school. However it has omitted two most important differences between the two processes to which recent research has pointed:

1　the nature of the speech acts transacted between the baby and its linguistic models compared with the (non-speech act or non-serious) transactions of the foreign language classroom
2　the role of 'awareness of language', and its effect on aptitude for secondary linguistic activities such as learning to read and learning other languages.

Speech acts

The notion of the 'total speech act' was introduced by the Oxford philosopher J. L. Austin in 1962 (*How to Do Things With*

Words). He drew attention to a category of utterances which are 'performative' (or 'operative') in the sense that the issuing of the utterance is the performing of an action. Austin distinguished (tentatively) five classes of performatives:

(i)   verdictives (to acquit, reckon, characterise, rank, describe etc., e.g. the giving of a verdict by a jury or umpire)
(ii) exercitives (to dismiss, choose, enact, command, advise, beg, e.g. a decision about how things should be, or advocacy of a particular course)
(iii) commissives (to promise, guarantee, adopt, agree, swear, etc., e.g. an announcement of one's intention)
(iv) behabitives (to apologise, to deplore, to commiserate and other ways of reacting to other people's behaviour, e.g. congratulations)
(v)   expositives (to show how words are being used to affirm, inform, testify, accept, interpret, etc., e.g. I concede).

Austin's professional concern, as a philosopher, was to argue that some utterances should be considered as 'actions' as opposed to statements of fact whose truth or falsity had pre-occupied philosophers and logicians hitherto. Thus, to declare '"I name this ship the *Queen Elizabeth*" is not to *describe* what I am doing or to *state* that I am doing it, *but to do it*'.

Austin's pupil J. Searle developed in *Speech Acts* (1969) 'the hypothesis that the speech act is the basic unit of communication'. He sets out, in effect, to answer Austin's question (in *How to Do Things With Words*): 'What are the different kinds of speech acts speakers perform when they utter expressions?' (p. 21). He adopts Austin's term 'illocutionary act' to characterise the acts of asserting, questioning, commanding (verbs like 'state', 'describe', 'warn', 'remark', 'command', 'welcome', 'argue', etc.). Austin claimed there were over a thousand such expressions in English (Austin, 1962, p. 149). Searle's insight was to distinguish, in the illocutionary speech act, two elements: the illocutionary force and the propositional content. This can be shown as follows:

$$\text{speech act} = F\,(p)$$

where F is the illocutionary force and p the propositional content.

Note that different speech acts, having different F, may share a common propositional content. In other terms: one and the same utterance may constitute the performance of several different illocutionary acts (Searle, 1969, p. 24). The following examples are adapted from Searle's instances to make this point plain:

w (p) = a proposition p uttered with the intention of giving a *warning*
e.g.: 'I'll be waiting for you!' (with a gun ?)
pr (p) = the same proposition p uttered with the intention of *promising*
e.g.: 'I'll be waiting for you!' (with the theatre tickets ?)

The common element in these two speech acts (the proposition) is a sentence which the linguist can analyse grammatically but, to quote Searle again:

the unit of linguistic communication is not, as has generally been supposed, the symbol, word or sentence . . . but rather the production of that symbol, word or sentence in the performance of the speech act . . . purely formal study [of language] is necessarily incomplete. It would be as if baseball were studied only as a formal system of rules and not as a game. (p. 17)

The special interest of this for language teachers is that the philosopher's account of the speech act links with what the sociolinguists tell us about mother-tongue acquisition. Halliday (1975) sees the first stage of this process as the mastery of certain basic functions of language each one having a small range of alternatives or 'meaning potential' associated with it. Six of Halliday's functions are extrinsic to language. They are:

Instrumental	'I want'
Regulatory	'do as I tell you'
Interactional	'me and you'
Personal	'here I come'
Heuristic	'tell me why'
Imaginative	'let's pretend'

Halliday adds a seventh function, the 'Informative', which is highly sophisticated, and does not develop until about the age of two years. It is intrinsic to language and definable only by reference to language. It is, however, the function that predominates in adult thinking about language and makes it difficult for adults to imagine the very different image that the young child forms of what can be done with language. We return to this difference between adult and child language in the second part of this chapter, when we examine the problem of the child's 'awareness of language'.

Learning functions, in Halliday's sense, is learning to transact 'speech acts'. The motor that propels language acquisition seems to be the drive to 'do things with words' as Austin put it.

But what happens if the language transacted (in the classroom) serves no function for the learner? It does not then consist of speech acts. Only 'serious language', Searle says, consists of speech acts having 'force'. 'I contrast "serious" utterances with play acting, *teaching a language* [our italics], reciting poems, practising pronunciation etc.' (Searle, p. 57). Exchanges in the foreign language classroom, then, for Searle, are not 'serious' language. They may have propositional content or reference and be susceptible of grammatical analysis but they are not uttered with intention to mean.

There is now clear research evidence that such non-serious utterances, spoken without 'force', are not retained effortlessly by the speaker/hearer as are true speech acts. This gives us an important clue which may explain why so many learners who acquired their mother tongue effortlessly fail to learn the foreign language.

Before we consider this evidence we may note in parentheses that some teachers of English have found useful the words 'text' and 'discourse' to distinguish between 'sentences in combination' (text) and 'use of sentences' (discourse). Widdowson (1973) has argued that if we are to teach language in use, we have to shift our attention from sentences in isolation on the one hand to the manner in which they are used to perform 'communicative acts' in discourse, on the other. This comes close to the distinction we are making between sentences and true speech acts, though it is not exactly the same. Foreign language teachers should welcome and learn from the advances made in English teaching by work on discourse analysis (Coulthard, 1977; Widdowson, 1978).

To return to the evidence that 'non-serious' language is not retained, Lois Bloom has shown how the child Peter (aged two-and-a-half) was incapable of *imitating* successfully sentences he had himself spontaneously produced the day before (Bloom, 1974, quoted in Donaldson, 1978). Similar findings are reported by Dan Slobin and Charles Welsh (1973) even when the imitation is asked for *immediately after* the spontaneous production. They suggest that, in spontaneous speech, the child has an 'intention-to-say-so-and-so' and that this intention supports the complex utterance. When the intention has faded the child must process the utterance as pure isolated language. This is a very different task because the child is not now using language in order to achieve some purpose. This is 'non-serious' language in Searle's terms. It reminds us of the pupil in the foreign language lesson.

'Intention to say' (Searle's 'F', Halliday's 'function') reminds us of what other writers have called 'drive'.

The child's drive – his need to relate and to be understood – is one of the central factors of his life. The intelligent interest which a student brings to the task of learning a second language is pale by comparison. There is only one way in which an adult can experience something approaching the intensity of drive which he brought to his first language, and that is by being in a comparable situation. An individual may find himself in a place where people speak a language he does not know, and where there is nobody to interpret. Learning in such cases can be incredibly fast. (Ingram, 1975, p. 286)

Not only does this 'drive' ('intention to say') *motivate* the utterance but, as M. Donaldson suggests, it sustains and supports the capacity to operate complex grammar rules. When the drive is missing, the grammar rules prove too difficult. This may explain the phenomenon that many teachers will have observed, the dramatic leap forward of the pupil's mastery of the foreign language as soon as he or she goes abroad. It is as if the *rehearsal* of the classroom (with no audience present, no curtain up, no real intention to do things with words) gives way to true *performance*.

The two levels: Carl Dodson

Another way of describing these two stages of rehearsal and performance has been proposed by Carl Dodson, in his two-level theory of foreign language acquisition:

The learner finds it difficult to reach communicative competence – that is, when the second language becomes a mere tool in the execution of an activity or the satisfaction of an immediate non-linguistic need – if he is not allowed to pass through two levels of communication. The first level, which can be called 'medium-orientated communication' is the stage where for any activity the child's mind is focussed mainly on the language itself. At the second level, which can be called 'message-orientated communication', the language tends to become a tool and gradually of secondary importance to the learner, whose main aim at that juncture is to communicate a message which is not about language. (Dodson, 1978, p. 48)

Dodson contrasts pupils 'using' language (to show teachers that they can use it) and 'making use' of language (to communicate a message). This recalls Widdowson's distinction between 'usage' and 'use' (Widdowson, 1978). Dodson is here, we should remember, discussing 'bilingual' schools in Wales where there is opportunity and motivation for English-speaking pupils to use Welsh with their Welsh-speaking peers in classroom games and other 'message-orientated' activities. In a later study (Butzkamm and Dodson, 1980) he has shown how 'level 2' or 'message-orientated' activities are also possible in the normal foreign language classroom. He takes up Littlewood's distinction (Littlewood, 1975) between 'role taking' and 'role making'. In the latter (as in Dodson's 'level 2' message-orientated communication) the speaker's attention is directed away from the language, on to the meaning. This (Dodson shows) was the principle formulated by Otto Tacke (1923) as 'Ablenkung vom Wort als Selbstzweck' (diverting attention from the word as an end in itself), 'stets ein Ausdruckswille beim Erlernen fremdsprachlicher Ausdrücke suggeriert wird, sonst haften die fremden Ausdrücke nicht' (a will to mean must always underlie the learning of expressions in the foreign language, otherwise the foreign expressions do not stick). Otto Tacke's principle of 'Ablenkung vom Wort als Selbstzweck' recalls the insistence of Felix Francke (1884) that language can only be acquired 'unconsciously'.

H. E. Palmer made the principle of subconscious comprehension one of the foundations of his programme: 'Of the vocabulary possessed by any person proficient in the use of a foreign language, a very small proportion has been acquired by conscious study, probably less than 5%; the bulk of his vocabulary has been acquired by subconscious assimilation' (Palmer, 1917, p. 131).

A hypothesis which links interestingly with the ideas of Tacke, Francke and Palmer, is the widely discussed 'monitor' theory of Stephen Krashen of the University of Southern California. He distinguishes between subconscious 'acquisition', which is 'the most effective and central means of internalizing language for adults as well as children', and conscious 'learning', which involves deliberate use of the 'monitor' which focuses on 'form' and checks for correctness (Krashen, 1977, 1981).

When immersed in the language, as is the baby getting L1 or the immigrant getting L2, the learner will 'acquire' the language by 'intake' from 'comprehensible input' (though 'intake' need not always correlate with 'input'). The learner 'creates' his own rules from the evidence given by the input. This recalls the Chomskyan hypothesis of an innate 'grammar searching device' or LAD (language acquisition device) which can search out linguistic 'rules' from even quite fragmentary input (Chomsky, 1965).

Krashen contrasts 'acquisition' which is subconscious, with the conscious learning of rules, followed by correction of error, by feedback or by teacher's intervention. Such consciously learned rules are stored in the learner's 'monitor', and are available for checking and correcting, though not for 'generating' the language.

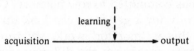

(Krashen, 1979)

Krashen allows a role for memorised chunks of the language picked up involuntarily from the 'input', even if they were not originally understood, and heard playing themselves back in the memory 'en bloc'. This phenomenon, which will be familiar to many learners immersed in a foreign language, Krashen calls the 'din in the head' (Krashen, 1983). An interesting link suggests itself between Krashen's theory and Otto Tacke's observation that a 'will to mean' makes the language stick in the head. Can it be that concentration on the *intention to mean* diverts the learner's attention from use of the 'monitor' temporarily?

Krashen, himself an outstanding linguist and a brilliant communicator, has made a great contribution to thinking about this central issue of how language is acquired. It should be said, however, that the underlying theory has been questioned. Psychologists have reconsidered the notion of a language acquisition device, LAD, and have asked if successful getting of the mother tongue does not call for a great deal more than the mere application of an inborn faculty. Jerome Bruner, of Harvard and Oxford, suggests that observation of children's language progress at the pre-school stage and when faced with learning to *read* shows that in addition to a LAD, a LASS (language acquisition support system) is needed, in the form of supportive adults able to spare the time, as Bruner puts it, to 'attend to what the child is attending to'. This view is now strongly reinforced by a wealth of careful research (Bruner, 1983; Donaldson, 1978; Tizard *et al.*, 1981; reviewed in Hawkins, 1984). Krashen's theory has been criticised from other standpoints. One weakness is that so far it is not supported by empirical evidence. Critics have asked whether it follows, even if 'comprehensible input' leads to greater comprehension, that *production* is thereby facilitated. Some psychologists maintain that comprehension and production involve quite different procedures (Forster, 1979; Bever, 1981; Pienemann, 1985).

And there are, surely, two very different kinds of production, speech and writing. Can Krashen's theory apply to both kinds? Clearly, when one is writing a letter, one has the opportunity constantly to review, correct, even to run over the paradigms of verbs that one has committed to rote memory. One can stop to search the memory for a gender, even look up a word in the dictionary. All this is 'monitor' work, yet true 'production'. Krashen, of course, recognises the difference between spoken and written production, but the true role of deliberate learning of 'rules' for the learner who is chiefly concerned with written production remains to be clarified. The foreign language teacher ought not to forget the impressive command of Latin and Greek shown by the products of our traditional classical sixth forms brought up on teaching methods which relied greatly on deliberate learning and the 'monitor'. The best of these classics scholars were required regularly to *compose verses* in Latin and Greek, calling on a formidable vocabulary and mastery of complex rules, both of syntax and prosody. Could our 18+ candidates in French and German do the same? The classics students were operating, of course, almost entirely in the *written* language, where the 'monitor' has full scope.

The theory advanced by Dodson, briefly summarised above, supposes, like Krashen's theory, two 'levels' or kinds of cognition. But Dodson sees his two kinds of cognition (concentration on 'form' and concentration on 'message') as constantly interplaying and reinforcing each other. 'Utterances are often a mixture of medium- and message-orientated communication' (Dodson, 1985, p. 332). This could better explain the clearly different roles played by rehearsal of consciously (explicitly) learned rules in *writing* as opposed to *speech*. We return to these two kinds of cognition in Chapter 9 where classroom activities to promote *both levels* in fruitful interaction are described in detail.

What our comparison of L1 and L2 learning has revealed so far is:

   i   a crucial factor in language acquisition is intention to 'do things with words' ('force') without which new linguistic expressions are not retained by the learner ii The role of 'level 1' language learning, has been seen by some as a foundation (as 'rehearsal' before 'performance') and by others as a monitor applied to what has already been acquired. It begins to be clear that a major defect of school language courses hitherto has been that the learners have remained at the 'level 1', except for the fortunate few who go abroad for a serious immersion in 'level 2' language communication and/or who read widely, looking for meanings *that matter to them.*

We now begin to understand why it is that most school language teaching fails, despite striking improvements in materials and incessant attempts by teachers to perfect their techniques, why those pupils who succeeded in the past were those who went abroad to study and why immersion courses proved so effective.

A further dimension has been added to the discussion by Earl Stevick (1976). Stevick, like Dodson, would not categorise foreign language transactions in black and white terms, as possessing, or not possessing, the essential ingredient of 'force'. Between the utterance which is pure 'rehearsal' and the authentic speech act, there may be a number of degrees of 'depth', the term used by E. Stevick to describe the degree of personal meaning in a given utterance.

Some learners, very strongly motivated or of outstanding ability, will triumph over lack of personal meaning in classroom transactions. One has recently seen Chinese students of English, brought up on a regime of plodding translation of arid texts describing the exploits of Chairman Mao, students who have been isolated by the 'cultural revolution' for years from communication with native speakers of English, yet who reach astounding levels of competence. The motivation and self-discipline of such students, their willingness to 'suspend disbelief', are awesome. They can transform every 'rehearsal' into a make-believe 'performance' by sheer mental discipline.

Such students are rare in our schools. We are thinking of the average pupil in the comprehensive school, indeed of the great majority of pupils, for whom we need to map out a programme of varying degrees of what Stevick has called depth. The learning activities will lie along a cline from formal drills, to teach the basic habits of pronunciation, intonation, structural patterns etc., up to language transactions that are true speech acts, spoken with force and intention to 'do things with words' and thus retained effortlessly. It is to this that our next chapter is addressed.

Before we examine this aspect of the way ahead, however, there is one more hypothesis to be considered in looking for an explanation of wholesale failure to learn foreign languages in schools. It is one prompted by our reference to the highly motivated and gifted Chinese learners: does the task call for special *aptitude*, and if so, can aptitude for foreign language learning be improved?

Aptitude for foreign language learning: the 'parental lottery'

It would be surprising if innate aptitude for foreign language learning (and for mother-tongue learning) did not differ from one individual to another. Differences in innate aptitude for other complex skills are vast. When Yehudi Menuhin played the Beethoven concerto in Berlin at the age of 12, in April 1929, the great physicist Albert Einstein came running across the stage to hug him and exclaim 'Now I know there is a God in heaven!' Nobody pretends that you or I could have made such music if only we had practised our scales harder! So it may be with language. Amazing cases of precocity in foreign language learning include, for example, John Stuart Mill reading Greek at the age of five. Seneca, Virgil, Livy and Cicero, whom we read as models, learned their Latin in school. Milton drafted papers more readily in Latin than in English. There are accounts of Victorian linguists who mastered as many as 200 languages. As the Robbins Report on Higher Education put it: 'No one who has taught young people will be disposed to urge that it is only the difference in educational opportunity that makes the difference between a Newton or a Leonardo and Poor Tom the Fool. But . . . it is equally wrong to deny that performance . . . is affected by nurture in the widest sense of that word (Robbins, 1963, p. 49).

Verbal aptitude is particularly vulnerable to nurture in the family, and the power of the school to compensate for lack of parental encouragement has been shown by repeated studies, from Plowden onwards, to be extremely limited. The effort to create a worthwhile comprehensive school system has been side-tracked by muddle-headedness and dogma concerning the range of human abilities. It has sometimes been assumed that differences of ability between pupils would go away if teachers pretended they were not there. This has distracted attention from the really iniquitous inequality suffered by children, namely the lottery of finding themselves in homes where the adults lack the capacity to act as parents.

The role of parent is the hardest any adult ever has to play. It demands willingness to give time and effort endlessly, tirelessly to the task of building the family into a cooperative, responsible team. It is an immensely difficult role in our society which many adults are too immature (and many unwilling) to take seriously. A great many children in consequence draw a blank ticket in the lottery.

The capacity to be a good parent is not the prerogative of any one social class though it does appear to correlate to some degree with the parental job, perhaps because some jobs call for the same qualities of maturity and unselfishness as are required for parenthood. It correlates, also, with cultural patterns. It is no accident that, for example, the incidence of juvenile delinquency among Jewish youth or Asian immigrant youth is relatively low, compared with other cultural groups whose traditions of family responsibility are weaker. Nor do crude measures of 'broken' homes correlate to a great degree with failure at verbal learning. Much more important, as Vygotsky showed (1962) and Mia Kelmer Pringle's life-work confirms, is the factor of adult time devoted to sharing activities and dialogue with children.

The parent is, for the first five years of a child's life, not simply the loved and unquestioned *model*, giving the child the main components, as Vygotsky showed, of the 'conscience' (inner, imagined dialogue with 'the other', i.e. the parent) that the child takes through life, but also the chief language informant on whom the child is almost wholly dependent. The language informant does not simply model a vocabulary and a syntax to which the child applies an innate 'language acquisition device' or innate cognitive 'functions' of 'assimilation' and 'accommodation'. As Saussure argued, acquiring the rules and habits of syntax, and a few thousand vocabulary items, is a relatively trivial intellectual accomplishment for the sophisticated human brain. What is not at all trivial is constructing a *conceptual* network whose categories have precise outlines, are clearly discriminated one from another, and have depth.

Children's surface similarities of vocabulary and syntax may mask great differences in the richness and precision of the conceptual infrastructure. It may take a lifetime to match our limited stock of relatively crude verbal expressions to even a small part of our cultural heritage of conceptual categories with subtlety and precision. The process of *matching* language to the constantly growing conceptual network is begun (again the insight was Vygotsky's) in the baby's dialogue with an unhurried, patient, attentive parent. It is through this dialogue that 'awareness of language' (see the discussion in Chapter 2) develops. But the parent must have the time (and energy and peace of mind!) as well as possessing the concepts to which the subtle match with language has to be made. (The education of school leavers for the responsibilities of parenthood – a sadly neglected aspect of education – is outside the scope of this book, yet without parental support the linguistic education given in the school, like so much else, will fall on stony ground.)

If parental effectiveness is a lottery, so is the chance of meeting, in school, teachers equipped professionally to devise appropriate remedies for pupils who have not developed awareness of language. The Bullock Report argued for the inclusion in teacher training programmes of courses in 'language in education' and offered in an appendix some model syllabuses. A beginning has been made in some college courses and university degrees by the inclusion of linguistics and sociolinguistics. It is possible that some teachers of English will in future go into schools knowing something of how children acquire language (both mother tongue and foreign languages), of language change, of dialects and of linguistic prejudice, and the rudiments at least of the vast literature on language and learning. Most mother-tongue teachers, however, will have graduated in 'English' which generally means English literature. How prepared are they to answer the questions that perceptive pupils ask about the place of language in society, or indeed to ask such questions themselves, let alone (for lack of thorough grounding in phonetics) to take an informed part in (say) the debate about the use of a 'teaching alphabet' to help slow readers.

Another handicap suffered by teachers who have followed conventional degrees in English literature is that they have not studied a foreign language in depth and through that study come to understand the values of a culture different from their own. They are unlikely, therefore, to reflect in their teaching, or share with their pupils, an active curiosity about what lies beyond the parochial linguistic horizon. Of course this is not true of all English teachers, some of whom set splendid examples of outgoing, enquiring attitudes to the linguistically unfamiliar. For the majority, however, foreign languages, like sociolinguistics, are a closed book. Is this not very serious, when in our cities we have many schools in which a dozen or more different mother tongues are spoken or in which a majority of the pupils may speak a West Indian dialect? It must be said that foreign language teachers, too, may display parochialism regarding the mother tongue or home dialect of their pupils. Is it not time that the two kinds of language teacher came together? A recurring theme in these pages is the need not only for joint degrees in English and a foreign language but for the opportunity for teachers so prepared to continue their cooperation when they join their schools. One way to begin might be by planning together a linking course in 'awareness of language'. This could be the bridge between these two elements in the curriculum which could be so mutually enriching and which at present have no contact with each other.

Meanwhile schools are ill-equipped to understand, still less to help, the child who, having drawn an unfortunate ticket in the parental lottery, misses the patient, relaxed dialogue with an informed adult on which school readiness and 'awareness of language' depend. What we must now examine is how this affects foreign language learning. Are 'awareness of language' and the capacity to acquire a foreign language in some way linked? What is 'aptitude' for foreign language learning?

Assessing aptitude for foreign language learning

The most successful approach to defining aptitude for learning foreign languages has been to construct tests which prove to be predictive of success of FL learning. When, by trial and error, test items that are highly predictive of future foreign language learning have been identified, the items are scrutinised to determine what cognitive capacities they seem to call upon, and it is hypothesised that the sum of these constitutes 'aptitude'.

The leading researchers in this field in the post-war period have been J. B. Carroll and S. M. Sapon whose *Modern Language Aptitude Test* was published in 1958. They found that IQ was a good predictor of foreign language learning, not surprisingly correlating between 0.34 and 0.53 with scores in the foreign language.

Other researchers have found similar correlations (Ingram, 1975, p. 276):

Learned and Wood (1938)   0.46
von Wittich (1962)   0.48
Pimsleur (1966)   0.46
Green (1975) (verbal I Q)   0.39 to 0.47

(Green's test included comprehension and writing but Green found correlations of only 0.13 to 0.18 between verbal I Q and oral tests.)

These correlations suggest that 'aptitude' has other specific components besides IQ. The studies of Carroll and Pimsleur agree fairly well together in identifying the following four components of aptitude:

1 Ability to match sounds with symbols, at speed
2 Insight into the pattern of language or awareness of the syntactical structure of sentences (Carroll, 1971, quoted in Ingram, 1975)
   (The reader is referred to our discussion of language 'awareness' in Chapter 2 and the evidence for its correlation with reading in the mother tongue)
3 Capacity to 'induce' rules from language met (closely related with insight into pattern)
4 Associative learning: both Carroll and Pimsleur include tests of rote learning in their aptitude measures.

The crucial abilities identified by the Carroll/Sapon and Pimsleur batteries as: 'insight into pattern/induction of pattern "rules" in grammar' have been further studied by Green at the Language Teaching Centre, York University.

Beginning with the York Study (Green, 1975) and continuing in prolonged trials with language learners of different ages, Green has found that language learning correlates consistently with the capacity *quickly* to accomplish two learning steps:

1 perceiving the pattern or regularity in a given display of language
2 inventing a new, analogous component.

Thus in Green's Swedish Grammar Test the student is given the instruction:

'the' is not a separate word in Swedish but an ending added to the noun. Read through the examples in the table below and try to fill in the missing word in the space opposite the arrow, e.g.

a book	*en bok*	the book	*boken*
a chair	*en stol*	the chair	*stolen*
a spoon	*en sked*	the spoon	*skeden*
a cat	*en katt*	the cat	←

After this opening item Green's test becomes progressively more complex, but the emphasis throughout is on the two cognitive steps: (i) perceiving pattern and (ii) creating 'analogous' appropriate new forms. This is, of course, the process well attested in studies of mother-tongue acquisition, exemplified by such 'creations' as 'Daddy *digged* the garden.' Here analogising from a wrongly perceived pattern (over generalising from too limited an experience of adult usage) is seen as an essential, creative step in acquiring the mother tongue.

This aptitude for perception/creation emerges in the studies of Carroll/Sapon, Pimsleur and especially in Green's recent work, as an important component of foreign language learning. The close similarity between perception of pattern in languages and the concept of linguistic 'awareness' discussed in works, already cited, by Donaldson, Mattingley and Bruner, is striking.

Interest in 'awareness' or 'insight into pattern' as an important component of foreign language aptitude (and of aptitude for learning to read) is heightened by work on STM (short-term memory). The study of memory has fascinated researchers since the dawn of psychology as a science in the nineteenth century. The father of modern psychology, William James, experimented tirelessly on his own (and his students') memory. Recent work on memory has followed two paths of particular interest to language teachers:

i study of the different kinds of memories stored ('episodic' memory, 'semantic' memory, etc.)
ii study of the mechanisms of storage and especially the 'processing' of incoming messages.

The first of these paths has led to interesting hypotheses which may prove of immediate relevance to classroom practice, though much of the work is still tentative. Psychologists now suggest that there may be more than one 'memory system'. For example, recall of a series of events ('episodic memory') seems to presuppose storage of a different kind from recall of meanings of words ('semantic memory'). Other systems have been proposed:

'action memory', 'geographic memory', 'person memory', etc. (Miller and Johnson-Laird, 1976).

There is evidence that girls at adolescence show superiority over boys in 'semantic memory' while boys are superior in 'geographic' or 'spatial' memory. Some teachers have developed ways of helping boys to exploit their 'spatial' memory in order to compensate in part for the unfairness of having to compete in verbal learning tasks with girls whose verbal learning age is, on average, 18 months in advance of that of boys at chronological age 12. 'Spatial' discrimination has been found useful, for instance, in teaching grammatical genders. (Gougenheim et al. (1965) remind us that the use of spatial aids to memorising was pioneered in France in the teaching of deaf and dumb children in the eighteenth century by the Abbé de l'Epée.) In our discussion of classroom techniques (Chapter 9) we shall return to 'spatial discrimination'.

Short-term memory

Research into the mechanism of storage also has clear implications for language teaching. Work on 'short-term' memory has been especially active following Miller's classic paper 'The Magical Number Seven' (1956). Miller proposed an elegantly simple model of storage in the memory consisting of a 'long-term' reservoir equipped with a 'short-term' vestibule or narrow sluice-gate through which all incoming messages must pass. The short-term receptacle is of limited capacity, i.e. the average adult can only accommodate a limited number (7 ± 2) of 'bits' of information at any one time and retains them only for a brief period (3 to 10 seconds?). Thus the listener receiving a verbal message might hold in his STM the preceding clause while listening to the next one. Some research (Caplan, 1972) suggests that once a clause has been decoded in STM its exact wording is not retained; what is 'encoded' in the long-term store is not the verbatim content but the meaning, unless by 'loop' repetition the verbatim, surface features are reinforced, as when learning by rote. As Slobin puts it: 'listeners begin "purging" memory of verbatim content after a sentence has concluded' (Slobin, 1979). This is a feature of STM that the foreign language teacher may not welcome!

Miller's calculation of the normal adult capacity of STM as 7 ± 2 'bits' or 'chunks' of information was based on the conventional tests using random digits, presented at a speed of two per

second, without 'bunching' or grouping into chunks by intonation or by some regularity of pattern.

Research on STM has been intense since Miller's seminal
paper. STM is given various names: 'primary memory' is used to
distinguish it from 'secondary memory' (the long-term store).
The term 'buffer memory' is also used and STM is also sometimes referred to as an 'echo box' or 'echo chamber'; these terms
usefully describe one feature of STM: it is not under conscious
control. It is as if messages reverberate, for a few seconds,
whether we like it or not, but quickly fade unless we take deliberate steps to attend to the dying echo, and process it in some way.
The function of the STM seems to be to hold in focus transient
features of the rapidly changing environment for long enough to
allow (relatively slow) mental processes to be brought to bear on
them. It forms a kind of 'work-table' (of limited capacity) in the
mind on which messages can be inspected and processed. More
recent studies of STM have suggested that there may be, in fact,
not two levels only ('short-term' and 'long-term') but a series of
levels of varying degrees of depth.

It has been established since the early days of IQ tests that
simple digit-span STM capacity is systemically related to both
chronological age and IQ. Digit span was one of the basic devices
used in early intelligence tests such as the Stanford-Binet and
Wechsler batteries. The span increases on the Stanford-Binet
scale from 2 digits at chronological age 30 months to 3 at 36
months, 4 at 54 months and stabilises in adulthood at about 7
digits (Olson, 1973). It can be increased by training, as Miller
showed, up to as many as 14 or 15 digits with specially selected
adult subjects.

Despite this systematic relation to IQ, however, Olson's experiments have demonstrated that STM capacity, measured by
crude digit-span tests, correlates poorly with foreign language
learning. In order to explain this Olson goes back to an observation of Miller (1956) that STM capacity can be increased by
processing the incoming message so that each bit of information
is enriched. This linguistic processing is learned and develops
with maturity. 'The performance deficits we find in younger
children's remembering are due to failure to organise, plan,
monitor and integrate their information processing' (Olson, 1973).
It is not that children *cannot* process incoming messages so
that they retain more in STM: 'children as young as 3 or 4

if not younger can employ many of the strategies they will later use routinely in remembering. *But unless prompted they do not'* (p. 151).

Olson concludes: 'language presents the earliest and most acute challenge to the child's ability to handle information in real time' (Olson, 1973). What if a similar challenge is repeated when the child meets the foreign language?

J. W. Oller has suggested (1972): 'Consider a model of the language processing mechanism which incorporates short-term memory constraints. If short-term memory is vaguely like a tape-loop which has a constant rate of fade-out, the only way that efficiency for storing elements on that tape-loop can be enhanced is somehow to get them onto the loop faster', i.e. by processing or enriching each chunk stored (p. 514).

The processing of the incoming message, whether in the L1 or the L2, seems to be a *learned process*. Processing implies encoding, organising, planning, monitoring. These (says Olson) are just the abilities the child most needs to learn, as he moves away from the enactive world of concrete objects in which his first simple grammars are practised into the adult world where verbal learning increasingly takes over.

Recognition of pattern, however, as measured, for example, by Green's aptitude test, may be the first step underlying such processing of the message. The rapid recognition that the pattern of the incoming message is similar to, or different from, a pattern already known; the ability quickly to categorise the message, distinguishing its key features, must precede more complex processing.

Two observations may be made at this point. The first is that the processing in STM may be helped by allowing time for it:

if further auditory material is introduced into short-term memory before the first material has faded from it, the later material will interfere with the person's ability to process and assimilate the earlier. Silence . . . gives the mind maximum opportunity to extract information from a short bit of aural input. In most of our [language teaching] methods the barrage of utterances from teacher and fellow students is like a handful of stones thrown onto the surface of a quiet pond: we are unable to follow the ripples from any of them because of interference produced by the others.

It is for this reason that in my attempts to use the Silent Way, I have learned to forbid any immediate repetition of new material spoken by the teacher. The enforced silence that surrounds the new words both allows and compels maximum attention and superior processing. The first individual or group production of this material comes about three seconds later (well within the span of short-term memory) in response to a fresh presentation of the visual stimulus . . . This use of silence means that the student derives more benefit per audible model from the teacher. (Stevick, 1976, p. 139)

The second observation is that processing of incoming messages involves mental activities that are common both to listening and to reading.

It is significant that Green's aptitute test, a purely pencil and paper exercise conducted in silence, proved just as predictive of listening comprehension as of reading comprehension, suggesting that both listening and reading make demands on 'insight into pattern'.

Cloze tests

This hypothesis is reinforced by J. W. Oller's work on 'cloze' testing. Closure procedures or completion exercises ('clozentrophy'!) have been practised in great variety by psychologists. The word 'cloze' was the invention of Wilson Taylor, an American journalist. It was, says Oller (1979), a corruption of 'close', a 'mnemonic or humourless pun' on the procedure familiar in Gestalt psychology as 'closure'.[1] In 1953 Taylor measured the readability of prose passages by replacing every *n*th word with a blank of standard length and asking a selected group of native speakers to fill in the blanks by intuition. The average score of the group gave a measure of the ease or difficulty of the passage. Taylor realised the possibilities of the procedure for foreign language testing as early as 1956 but its development began seriously in the late 1960s and is closely associated with the name of J. W. Oller. Oller's researches have shown, among many other interesting features, that the distance between the deleted words is significant. The shorter the distance the harder the test. 'With native speakers deleting words more frequently than one out of five creates a test of such difficulty that much discriminatory power is lost. To delete words less frequently than one in twelve, on the other hand, does not substantially change the quality of the test . . . random deletion of a certain percentage of words yields similar results, but is considerably less convenient to use' (Oller, 1972, p. 504). Some studies have shown that when 'acceptable responses' are scored as correct (i.e. the exact 'missing word' is not required) the results correlate significantly better with other performance scores in English than when the exact missing word is required.

The most interesting feature of the cloze test of second language proficiency for our present discussion is that it has been shown repeatedly to correlate best with listening comprehension (Oller and Conrad, 1971; Oller, 1972, 1979). It is surprising that (as with Green's aptitude test) a pencil and paper test conducted in silence should correlate so highly with *listening* comprehension measures.

Oller's explanation is that there is a common factor called into play by both the written gap-filling of the cloze test and the listening comprehension, namely a 'grammar of expectancy' (or 'pragmatic expectancy grammar'); expectancies about syntax and semantics within context lead to hypotheses which can be confirmed (or disconfirmed) with only a small portion of the cues in the text. This is very close to the 'insight into pattern' that is tested by the Green aptitude test and by Carroll's 'grammar sensitivity' measures. It is also a vital part of the (learned) ability to process incoming messages that Olson has identified. This processing, it will be remembered, explained the low correlation found by Olson between crude measures of STM capacity (based on random digit span) and foreign language learning. Olson argued that the successive bits of information in a message in the foreign language are not random but are more meaningful to some listeners than to others. Listeners who are able to see the pattern more quickly and confidently *can hold more of the message in the short-term memory.*

Three lines of research converge

We might show the way in which the three lines of research (in aptitude testing, STM and cloze testing) converge by a diagram.

The evidence from all three research areas points to an underlying factor in foreign language learning closely similar to what we have earlier called 'awareness of language'. The significant thing about this 'awareness' is that it differs markedly from one learner to another, that it is to some degree dependent on home background (Donaldson, 1978) and that, in Olson's words, 'children as young as 3 or 4 if not younger can employ many of the [processing] strategies they will later use routinely in remembering. *But unless prompted they do not.*'

At present little is done in school to prompt children to learn to process language. They are thrown into the battle to crack the

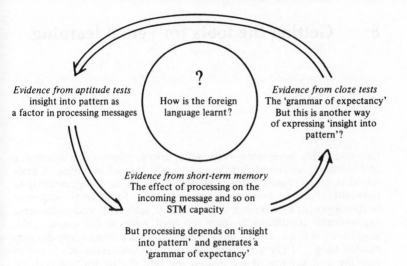

Evidence from aptitude tests
insight into pattern as
a factor in processing messages

?
How is the foreign
language learnt?

Evidence from cloze tests
The 'grammar of expectancy'
But this is another way
of expressing 'insight into
pattern'?

Evidence from short-term memory
The effect of processing on the
incoming message and so on
STM capacity

But processing depends on 'insight
into pattern' and generates a
'grammar of expectancy'

reading code of the mother tongue without training in awareness of language. The same process is repeated when the time comes to face the foreign language. Only children whose homes instinctively provide awareness training survive the linguistic Passchendaele of secondary schooling. Teachers of English and of foreign languages thus face a common problem: the existence of a vacuum at the centre of the curriculum, where systematic training in language awareness ought to be.

To sum up: by asking questions about the learning process we have identified two major reasons which may explain why foreign language learning in school fails, except for exceptionally motivated pupils:

1 absence of 'intention to mean' ('force', 'drive') from language transacted in the foreign language classroom
2 lack of preparation in awareness of language (insight into pattern) on which depends the ability rapidly to 'process' incoming messages.

Somehow these two important missing ingredients must be restored to foreign language learning in the comprehensive school. A possible strategy for doing this is described in the next two chapters.

NOTE

1 Wilson Taylor himself credits Charles Osgood with inspiring the development of 'cloze' procedure in the first place (Oller, 1979).

8   Getting the tools for verbal learning

the song of the male white-crowned sparrow, which has a distinctive and elaborate acoustical pattern, is normally learned in nature. A male raised in social isolation from five days of age with no opportunity to hear other sparrows develops an abnormal song. To correct the sequence of development into normal channels, it is sufficient, under the same experimental conditions, to play recorded songs to the young male, about sixty songs a day for three weeks. He will subsequently develop normal song . . . There is normally a delay of several months between learning and singing. If we deafen the bird during this interval, he subsequently develops a highly abnormal song. Thus he has to be able to hear himself if he is to translate what is learned into the motor pattern of song. If, on the other hand, the deafening is postponed until song development is complete, then it has little or no effect on the motor pattern.

> Peter Marler; Speech Development and Bird Song: Are there any Parallels? 1973

Our brief review of the history of language teaching made it clear that we should resist the temptation to grasp at any more panaceas. Instead we should try to construct a coherent programme of language education. This would begin in the primary school and might have the following four components:

1   a deliberate attempt to give all pupils the tools for verbal learning in the primary school
2   the provision of a course in 'awareness of language' in the secondary school bridging the space between mother tongue and foreign language(s)
3   closely linked with the language course and with the study of English in the secondary school an apprenticeship in learning a trial language, frankly accepting that no English-speaking pupil's adult foreign language needs can be predicted before the age of career choice is reached. The teaching methods used in this apprenticeship should reflect the research on 'aptitude' and on 'speech acts' reviewed in Chapter 7.
4   the opportunity to acquire at the post 16 stage in sixth forms and in further education the language *of choice* by intensive methods (IL)

In this chapter an attempt will be made to describe the first two components of this programme, offering practical examples of some of the learning activities called for at each stage. The third and fourth components are similarly described in Chapter 9.

The primary school stage

Everything depends on laying good foundations. In the past we have marched the troops, untrained and lacking the right tools, into the battle to learn to read their mother tongue and later to learn a foreign language, as into a linguistic Passchendaele.

There are experienced and sincere teachers of English who are opposed to deliberate attempts to teach pupils to listen and to match listening to looking. The Bullock Committee (1975) was divided on the question: 'In our view the ability can best be developed as part of the normal work of the classroom and in association with other learning experiences. But deliberate strategies may be required, for it cannot be assumed that the improvement will take place automatically.' What we are proposing is just such a deliberate strategy. The tragic figure of something over two million adult illiterates in England and Wales after 100 years of compulsory primary schooling suggests that deliberate strategies are needed. We accept the argument of Furth and Wachs (1974) that children need to learn 'thinking with the ears'. The limitations of the ear as a channel for learning are obvious:

1 sound input fades within seconds, unlike visual input, and what is not retained in the short-term memory cannot make any impression
2 the ears are not directional or mobile like the eyes
3 the ears cannot focus like the eyes, which accurately measure distance, speed etc.
4 the ears cannot cut off input at will, unlike the eyes; the trick of switching off internally is learned early and habits of defensive non-listening need to be unlearned.

Listening games

Furth and Wachs stress the need for listening games to be discovery games, with the right answer never given beforehand. Listening must develop at the child's own speed. We would add that, though a programme of 'thinking with the ears' can begin with activities such as Furth and Wachs suggest, the aim should be to incorporate as much listening for *meaning* as possible and wherever possible to link the listening programme with other learning experiences.

Furth and Wachs suggest a series of classroom games designed to develop discrimination of pitch, intensity, duration, pause, component sound(s), rhythm. Skills to be practised are: recall, location (of a given sound in a string of sounds), identification, innovation (child creates a word on a recognised pattern), addition and substitution of sounds.

A couple of illustrations may show the kind of games Furth and Wachs propose.

The rhythm game: Children learn progressively more complex discrimination of rhythms (starting with rhythms of hand clapping, tapping on wood, beating drum or empty bottle, etc.). After learning to imitate and discriminate different rhythms they learn a graphic notation in which to record rhythms. Now they write down rhythmic messages and go on to follow a written message on the blackboard while listening to a version played by the teacher or another pupil. The two versions seen and heard are compared. The game is progressively complicated by the introduction of different sounds which must be distinguished in the written notation. The pupils then invent their own messages, writing them on the blackboard for others to play.

The sound pattern game: Children learn to discriminate between different sound sequences in syllables and words. Nonsense words are presented such as BAL, LOM, ILZ. Children must locate specified sounds given either before the word is heard or (a harder task) after hearing the nonsense word. There are innumerable variations possible, including spotting words from a sequence which do not contain a given sound, or substituting whole syllables for single sounds. Again the introduction of a written notation when pupils are ready for it sharpens the challenge and allows many variations to be played, including pupils replacing the teacher and inventing games for the class to play.

Our experience in using the games over a number of years with slow readers at summer school suggests the following rules:

1 The games should be used sparingly for a short time each day.
2 The teacher should listen sensitively to children's performance and continually try to stretch listening discrimination to the limit of what pupils can achieve, while ensuring that every pupil gets some reward from successful achievement.

3   To make this possible each session should begin with a game that all pupils can do confidently but should move quickly to activities that are harder. It is the sense of growing mastery that is rewarding and pupils are acute judges of what they feel proud, and rewarded, to have done.

4   Each session should be broken down into no more than five or ten items with the reward of success after each group of items, immediate feedback of encouragement to those who found the game too hard and an attempt to make sure that pupils who failed understand what they have to listen for.

5   Learning to observe absolute silence in order to hear the problem or message is a valuable part of the programme.

6   'Cue' words or messages are hard to seize first time. To help the slower listener cues can be given twice to begin with. In every session, however, there should be practice in once-only hearing, to wean pupils from lazy habits of never focussing first time.

The intention of the Furth and Wachs games is 'to develop the child's ability to focus attention on and derive information from auditory stimuli'. Our experience with such games has shown that listening largely depends on knowing what to listen for. As with so much learning, expectations are all-important. When our pupils approach the task of learning a foreign language they will need to be armed with accurate expectations as to the new sounds that they will hear, new stresses, new intonation patterns, etc. As pupils approach the secondary school, therefore, new elements will be added to the programme:

1   discrimination of complex consonant clusters, stress patterns, etc.

2   listening for meaning to which more and more time is given

3   discrimination of sounds in foreign languages; here particular attention will be paid to languages spoken as mother tongue by ethnic minorities in the school and to sounds that occur in dialects represented in the school which differ from standard English

4   more and more attention will be given to the sounds that pupils must expect to meet in the foreign language offered in the secondary school

5   a phonetic script will be introduced in which pupils can record the new sounds they hear; this should be as simple as possible and ideally it should be invented by the pupils in discussion, the advantages and disadvantages of particular symbols proposed for particular sounds being discussed as a valuable part of the learning. (An example of such a simple script is given in Appendix B.)

6   pupils will learn by heart simple jingles, verses, songs, nursery
rhymes, greetings, etc. in Spanish and French and possibly in
German and Italian. They will also learn and record in their own
phonetic script the numbers up to 100 and the days of the week
and months in these languages. They will use their phonetic
script to record the words of Christmas songs, etc. that they
learn in other languages, including some songs in the languages spoken as mother tongues by ethnic minorities in the
school. The phonetic script should also be used to record greetings, counting etc. in the ethnic minority languages with children helping each other in pairs to get each other's phrases
correctly transcribed.

It is appreciated that some teachers, especially those with
responsibility for slower learners, may, while accepting the need
for thinking with the ears, have reservations about introducing
even a simplified phonetic script in case it complicates pupils'
reading problems in English.

It is perfectly possible to omit this part of the programme if
teachers prefer. Only trial and error will show what a given class
can enjoy. The phonetic symbols should in any case be introduced very gradually so that the consistent matching of symbol
to sound builds confidence. Where the sound is a common one in
English the symbol chosen can usefully be a spelling that pupils
will most often encounter in English.

It may be useful to give some examples of games which help
pupils to match sounds to symbols.

Discrimination of consonant clusters: Pupils listen to the two
sounds: 'ch', 'sh'. They draw a simple grid. They then listen to
words or phrases containing the two sounds and they indicate
by writing 1, 2, 3 etc. the order in which the sounds were heard.
For example:

	ch	sh
fish and chips	2	1
Cheshunt	1	2
Ashchurch	2 3	1
Which shape shall I choose	1 4	2 3

The game can now be played with less familiar Spanish or French
pairs:

[u] *v*. [y]; [l] *v*. [ll]; [œ] *v*. [ã]; [n] *v*. [ñ]; [é] *v*. [è], etc.

A variant is: pupils look at a completed grid and listen to cues, marking the grid 'right' or 'wrong'.

Discrimination of tonic stress patterns: Pupils listen to the pattern of stressed and unstressed syllables in:

*Bir*mingham   / o o

They then listen to the following towns and say whether or not they have the same stress pattern:

(i)	*Man*chester	/ o o	same
(ii)	*Dar*lington	/ o o	same
(iii)	Dun*fer*mline	o / o	different
(iv)	Llan*gol*len	o / o	different
(v)	*New*castle	/ o o	same
	but		
(vi)	New*cas*tle	o / o	different

With very slow readers it may be necessary to practise a good deal of cutting words up into syllables before stress patterns are compared.

Pupils repeat the game with less familiar names:

Compare:	*Lon*don	/ o
	*Bris*tol	/ o

With:			
(i)	Pa*ris* (French pronunciation)	o /	different
(ii)	Ma*drid*	o /	different
(iii)	*Ex*mouth	/ o	same
(iv)	Ber*lin*	o /	different
(v)	*Frank*furt	/ o	same

Pupils then listen to names and write their own notation of the tonic stress:

Aber*deen*	o o /
Aber*yst*wyth	o o / o
Constanti*no*ple	o o o / o
*Wash*ington	/ o o
*Lea*mington *Spa*	/ o o /

Pupils now invent their own games for the rest of the class.

Cross-modality perception: music and movement
Such games as these give practice in 'cross-modality' perception
in which there is a dialogue between the eye and the ear. We
know (Geschwind, 1964) that such cross-modality perception is
closely linked with language skills. It is something for which
humans ('articulate mammals') have special aptitude. Other
mammals do not have the requisite associative areas in the cortex
of the brain to facilitate cross-modality tasks. Many of our pupils
find it difficult. The attack on reading will clearly make heavy
demands on confident and accurate cross-modality matching.
When the foreign language is met any lack of confidence or speed
in such tasks will prove a severe handicap.

It will be obvious that the 'thinking with the ears' that we are
seeking to develop closely concerns teachers of music also. There
is some evidence that training in discrimination of musical pitch,
intonation, etc. has a positive effect on reading readiness. Ideally
a joint programme will be worked out by a board of studies in
each school in which teachers of music and movement join with
teachers of language.

Typical music and movement extensions of the auditory games
might be:

1   Pupils listen to two tunes played on different instruments; are
    the tunes identical or not?
2   Pupils listen to drum beats or watch a movement, then beat a
    matching drum rhythm.
3   Pupils listen to popular melodies and decide how many beats to
    a bar.
4   Pupils hear a tune with a silent section; they decide for how
    many beats the *silence* lasts.
5   Pupils sing a song; on a signal they are silent but continue to
    'sing' soundlessly without breaking the rhythm; on a second
    signal they continue singing aloud, at the point they would
    have reached (a tape-recording, with volume control, may be
    used to test pupils' timing).
6   As 5., but pupils do rhythmic movements to music which they
    continue while volume is turned down without varying the
    rhythm, until the music is heard again.
7   Pupils compare rhythm and tonic stress of speech with a piece
    of music; they correct mismatches proposed by teacher, etc.
    (e.g. as in a bad song setting).
8   Pupils invent words, phrases, to sing to the rhythm of music
    heard, first practising matching the rhythm of morse code
    signals: for example,

(a) (morse code: Q) – – · – = God save the Queen.
    (morse code: K) – · – = And the King.
(b) (Beethoven's Fifth Symphony, opening figure)

'I hear a knock. What can it be?'

(c) (Schubert's Unfinished Symphony, entry of second theme)

'This is the second tune, the second tune played on a cello.'

9   Pupils make up a tap dance to match music or a castanet rhythm
    or a dance with tambourine or a triangle accompaniment, etc.
10 Pupils working with Carl Orff methods practise matching
    musical rhythms to prose and verse passages. One pupil speaks
    (sings) while the others play.
11 Pupils are allotted 'call signs' (rhythmic patterns of drum
    beats), two or three pupils to each different call. The pupils sit
    listening while teacher 'summons' them with their 'call sign';
    the first pupil to respond correctly to the call wins a point;
    wrong reactions lose a point. The game is then played with
    melodies, later with chords!

Listening for meaning

A special word should be said about the role of meaning. While
the listening 'tools' are being sharpened it is essential to develop
confidence in listening for meaning. The following examples will
indicate the kinds of activity that should be practised daily and
which take on increasing importance as the programme
advances:

1   Pupils study a picture while commentary by teacher (or on tape)
    is heard. Pupils note the discrepancies in the commentary (e.g.
    wrong number on door of gate or wrong number of windows in
    house described, chimney not smoking, postman not wearing
    cap). Pupils at first 'buzz' mistakes; later they note mistakes and
    report at the end.
2   Pupils read a story silently. Then teacher reads the story mak-
    ing deliberate mistakes which pupils must listen for: e.g.
    teacher substitutes for one adjective another of different mean-
    ing, or omits a negative, or changes a date.

3   Pupils study a draft letter that a secretary has just typed. They then listen to a tape-recording of a conversation between the secretary and her employer in which the employer points out some errors. Pupils correct the draft letter.
4   Pupils listen to a dialect recording and pick out sounds or words that are not in their own dialect, giving equivalents if any.
5   Pupils listen to 'ambiguous' statements and re-phrase them to avoid ambiguity, e.g.
      'ship sails to-day': (a) the ship will sail to-day
                           (b) send the sails to-day by ship
6   Pupils hear riddles and explain them, e.g.
      Q. Why is a farm gate like a moth flying round a candle?
      A. Because if it keeps on its 'inges, it swings.
      (Because if it keeps on, it singes its wings.)

(See Hawkins 1984 for a detailed syllabus of listening activities.)

Need for one-to-one dialogue

For very many of our pupils the lack of the tools for verbal learning will be specially acute because they have been denied the opportunity for dialogue with an informed, patient, sensitive adult. Somehow the precious, individual 'adult time' must be given back to such children. In some schools they may well be in the majority. Only by bringing in adults in great number, to act as aides under the direction of teachers *trained to use them*, can the need be met. This may be the biggest challenge to primary schools in the 1980s if we aim to offer anything like equality of opportunity in education. The programme of preparation for verbal learning that we have outlined would be seriously incomplete and unprofessional unless it incorporated the provision of individual *one-to-one dialogue* with an adult for a large part of every day. We have indicated earlier that students in full-time study offer the obvious reservoir from which such adult volunteer tutors must be drawn. It will be a test of our commitment to democracy, whether students and teachers can meet such a challenge.

'Awareness of language' in the secondary school

The progressive programme of education of the ear that we have been sketching continues without interruption at the secondary level. Many of the listening activities that we have described can be extended and developed for older pupils. They should prepare pupils for the course in 'awareness of language' that we propose as part of the 'trivium' (mother tongue/foreign language/linking subject) which pupils will follow throughout the secondary years.

The new element in this 'trivium' which binds the other elements together is the course we have called 'awareness of language'. It is intended

1 to offer a bridge linking English with the foreign language and a neutral or common ground for the discussion of language. In schools whose pupils speak a variety of mother tongues or non-standard dialects the need for such a common ground is urgent but its usefulness is not restricted to such schools.

2 to equip pupils with aptitude for language learning by deliberately fostering the capacity to 'process' verbal messages (see discussion in Chapter 7).

3 to provide a firm base, a responsible board of studies, library resources and prestige for the teaching of 'language across the curriculum' which will languish unless built into the timetable and given this status.

Although the concept of a course in 'awareness of language' is a new one there is already a considerable body of experience to build on. Several hundred schools in the UK have introduced such programmes (Donmall, 1985) and there have been parallel developments in the USA ('exploratory language programmes') and in Australia ('introductory language programmes'). There is now a good deal of published material for teachers to choose from, while several LEAs (notably ILEA and Sheffield) have produced their own materials.

The Cambridge University Press Series 'Awareness of Language' (see Appendix C) offers seven topic books for pupils and a teachers' book. It is designed to promote discussion in class and activities (in groups, pairs or solo) exploring questions such as:

What makes human language so special?
Can we communicate without words?
How does language work to convey meaning?
How is language learned by the baby?
Is learning French in school different?
How do speech and writing differ?
Where did our kind of writing come from?
Is it the only kind of writing?
Is it harder to learn to read in English than (say) in Spanish?
What does the language map of the UK look like?
Where does English fit in the language map of the world?
Where did English come from and how is it changing?
Why do some dialects have higher prestige than others?
Why do we use some words in the playground that we would not use to our Headmistress? etc.

When these questions are discussed in class (and at home, through projects involving parents) the presence in class of pupils from a variety of language and dialect backgrounds can be made a source of strength and enrichment, rather than one more problem for the hard-pressed teacher. Each school will, of course, select the themes it prefers to concentrate on and the order in which they are tackled. In making their selection teachers may find the following guidelines useful:

1   The discussions and activities should seek to relate the pupils' growing 'awareness' of the mother tongue with the first exciting steps into the foreign language begun in the secondary school. The opportunity for cross-language comparisons and contrasts is not limited to the vocabulary, the grammar and the sound systems of the two languages. Pupils will enjoy comparing also the *process of acquisition* of the mother tongue with the classroom learning of their foreign language, to the benefit of both. If teachers of English and teachers of the foreign language (including teachers of the heritage languages in the community) can work together on the programme pupils may be helped to become aware of the insights that each language can offer into the others.

2   The discussions ought also to lead pupils towards a greater awareness of the role of language in learning and of the ways in which our language 'permits us to become the persons we are'. The equally important role of language in society should also become clearer, especially the operation of linguistic prejudice and snobbery. Perhaps most important of all, the role of the family, especially the vitally important early one-to-one dialogue between parent and child, will be brought out, in preparation for later discussions in 'Preparation for parenthood courses' with school leavers.

3   In schools with pupils who speak the heritage languages at home the discussions of language awareness will offer opportunities for exploration of language in which all start equal, all have a contribution to make, and in which *difference* of language background is a positive enrichment, because it helps to bring out important truths about language.

Perhaps the guiding principle throughout should be that, whatever the theme under discussion, or the activity engaged in, pupils should be encouraged to bring to it insights that they have themselves got from both kinds of language experience they have enjoyed, their mother tongue learning and their contact with other languages, in school or in the community. This is why we stress that when possible the Cambridge approach to awareness of language should run side by side, during the first two years of the secondary school, with the pupils' foreign language learning, rather than, as in some programmes, being brought in as a self-contained module of learning, *before* foreign language study begins. And that is also why we urge that where possible teachers of English and foreign language teachers should come together, leaving their sealed-off boxes, and *jointly* plan and teach the exciting new linking course, helping each other, and learning from each other.

9   Foreign language learning in school: rehearsal or performance?

> Other things being equal, the *deeper* the source of a sentence within the student's personality, the *more lasting value* it has for learning the language.
>
> Earl W. Stevick, *Memory, Meaning and Method*, 1976

We come finally to the key problem: how to teach the foreign language. We assume that the primary school has provided the tools for verbal learning in a more systematic way than hitherto, with the requisite one-to-one dialogue that a large number of children (denied it at home) will need. We assume also that throughout the secondary course the study of a foreign language will be closely linked with the mother-tongue teaching by the bridging course, 'awareness of language'.

Against this background we propose a foreign language course having two components, each with its own methods and objectives and assessment: an apprenticeship (up to about age 16) of a trial language followed by intensive acquisition by immersion methods (IL) of the language of mature choice from a menu provided at sixth-form or FE level. (Of course, many pupils may well wish to continue the study of the apprenticeship language, possibly by going abroad or on 'reciprocal courses'.)

It is necessary first to say a word about the teaching conditions. Foreign languages cannot be taught in a vacuum. There is a minimal framework within which it is fair to ask language teachers to do their very difficult job.

The framework

i. LEA support

Language teachers deserve at least the following support from their employers the LEA:

250

(a) appointment of a specialist language adviser qualified to bring together foreign language and mother-tongue teachers and committed to provide a full programme of in-service training

(b) a well-equipped resource centre acting as an out-station for the Centre for Information on Language Teaching in London

(c) active teachers' workshops to devise materials, especially for the course in awareness of language

(d) firm commitment to the employment of native assistants in all schools

(e) active promotion of pupil and teacher exchanges with European schools

(f) commitment also to close partnership between schools and institutions which train teachers, to facilitate training courses that are classroom- rather than lectureroom-based (see recommendations in the Epilogue)

(g) acceptance of the need for induction arrangements such as the James Committee (1972) recommended

(h) commitment to the James Committee's proposal of one term's sabbatical leave after each five years' service, to enable language teachers to return to their real laboratory which is the foreign country.

ii. *School support*

(a) Within an L E A offering such minimal professional support the school would be expected to study carefully the special needs of foreign language teaching and provide for them just as meticulously as they do for (say) chemistry or woodwork. It would probably be agreed that for serious language work the following would be the least that ought to be provided:
acoustically adequate teaching rooms furnished with tape-recorders and wall loudspeakers of good quality for class listening; cassette-players sufficient for one to every two pupils (see later discussion of teaching methods); a listening library; slide projector and overhead projector; dim-out blinds; extensive wall display area for maps, 'window on the foreign country', etc.; ample storage space for teaching materials, visuals, backcloths, models, shop equipment, etc.; classroom library in each teaching room including collections of plays, magazines, readers, etc., to be taken home by pupils.

(b) There should also be a policy on timetabling subjects which takes sensitive account of the unique needs of teachers who have to plant their seedlings in a gale of English.

(c) The kind of exchange programme with the foreign country (the true language laboratory) on which a proper apprenticeship should be based needs the active support of the school authorities (e.g. by promoting saving for travel schemes, initiated as soon as pupils join the school; by educating parents in the need for such educational travel and the need to plan ahead for it, and by making professional arrangements to ensure that no pupil is debarred from this essential part of the language course because of home background).

(d) The cooperation between mother-tongue teachers and teachers of the foreign language will depend on the good will and good sense of individuals but the encouragement of school authority will also be needed.

(e) The subject 'awareness of language' as a bridge linking mother tongue and foreign language should be given its recognised place in the timetable and its own resources.

(f) The timetable should also allow for a variety of arrangements for intensive immersion sessions in the foreign language; full support should be given to residential or semi-residential weekends, reciprocal courses with linked schools or within consortia of schools, the tutoring of younger pupils in intensive sessions by teams of older pupils under the guidance of the teacher, etc.

(g) There should be a flexible menu of languages offered at sixth-form level in intensive courses; the languages offered should include the languages spoken by ethnic minorities in the school, as well as the main European languages.

The comparatively modest cost of this programme should be compared with the sums demanded as of right by the natural sciences.

iii. Departmental support

Even with the best support from L E A and school authorities the impact of the subject will depend on the professionalism and cooperation of the team in the department. The functions of the head of department are lucidly set out in *HMI Matters for Discussion 3* (HMI, 1977). Following the lead given by HMI we may say that the responsibilities of the head of department should be written down in the conditions of service which are accepted by both sides on appointment to the post. It would probably be agreed that the head of department:

(a) prepares and keeps up to date a written statement of objectives backed by a detailed syllabus of learning activities for each age group and within each age group for each 'aptitude' range

(b) allots himself/herself a generous measure of the more difficult teaching assignments

(c) regularly observes the teaching of junior members of the department and is observed by them

(d) takes a lead in inter-school exchanges and in keeping up to date foreign contacts

(e) reads actively and attends in-service courses and workshops

(f) arranges regular departmental meetings and seminars

(g) builds a departmental library of teaching materials and aids including a listening library, clearly catalogued and flexibly available to all

(h) keeps a record of the progress at least monthly of every pupil.

We make the further assumption that the foreign languages department forms part of a wider language faculty. The main partners in this faculty would be the teachers of English (and of other mother tongues taught in the school) and the foreign language staff. They should be joined regularly by the teachers of music and movement, arts and crafts and by representatives of the sciences. All of these have much to contribute to a course in 'awareness of language' and there are some aspects of foreign language teaching (e.g. in the planning of a 'reciprocal' intensive course with the linked school calling for interesting language learning activities for the pupils from abroad), in which the contribution of teachers across the curriculum could be invaluable.

iv. Parents and the community

Whatever the L E A, school authorities or teachers individually may do, the decisive influence on pupils' motivation will come from the parents' attitude *and example*. Leaving aside sheer parental inadequacy (a factor greatly underestimated by many commentators who blame schools for matters over which they often have no control) the attitudes of most parents reflect those of employers (and trades unions), and of those who select for higher education. Eventually public opinion shapes what pupils learn, regardless of what schools offer.

There is, however, much that schools can do by working through parents. There have been interesting experiments in enterprising schools in offering language classes to parents who wish to make a start at the same time as their children. The prospect of a whole family working at its Spanish homework together is an exciting one. Even more interesting is the possibility of parents and children embarking together on a new language intensively when the children reach 16+ and make a deliberate choice of a language for adult use. One L E A has already arranged courses abroad for whole families wishing to combine a holiday with intensive study of a language.

Even if parents do not themselves study they can be kept interested and informed by open evenings and demonstrations (just as the parents of young string players are encouraged through the painful early stages by concerts in which simple pieces played on the open strings give the young players the chance to shine and the parents to hope against all the evidence of their ears!).

How should it be done?

Against the background sketched above how should the apprenticeship be planned? The research reviewed in Chapter 8 gives us two starting-points:

1 it is a fair inference from research on aptitude for language learning that under normal school conditions what determines progress is insight into pattern in language
2 observation of pupils' often startling progress as soon as they go abroad, reinforced by the evidence of intensive immersion and reciprocal courses, leaves little doubt that language is retained far more easily when the learner transacts real speech acts, that is, he really tries to 'do things with words', to use Austin's phrase.

How do these two lessons from research and observation relate together?

We should be careful not to present too black and white a picture when research is at an exploratory stage. Some learners do seem to be able to make progress by quite mechanical exercises, applying what Krashen has called the 'monitor'. In the previous chapter we referred to our observations in China when sheer awesome motivation triumphed over methods which turned upside down every rule in our teacher training courses. With very little opportunity for true speech acts in which personal meanings are expressed and in classrooms cut off from the speech communities where the foreign language lives, some students, highly selected and superbly gifted, manage to peform magnificently in the foreign language.

Could the explanation be that the two factors we have identified subtly interact? That learners gifted with a marked aptitude for insight into language pattern can learn even by means of activities which do not involve conveying personal meanings? And might it be the case that for the average learner the foreign language will not stick unless (as happened when the mother tongue was acquired) it is used to transact real speech acts, conveying personal meanings that matter to the learner?

If this is the conclusion to which our present knowledge points, the way ahead seems clear. We should do everything we can to awaken and develop insight into pattern while providing as much opportunity as possible for pupils to alternate their formal studies of language structure with activities which call for the expression of personal meanings and the solving of personal problems.

The first objective will be secured in three ways: the primary school preparation for verbal learning; the secondary school course in awareness of language; the insistence, in the foreign language classroom, on presenting pattern in as attractive and clear a way as possible and arousing pupils' curiosity about the contrasting patterns of the mother tongue and the foreign language.

The second objective will be attained if we can devise activities in which the pupils' attention is not focussed on the form of the message but on a real concern with achieving some result by use of the language *which could not have been achieved by the use of English.*

The search for such activities presents the chief challenge to modern language teaching in the comprehensive school, where the great majority of pupils will not have outstanding motivation or aptitude. We are only at the beginning of the road. What follows is an attempt to describe the various levels of meaning that our activities in the classroom might reach and to suggest examples to illustrate each level. The analysis is offered tentatively as a contribution to discussion and to encourage teachers to apply the categories in the teaching and so to refine and improve the model. Two points may be worth stressing:

1   It is not sufficient, if we are seeking to promote 'discourse' or true communication in the foreign language classroom, to concentrate on the selection of a syllabus, however 'functionally' motivated, since the most functional utterance (potentially) can be turned into a formal drill with the learner's whole attention given to the form. Much more difficult is to set up situations and activities in which the learner really wants to do things with words, to change the world in some way that matters at that moment.

2   At the same time by giving an equal place to studies designed to build insight into pattern and trying to alternate between such activities and true speech acts we meet an objection that has been made to the 'functional syllabus', namely that the learner is not helped if grammar is introduced in a haphazard way.

Four levels of personal meaning or 'depth'

There may be an infinite number of gradations between the utterance which is purely formal, devoid of any intention to achieve a result but spoken as a drill, and the spontaneous speech act with no thought of whether the form is correct or not but simply aimed at solving a problem. It will probably be helpful to teachers to keep the analysis as simple as possible. Dodson (1978) suggests a two-level categorisation: medium-orientated and message-orientated utterances. Stevick (1976) proposes a number of levels of 'depth' of meaning. Our analysis suggests something between the two. The first step in trying to shift from formal language transactions devoid of 'force' to speech acts and so to more effortless retention of the new language, is to recognise, for any particular classroom activity, what level of meaning (pupil's personal meaning, not teacher's or text-book's meaning) the activity calls upon.

We may distinguish without undue complication four different levels of meaning in foreign language learning. Note that these are levels not of difficulty but of 'depth' (in Stevick's terms) of meaning. It is possible to devise easy or more difficult activities at our level 1 just as one can envisage harder or easier activities at our more meaningful third or fourth levels.

Level 1 (concentration on the medium)

Production: Activities in which the pupil concentrates on manipulating the sounds and the grammar patterns, as in a paradigm drill.

Reception: Activities in which the pupil's attention is focussed on the structural patterns of the language heard or read, as in games matching sounds to spellings, or picking out (say) the future tenses in a passage.

Level 2 (message-*relaying* as rehearsal for eventual performance)

Production: Activities in which language is produced with meaning but it is not the pupil's meaning; it is not generated by the pupil's wish to find out or to effect some result. Rather phrases are relayed dutifully from text-book to teacher, as a rehearsal in case on some future occasion they should be needed. A typical example might be picture composition as in the 16+ examination.

Reception: Rehearsal activities in which the pupil focusses attention on the meaning of a text, complying with the teacher's instruction, not because the text contains a meaning that the pupil wants to get at to satisfy a felt need. A typical example might be the 16+ comprehension test. Note that in the traditional secondary course very few pupils proceed beyond this level. The 16+ examination is almost entirely conducted at this level – the only part of the examination in which the *pupil*'s individual meanings play a part is the short oral test. It is significant that this latter element has traditionally counted for few marks and that standards of performance have been extremely low. Even in the days of the grammar schools only those pupils who went beyond our level 2 (i.e. went abroad and/or read significantly in the sixth form) ever succeeded in performing effectively or retained more than a few phrases from their five-year course.

Level 3 (conveying a personal message but still with an element of rehearsal)

Production: Activities in which the pupils' own individual meanings are conveyed but prompted by the (English-speaking) teacher and within the constraints of classroom and timetable; interrupted by the 'gale of English'. Pupils still have to suspend disbelief regarding the need to use the foreign language (a make-believe that some adolescent pupils, especially boys, find difficult). An example would be the filling-in of a personal *carte d'identité* as for disembarkation, but knowing that one was doing so as part of a lesson.

Reception: Activities in which the pupils' own preferences and interests motivate the choice of what to listen to, or read, but there is still the artificiality of playing a game of make-believe in not using English. The ulterior reason (learning the language) is still the main motive, not getting the message. An example might be listening in class to personalised messages recorded by the native assistant.

Level 4 (the level of true 'speech acts': real performance)

Production: Activities in which the pupil takes the initiative (as in learning the mother tongue) to satisfy his own felt needs and, *because he is faced with a native speaker*, has a compulsion to speak the foreign language. Utterances at this level have 'force', in Searle's terms, and as our earlier discussion has suggested they are more likely to lead to retention for that reason. The best example is, perhaps, the pupil, genuinely lost in Paris on his first school visit, who asks the *agent* the way to the Gare St Lazare. He will never forget the ensuing dialogue!

Reception: Activities in which the pupil listens or reads in order to satisfy a need *that he cannot satisfy in the mother tongue*. All trace of rehearsal is absent; there is no ulterior motive. An example is the pupil in the foreign country reading the weather forecast to find out if tomorrow's picnic will be cancelled.

Having identified our four levels of 'depth' (and so of probable retention) we have three main tasks, as teachers:

  (i)   to ensure that the lower-level activities, in which attention is concentrated on the medium, are rewarding and effective in developing insight into pattern which is essential for rapid processing of incoming messages
  (ii) to shape the whole course as an apprenticeship in which the learner experiences *all* the levels of learning including completely message-orientated (our level 4) activities – unlike most existing courses which stop short at the level 2, rehearsal stage (e.g. the 16+ examination) or in which level 4 activities are extras fortuitously tacked on for a very few fortunate pupils
  (iii) to set to pupils of differing aptitudes correspondingly demanding objectives.

This can probably best be managed by using a series of 'graded tests' to be taken by pupils when they are ready for them (like the 'grades' in violin, piano etc.). Our graded tests, however, would not be simply tests of *performance*. Just as the music grades include, together with performance, tests of 'theory', 'harmony', etc., so the language graded tests must reward:

  (a) growing ability to perceive pattern and to process the language – the key to comprehension (see Chapter 7)
  (b) developing understanding of the way of life of the foreign country.

How to begin: enactive learning
Just as the mother tongue was learned *enactively* for the first

seven years, it will be retracing a familiar learning path and helping slower learners if we introduce the foreign language by associating it with objects, games and actions in the classroom, rather than by projecting pictures on a screen which requires pupils to remain static and passive. 'A situation where pupils are desk-bound and are required to utter teacher-directed responses can only lead to the exclusion of paralinguistic behaviour in both pupils and teachers' (Butzkamm and Dodson, 1980). Learning via pictures (the 'iconic' stage of learning) is a relatively sophisticated stage, reached at about the age of seven in the mother tongue, and should follow the enactive stage in foreign language learning also.

The teacher might prepare the classroom for 'learning by doing' by collecting in two large suitcases the objects needed to establish the basic vocabulary of some 300 words. This will include the names of all the commonest classroom objects, articles of clothing, toys, teacups, plates, cutlery for serving meals, etc.

Ideally, too, the classroom will be equipped with 'shop counters', a model street, etc. The problem of setting the scene in which it seems natural to use the foreign language must be faced. A solution (which the present author saw brilliantly exemplified in a Swedish school) is to arrange (quite inexpensive) pulleys in the ceiling of the classroom on which, as on an old-fashioned kitchen clothes-dryer, different backcloths can be lowered as needed to create the illusion of café, hotel, cinema, station, etc., and later hauled out of sight. The same Swedish classroom was equipped with a permanent clothes shop in the corner where coats, hats, gloves, scarves, etc. could be tried on, before the long mirror, and discussed. There was also a permanently wired telephone from one corner of the room to the other as well as built-in wall loudspeakers, wired to the tape-recorder. The shelves were stocked with readers suitable for every level from the first year upwards. There was also a listening library which was constantly added to by commissioning tape-recordings on specified topics from a linked school. Such a classroom is not costly to equip. It calls for imagination and the cooperation of pupils and their families in bringing in items from their journeys abroad.

Our task at the enactive stage is to establish the initial vocabulary and especially (the critical step) confident manipulation of the *gender* of the new names.

Gender

The first step is to use whatever clues we can to categorise each object as either feminine or masculine. There are many ways to do this. One well-tried successful way is to use colour and spatial clues. The two suitcases in which the objects are located are labelled F and M and coloured red and blue respectively. From the start suitcases are always placed on the table facing the class with the 'F' suitcase on the pupils' right (teacher's left). Objects taken out of the cases are always returned to the suitcase to which they belong and pupils are trained to be watchful for mistakes (intentional or not) by the teacher when packing objects away. Pupils use blue and red ballpoint pens distributed by monitors, using the foreign language as part of the classroom drill ('Je n'ai pas de stylo bleu.' 'No tengo un bolígrafo azul'). They divide each page of their exercise book into two columns. All F objects, when their names are learned, are drawn in red in the right-hand column, 'M' objects in blue in the left-hand column. The teacher keeps a piece of red chalk in the 'F' suitcase and always uses red chalk to draw 'F' objects or write their names on the board.

The intention is to combine spatial imagery and the colour code to identify feminine and masculine objects as belonging to their respective categories by continual reinforcement during the first year or two of the course. Grammatical gender is a completely new concept for English pupils. It is for them the chief contrast with Spanish/French. It is essential that the gender of the basic vocabulary should be rock-solidly known, otherwise the pupils never confidently learn to substitute the object pronoun. Doubt inhibits lively response. When adjectives are met a further uncertainty arises. Attempting to master agreement of the past participle often gives the *coup de grâce* to a dwindling relish for walking on such thin ice. It is failure to establish such a basic pattern as gender that produces growing bewilderment as pupils move towards reading and writing.

The solid objects in their respective boxes are further exploited by 'enactive' games:

counting the objects as the teacher lays them out or as they are handed round the class;

'packing their bag', each pupil remembering the objects already packed, and adding one (helped by the teacher who writes on the board the initial letter of each object as it is packed);

'laying the table' for tea with cups, cutlery, etc.;

playing 'Kim's game' with objects on a tray;
asking teacher for objects from the box, receiving an object if gender and
pronunciation are right, trying to beat the previous record;
'setting up shop' and buying and selling objects for cash;
drawing in notebooks the objects demonstrated silently by teacher *using
the appropriate colour* to show that gender is known;
learning common prepositions by placing objects on, under, in, behind,
etc. the box/table and playing the game 'oui/non' in answer to the
teacher's questions ('La tasse est sur l'assiette?' etc.).
Common adjectives, including colour adjectives, can be practised in a
similar game.

When objects are drawn in colour in notebooks the *outline* only is
drawn in blue (masculine) or red (feminine), the drawing being
filled in with the colour indicated by the adjective. Neither the
spatial code nor the colour code is an essential part of the enactive
stage. The essence is in doing things with tangible objects. Some
teachers, especially of very able pupils, may prefer to dispense
with the spatial and colour reinforcement of memory. If these
aids to categorising objects by gender are used they will probably
be phased out by the end of the second year. They may then
usefully be brought back from time to time, e.g. when the problem of the agreement of the past participle in the *passé composé*
with *avoir/être* is met, or to enliven dictation exercises, concentrating pupils' attention on 'agreement' patterns.

The initial vocabulary and grammatical gender are further consolidated by the game of 'Happy Families' (using cards grouping
the vocabulary in families of things to eat, to drink, to wear, to lay
the table, to use in school, etc.). The objects are illustrated on the
playing cards using the red and blue colour code, so that whenever pupils ask for them they get the gender right and form good
habits.

The game of 'Picture Bingo' using the same illustrations (again
colour coded) further establishes the basic enactive vocabulary.

When the written form of the objects is learnt (and this should
not be unduly delayed, the only rule being to establish the pronunciation of each object firmly before trying to spell it), it may be
found helpful to reinforce spellings by playing a game of 'Twenty
Questions', in which pupils guess the object the teacher is thinking of by putting questions: 'Est-ce masculin? De quelle couleur?'
'En quoi?' narrowing the search at each question. The winning
pupil then spells the word on the blackboard in the appropriate
colour.

Classroom activities at the four levels of meaning

Once pupils are launched on the enactive learning the teacher will introduce a programme of learning activities with the dual aim of:

   i   strengthening insight into pattern and building an ever more confident 'grammar of expectancy' on which rapid processing of incoming messages depends

   ii helping pupils to utilise the (increasingly automatic) patterns (level 1) to express meanings suggested by the text-book (level 2) and then to express personal meanings (levels 3 and 4) through which language is rapidly retained and emancipated.

All four levels will probably be in use in any one week. The teacher may even move from one level of meaning to another within the span of a single lesson. However there will be an increasing emphasis on level 3 and 4 activities as pupils move beyond the second year of the course. Activities traditionally associated with level 2 (e.g. those normally examined in the past in the CSE and GCE examinations) will give way to level 3 and 4 activities in the fourth and fifth years (see Appendix A). However, even at the fifth-year stage, there will still be a place for some level 1 and level 2 activities and possibly for some level 2 testing at 16+. We stress that our levels are kinds of learning, not stages of difficulty. Apprenticeship requires increasingly confident practice at all four levels. It also calls for tests appropriate to each level to be used to sanction the learning. Pupils who have spent several years merely relaying meanings (level 2) as in current 16+ tests cannot be expected to produce true 'speech acts' without transitional experience at levels 3 and 4. At the same time there will be a place in tests, at all stages up to 16+ and possibly beyond, for questions calling for insight into pattern alongside tests of performance.

Our four levels of depth of meaning are as follows:

Level 1: medium-orientated activities (no attempt to 'do anything' with language except manipulate it for its own sake)

Production:

   i   All audio-lingual drills (e.g. substitution drills and paradigm drills) cued by *verbal* cues (i.e. not 'contextualised') fall into this category, as do

   ii Reading aloud

iii Recitation of set passages learned by heart
iv Gap-filling exercises (e.g. the pupil is given a text of a popular song to study while he listens to a recording of it on tape. The endings of all the verbs are omitted in the text and the pupil writes them in, cued by the recording)
v Counting up to 100; recitation of days of the week, months, etc. mechanically
vi Reciting the phrase (or proverb) of the week. It is a sound practice to commit to memory one model phrase each week. The model phrases are chosen to provide a menu of patterns covering the year's work. They are copied into notebooks week by week and cumulatively revised. Each phrase becomes a model, constantly referred to when other, analogous phrases are met or have to be produced. The phrase of the week remains visible all week at the top corner of the blackboard. From time to time pupils are called on to recite previous 'phrases of the week'. Typically, phrases of the week would rehearse: principal question forms, use of object pronouns and relative pronouns, use of partitive (French) and indefinite articles, main irregular verb forms (especially past participles), irregular adjectives, common idioms, and the various forms in '–ing' etc. The intention is that the growing 'capital' of model phrases, solidly known, becomes a corpus of patterns from which pupils can induce the grammar of expectancy that they must continuously enrich
vii There is no reason why level 1 activities, which have a necessary place, need be boring. For example, once the basic question forms have been learned an enjoyable game to take the tedium out of rehearsal is to begin the lesson with 'an attempt on the two-minute record'. The teacher challenges the class to put as many (different) questions to him/her as possible in the space of two minutes. An egg-timer is used which rings after two minutes. A tally is kept on the blackboard. One point is allowed for each correctly phrased question. As the tally is seen reaching the previous record target, the class strives to invent new forms of old questions, while the egg-timer ticking away gives urgency to the pupils' efforts. If the previous record is beaten the teacher offers the class a chance to repeat the attempt in the last five minutes of the lesson. If the record is again beaten the class is rewarded by being excused homework! Many variations of this game are possible:
(a) an answer to each question may be required from another pupil, to score a point (one should perhaps categorise such answers as coming in our level 2; this variant is therefore on the borderline between two levels of meaning)
(b) the teacher puts the questions and pupils score points for rephrasing the question
  e.g.
    teacher: 'Quelle heure est-il?'
    pupil: 'Il est quelle heure s'il vous plait?'

    (c) the teacher requires answers from all pupils in turn in order to prevent the less energetic pupils opting out of the record attempt

    (d) the teacher requires only phrases which are imitations of the pattern of the phrase of the week, etc.

viii A way of enlivening pattern drills is to ask pupils to compose their own drills to establish specific points. Pupils often learn more insight into pattern by composing a drill than by reciting the text-book drill with minds possibly wandering. A very useful class or homework task is: 'Compose a drill (or design a wall poster) to help younger pupils to learn this pattern that you have just met, possibly using a colour code to bring out the structure'

ix Another alternative to the audio-lingual drill is the 'substitution frame' first proposed by Harold Palmer (1921) as a way of building sentences. A variant of this is to offer pupils 'gapped' sentences and invite suggestions for filling the gaps. Given a number of fillers, the pupils arrange them in order of probability.

Level 1

Reception

i Many of the 'education of the ear' games (Chapter 8) fall into this category. (Examples are chosen from French as this will probably be the language familiar to most readers.) An example of a useful 'matching sound to symbol' game is to teach the three 'e' vowels in French by numbering them

    1 [e] spelled *é, et* (and), *ez, ed, ai* (for some speakers – *ais, – ait*)

    2 [ɛ] spelled *è, ê, elle, ette, ais, ait, – et* (ending e.g. jou*et*)

    3 [ə] spelled *de, se, me, te, le, etc.*

Pupils are given lists of words written without accents (*un eleve, Helene,* etc.) and they insert accents (*and* the number of the vowel) while listening to the teacher's pronunciation, thus:

élèv(e)
1 2 (3)

ii Another valuable receptive activity at the 'formal' level is practice in perceiving 'pattern' in new language heard or read. A typical listening activity would be the presentation (aurally) of the present tense of two verbs such as *lever* and *jeter* which sound:

[lɛv]	[ləvõ]	[ʒɛt]	[ʒətõ]
[lɛv]	[ləve]	[ʒɛt]	[ʒəte]
[lɛv]	[lɛv]	[ʒɛt]	[ʒɛt]

The pattern ([ɛ] when the tonic stress falls on the root of the verb, [ə] when the tonic stress falls on the ending) should be *discovered* by the pupils. They can then listen to another instance of this 'root-changing' pattern which is such a common feature of the French irregular verb (as it is of the Spanish verb):

pouvoir and *vouloir* [puvwaʀ, vulwaʀ]

[pø]	[vø]
[pø]	[vø]
[pø]	[vø]
[puvõ]	[vulõ]
[puve]	[vule]
[pœv]	[vœl]

[ø, œ] whenever the root vowel is stressed;
[u] when the *ending* is stressed as in
vouloir, voulons, voulez

iii Perception of *spelling* patterns is equally important (and rewarding). Once perceived aurally the pattern (of root-changing vowel) can be listened for in other verbs (*appeler, répéter, mener, venir, tenir, prendre,* etc.) and then the patterns of spellings which represent the change of vowel sound can be compared:
  e alternating with *è* (*e* with *elle, ette*) as in *lever, je lève; jeter, je jette*)
  è alternating with *é* (*répète* with *répétons*)
  eu alternating with *ou* (*veux* with *voulons*)
  iens (t) alternating with *e* (*viens* with *venons* etc.)
  (even a complex verb like *aller* with its three Latin roots can be seen to obey the same underlying rule).
iv Similarly pupils can be asked to compare patterns across languages, for example at a very superficial (aide-mémoire) level compare the ending in the singular of many irregular verbs in French with English:

French: *je* –*s* (*mets*)   English: I –t (put)
         tu –*s* (*mets*)   you –t (put)
         il –*t* (*met*)   he –s (puts)

v Pupils make a wall poster to illustrate the contrast between the order of words in French and English negative statements with pronoun object(s).

Level 2: message-relaying activities (now meaning *is* conveyed but not because the learner wants to achieve some effects on his own by the language spoken or heard)

Production: At this level pupils relay messages; the language is 'message-orientated' but it is somebody else's message, not the pupil's own.

i This is the level of 'role-taking' not 'role-making'. Pupils are placed in 'survival situations' and they rehearse language to be used (eventually) if ever they are in certain situations (e.g. ordering a hotel room, a drink, a ticket; asking the way; making purchases). The task is commonly based on work cards containing supporting vocabulary. Role-taking works well when pupils cooperate in pairs, using matched work cards, with questions and corresponding answers. This paired work, inexplicably neglected in favour of the far less feasible 'group work', is the secret of successful classroom dialogue. (See McMunn, 1914 for a complete teaching strategy based on work in pairs.) Most pupils, however, trained in the classroom tradition of each man for himself, need careful re-training in paired working. The training can take as long as a term but it brings great rewards.

ii The other typical activity at this level is guided composition. In its commonest form this relies on picture stimulus, the staple composition test in the traditional 16+ examination. Such activities have an important place, but teachers will remember that retention and rapid learning depend on language transactions motivated by the pupils' *own* intention to mean. Guided composition is a half-way-stage only.

iii Level 2 activities that have been less commonly used are:

    (a) making phone calls, a work card gives a message in note form; the pupil makes a phone call (using a model instrument in the classroom) and conveys the information listed on the work card

    (b) giving instructions, e.g. for a journey, detailing date, time, route, changes, etc.

    (c) working from a train timetable and platform indicator the pupil answers questions about particular destinations

    (d) describing, e.g. the appearance of partner, of teacher (build, hair, eyes, glasses?, dress) or actions, performed by partner or by teacher

    (e) giving a commentary on slides, teacher shows half a dozen slides (e.g. of a market scene) and gives a simple commentary (twice), then a pupil volunteer makes the commentary.

iv Level 2 activities at a more elementary stage include (meaningful) work with numbers, e.g.:

    (a) variations on mental arithmetic: teacher holds up two numbered cards: pupils subtract the lower number from the higher and call out the answer; or teacher holds up clock face and calls out a figure in minutes: pupils add the minutes to the time shown on the clock and call out the time

    (b) teacher shows, or projects on screen, a calendar for the current month showing days of week and dates: he calls out a date and pupils say on which day of the week it falls; or pupils find date of national *fêtes*, etc.

v   An extremely valuable activity at this level which can be made
     very simple for beginners, or more demanding for older pupils,
     is the 'contextualised' language drill (we owe the original con-
     cept to Dakin, 1973). In such drills the response is cued by
     signals from the context, e.g. 'Listen to this noise and say
     whether Paul is typing a letter, playing the violin, riding a horse
     or driving his car.' The tape-recorder then plays the sound of
     typewriter and the pupil answers appropriately. In more de-
     manding versions the initial question is open-ended and does
     not suggest any possibilities to the pupil. Obviously this activ-
     ity involves both production and reception, if the instructions
     are in the foreign language. A similar activity can be invented
     for beginners using simple drawings as cues, where there is no
     input of foreign language, only response to the picture cues.

vi Perhaps the most productive level 2 activity which provides a
     'transition' to the expression of more personal meanings de-
     scribed under level 3 is the 'internal translation' of a text using
     different language to convey the meaning. An excellent ex-
     ample of this activity suggested by R. Dunning was quoted in
     Schools Council Working Paper 28 (Schools Council, 1970,
     p. 77)
        Many varieties of 'internal translation' are possible. An
     elementary example, used by Hawkins and Howson in *Le fran-
     çais pour tout le monde*, may be quoted:

   The pupils read a text containing *inter alia* the expressions:
   Oh, pas mal, tu sais
   Veinard!
   elle est de fabrication japonaise
   pas trop chère . . .
   One of the exploitation exercises is as follows:
   Dites autrement (cherchez les réponses dans le texte):
   Oh! comme ci, comme ça!
   Que tu as de la chance!
   Elle est fabriquée au Japon
   A un prix raisonnable . . .
   Later – in the revision section some weeks later – pupils can be
   asked:
   Dites autrement: Oh! pas mal, tu sais!
                      Veinard! . . .'
   and on a still later occasion:
   How many ways can you find to express the idea of:
   Assez bien, tu sais
   Que tu as de la veine! . . .

vii Finally a 'productive' activity that has been neglected is com-
      posing *clues* for (but not solving) simple crossword puzzles –
      rather than asking pupils to compose or solve puzzles, it may be
      found better for the teacher to make up a puzzle, the pupils
      being asked (in pairs) to compose clues to the words of the

teacher's puzzle. The best clues are then selected and the class puzzle is given to the native assistant who is timed in his attempt to solve it. (*Solving* puzzles is a level 3 comprehension task, discussed in a later section.)

Level 2

Reception: This is the level of the 'comprehension exercise' in all its forms, both spoken and written. There is an abundance of these in the traditional courses and examples need not be given here. It may be worthwhile to suggest some variations on the theme:

i   At the beginners' level a good game to rehearse vocabulary (and genders!) without tedium is to display a number of objects whose names have been learned. The teacher names all the objects in turn *except one*. Pupils name the missing one (with gender!). The game can be played as a test; pupils write the missing name (in red or blue to emphasise retention of gender). Later a volunteer pupil can be asked to call out the names.

ii   The game can be played with numbers (teacher counts up to 20 missing out a number; pupils, in silence, note the number missed; the game is played five times with a different number missed each time. This enables the teacher to discover which pupils are less confident). A variant is to omit two (or more) numbers in a longer count. A similar game can be played with the months. Similarly the clock face can be shown and the teacher says a time. Pupils note *faux* or *vrai*.

iii   The game of right and wrong can be played with teacher's commentary on a picture – the deliberate mistakes are noted.

iv   A written text is compared with a spoken version which departs from it in places – the discrepancies are noted.

v   A written text is studied and a spoken commentary is listened to which suggests certain corrections in the text. The following is an example (Ex. 18, p. 134) from *Revision French* (Hawkins and Howson, 1979):

Read the business letter below. Note the details (date, name of the firm, of the writer and of the addressee, nature of the business, etc.). Then listen to the dialogue on the tape. With the information provided in the taped dialogue, rewrite the letter as André would correct it.

Messieurs Charles Barré et Cie.   le 14 juin 1979
16 rue de la Paix
157924
Bordeaux
Gironde

Messieurs,

    J'ai le plaisir de vous passer la commande suivante:
144 bouteilles de votre Château Balzac (rouge, V.D.Q.S., premier cru, 1972) au prix de francs 9 la bouteille moins 3% d'escompte pour

paiement immédiat. Je vous saurai gré de bien vouloir exécuter cet ordre au plus tôt et d'expédier la facture comme d'habitude à l'adresse ci-dessous. Le montant de la facture sera réglé par chèque sur Crédit Lyonnais dès réception du vin en bonne condition.

Agréez, Messieurs, l'expression de nos sentiments les meilleurs.

André Carnot
Marcel Carnot et fils
13 Avenue de la Guerre
Bruxelles 11e

Taped dialogue

— Allô! Allô!
— Allô! André Carnot à l'appareil.
— Ah! c'est toi André? Ici ton papa.
— Bonjour papa! Ça va?
— Oh oui! Ça ne va pas mal. Mais écoute André — cette lettre à Jacques Barré à Bordeaux, tu l'as expédiée?
— Pas encore papa. Je l'ai fait taper hier après la dernière levée. On l'expédiera cet après-midi.
— Oui je sais. Je l'ai lue hier soir quand je suis passé au bureau. Tu as fait plusieurs fautes, André, qu'il faut corriger.
— Des fautes papa? Je sais qu'il faut changer la date, car c'est le quinze aujourd'hui, mais c'est tout, n'est-ce pas?
— Mais non, mon petit. Regarde l'adresse. Tu as mis Charles Barré, n'est-ce pas? Il s'appelle Jacques, le type. Et puis c'est au quinze rue de la Paix et non au seize qu'il a son bureau.
— Peste! Tu as raison papa. J'ai ici sa dernière lettre.
— Puis Bordeaux c'est 33000 et non 157924. Et vous avez commandé 144 bouteilles de leur Château Balzac '72, n'est-ce pas?
— Oui papa.
— Et bien, c'était le '73 que je t'avais dit, idiot!
— Oui papa!
— Et quel escompte as-tu demandé?
— Trois pour cent papa!
— Stupide! Mets trois et demi. Nous payons toujours à temps. A propos, tu a mis notre numéro de téléphone après notre adresse?
— Non papa!
— Mets-le. Bruxelles 75-99-71.
— Oui papa. C'est tout papa?
— C'est tout. Mais fais vite! Et fais attention André. Les fautes, ça coûte cher.
—Oui papa. A bientôt papa.
— A ce soir André!

It will be obvious that it is at this level that the tape-recorder comes into its own. The immense potential of the tape-recorder for level 2 activities has scarcely been exploited. It is possible to identify ten different uses to which the tape-recorder can be put and it might be useful for a school language department to check periodically how many of the ten are consistently exploited. They are:

1 Listening comprehension in all its many forms
2 Using the recording as a model for learning prose and verse by heart (rote learning is hazardous, possibly counter-productive unless based on a native-speaking model, when it deserves more time than it has been given hitherto in most schools)
3 Gap-filling (e.g. listening for key words and phrases in popular songs)
4 Comparing a text or a picture with the spoken version, noting discrepancies
5 Variations on the theme of reconstruction of text after listening once or twice and given cues of different sorts
6 Taking a role in a dialogue (a group of pupils listen twice to a dialogue; on the third hearing the volume is turned down without warning and one pupil, on a signal from the teacher, takes the part of one of the speakers, saying what he or she was about to say)
7 Commentary on a series of eight or ten slides. The commentary can be at a very elementary level suitable for beginners or at sixth-form level. After the slides have been seen twice, and the commentary has been listened to, with difficult phrases written on blackboard, the slides are shown again with a pupil giving the commentary. (Note that this typical level 2 activity can be made either very easy or very demanding.)
8 Regular sessions of *'phonétique corrective'* to avoid the 'erosion' of French/Spanish vowels or intonation by the gale of English
9 Listening to cassettes sent from the linked school
10 (A variation on 9) recording a playlet or dialogue composed by the class in the foreign language. This is sent on cassette to the linked school who *re*-record it (correcting infelicities) and send it back for the authors to compare the two versions and learn from the comparison.

Level 3: activities involving personal meanings, but motivated still by the intention to learn language

Production: The step from level 2 to level 3 is a big one. It has sometimes been referred to in the past as emancipation of language from the context in which it was first met, and its application to the learners' *own* meanings.

We can help the learner to take this step if from the beginning we insist on manipulating each new bit of language and using it in new contexts and to serve personal meanings. It may not be an exaggeration to say that one of the teacher's most challenging tasks is to help pupils to move, in classroom dialogues, from level 2 to level 3 responses. Both are necessary. The pupil must first imitate the model answer. But too often teachers allow the pupil to stay at the stage of relaying the model answer, instead of moving to the next level.

i   Butzkamm and Dodson (1980) give a simple example. To ask a pupil 'How old are you?', when all the pupils are about 12 years old and the pupil knows that the teacher knows this, is not 'communication'. However, they go on; 'there is still scope for real or simulated surprise accompanied by appropriate para-linguistic behaviour. For example: "Oh, you're only eleven. But you are a big boy. I thought you were twelve. (Aren't you twelve?) When is your birthday?"'

ii In this connection, Stevick (1976) quotes an interesting feature of the course *Liberated Spanish* by Keith Sauer. 'From the very beginning students are taught words and structures that will enable them to *disagree* with one another.' Disagreeing, says Stevick, is powerful 'stroking', in Transactional Analysis terms. Disagreement is personal and singles out the speaker. Have language teachers unduly neglected disagreement in classroom dialogue?

iii Another example of moving from relaying mean to personal meaning: pupils are forming sentences with 'I would like to . . .'

> Pupil: 'I would like to eat my supper.'
> Teacher: 'Why! are you hungry?
>   Hey! I think you are eating now!
>   Open your mouth! Oh! he's not eating!'

(adapted from tape-script in Butzkamm and Dodson, 1980)

iv Another example particularly suitable for beginners is writing simple illustrated stories. A version of this game developed imaginatively by Graham Sedgley at Royton and Crompton School, Oldham, involves each pupil inventing his or her own mythical monster which is depicted in large attractively coloured drawings having a series of far-fetched adventures. At the foot of each full-page drawing the pupil writes a single sentence of explanation, narrative or dialogue (in French), consulting the teacher if help is needed with vocabulary. There is considerable tolerance of error. The drawings are later bound into a booklet and given attractive covers and often witty titles. (We referred in Chapter 4 to Otto Jespersen's advocacy of drawing in the language classroom, with pupils instructing each other what to draw; such a game is developed brilliantly in Jim Wight's *Concept 7–9*, Schools Council, 1973, to promote use of English.)

v   Also for beginners: each pupil brings to school a photograph of himself/herself. These are pasted into notebooks and labelled *moi/yo*. The pupil then appends a description, including likes and dislikes. An alternative version is to fill up a *carte d'identité* for disembarkation, or to register at a hotel.

vi In place of the usual guided composition about fictitious characters the pupils are asked to read an account by the school native assistant (or teacher) of how he/she intends to spend next week-end; they then write their own short essay on: 'My next week-end', adapting the vocabulary and structure of the model.

vii The game of 'newspaper reporter' calls in aid the native assistant. After rehearsing suitable questions in class (and 'passing out' as competent) pupils meet the native assistant, in small groups, and put their question, as reporters, in order to obtain a story which they later write down and 'telephone' to their office, while the rest of the class listens. This activity can be played several times by a given group with the same visitor, each session concentrating on a different area of interest:
   (a) family background, education, experience
   (b) likes and dislikes (food, drink, music, reading, leisure)
   (c) what he/she did last week-end
   (d) plans for the holidays
   (e) job; reaction to British schools etc.
   (f) life in the region from which he/she comes, etc.
   This game of 'interviewing the stranger' can scarcely be played too often. It would be well worthwhile for schools to advertise locally for native speakers to come in to be interviewed! It helps if pupils themselves prepare the questions in the 'rehearsal' sessions, if necessary seeking help in correcting grammar etc. The questions should be felt to be pupils' own questions.

viii Another generally neglected level 3 activity which many pupils will enjoy is the exploitation of 'models' to make personal statements. A simple example may make clear the possibilities of this activity. A group of pupils read the famous ballad quoted by Don Quijote:

Romance de la Constancia

Mis arreos son las armas;
Mi descanso es pelear;
Mi cama las duras peñas;
Mi dormir siempre velar . . .

(my ornaments are arms, my rest is in the fight, my bed it is the hard stones, my sleep perpetual watching . . .)

A pupil in his 4th year of Spanish (facing an examination) went home and wrote:

> Mis arreos son los libros;
> Mi descanso es estudiar;
> Mi cama las traducciones;
> Mi dormir es trabajar . . .

ix The model need not, of course, be in verse. It should be part of the level 3 programme for pupils to study several model letters, of varying degrees of formality, on which they base versions of their own, addressed to real recipients, expressing the pupil's own meanings but utilising the sentence patterns, though not the vocabulary, of the originals. So far as possible recipients should be chosen to whom the pupil has something to say in the foreign language. Two obvious possibilities are the native assistant and the linked school. It should be an important part of the fourth- and fifth-year programme for pupils to write a (very short) personal letter (fortnightly?) to either the school assistant or the linked school.

x The assistant's periodical letters to each class (and replies from the linked school) published on the wall newspaper and discussed in class provide the model phrases. Pupils below the fourth and fifth years should, of course, also be encouraged to write regularly to the linked school, but their letters will most usefully be in English, thus providing valuable comprehension tasks for the pupils abroad, whose own letters in return (in the foreign language) will give useful practice in reading.

xi The acting of playlets in which pupils introduce each other, using real names and real likes and dislikes, mention their teacher, discuss coming events, etc., while keeping to the vocabulary and structures they know. Some delightful tape-scripts of such improvised dialogues are quoted in Butzkamm and Dodson (forthcoming). The example is of German pupils learning English:

Pupil 1: I am Jane
Pupil 2: I am Julia
Pupil 3: I am Frances
Teacher: Jane, Julia, Frances. Well, what's your family name? Are you sisters?
Jane: I am Jane Duff
Julia: I am Julia Benson
Frances: I am Frances Hiller
Teacher: And the title please? [i.e. what is your playlet called?]
Team: 'The Cream Buns'
Jane: Does your sister give a party next week?
Julia: Yes she does
Jane: Do you help her to prepare it with your friends?

Frances:	Yes, we do. We help her. We must fetch the re-cords from Eileen. She has very good pop music
Jane:	What about your parents. Do they like to dance for pop music?
Frances:	Yes, they like to dance
Julia:	I think Aunt Agatha comes too
Frances:	Aunt Agatha? Oh no! Does she also dance?
Julia:	Sally is coming. She has so many cream buns. Yum! The cream buns are wonderful
Jane:	Oh no! The cream buns are for the party
Team:	The end!

An important point made by Butzkamm and Dodson is that in this activity 'approximate' language must be accepted. ('Do you give a party' etc.)

xii A final example is the 'daily comment' or the 'class report'. Some teachers train their classes to volunteer a sentence with which to begin the lesson each day. This can take the form of a comment (on the weather or the day's events) or a 'recap' of something that happened yesterday. It is useful to take the proffered sentence, write it on the board, and use it to draw analogies with other phrases. It is unlikely to be easily forgotten by its author and can usefully be used to reinforce learning of analogous patterns.

Before the end of this section a word of caution may be in order. Although we are advocating moving, in classroom transactions, from level 2 to level 3, this should not be taken to mean that level 2 can be by-passed. It is an essential stage, though insufficient if pupils stay there (as most have hitherto done). There is no profit in throwing pupils without preparation into the 'deep end' of 'communication'; this leads to bewilderment identified by Harold Palmer (1921) as the chief teaching error to be avoided. As Butz-kamm and Dodson stress, pupils 'find it extremely difficult to participate effectively in communicative activities without pre-viously practising and internalizing foreign-language sound chains'.

It is for this reason that we would emphasise the need for teachers to be trained to analyse more systematically the levels of communication and the kinds of language transactions that they set up in the classroom.

Level 3

Reception
i It will already be apparent that the role of the assistant at level 3 is all-important. If language learning is to be individualised it

can be managed only by making the assistant available for dialogue with as many pupils as possible. How is this to be done? One answer is by issuing to pupils their personal tape-cassette and re-thinking the role of the assistant.

The assistant is not qualified as a teacher and has no training in class management. The common practice of allocating groups of pupils to the assistant for weekly 'conversation classes' is unproductive and wasteful of the assistant's time. We suggest a totally different approach. The assistant is the language informant. He or she should be given specific language production duties, chief of which would be:

(a) daily recording on cassette of a news bulletin in the foreign language, which is based on the BBC early morning news (in English) (i.e. quoting items that pupils will have seen in the morning headlines)

(b) recording on cassette once per month for every individual pupil in year 5 a series of questions in the foreign language about recent events in the school or in the news. (For 100 pupils this means 25 individual recordings in a week or 5 per day – equivalent to, at most, 1 hour per day of recording – not an impossible load)

(c) listening to the replies that each pupil records – based on items in the daily news bulletins – and attaching to each cassette a brief written comment to help the pupil correct mistakes

(d) regular recording of 'comprehension passages' to build up a listening library

(e) recording once per week a message for 'group comprehension' addressed to each of the fourth- and fifth-year classes, in which pupils are referred to by name and are therefore motivated to listen to what is said about them personally.

Some schools are already beginning to use the assistant and the cassette-recorders in ways like these. An excellent example is the imaginative exploitation of the daily news bulletin by David Cross at Archbishop Michael Ramsey's School, London. There the 7 a.m. BBC news was made the basis for a French news bulletin on cassette which was recorded in time for the first morning lesson. The immediacy of the events, and the fact that the pupils had heard or read the headlines the same morning, lent special interest to the recording. David Cross exploited the recording by means of questions (using an overhead projector) put to the class after listening a couple of times to the cassette. A 'gapped' version of the main items was then projected on to the screen for pupils to reconstruct the headlines.

ii If the cassette is to be exploited fully at level 3, schools will need to train pupils in its use. We suggest that in the fourth and fifth years of the course, when level 2 activities give way more and more to levels 3 and 4, each pupil should be issued with his/her personal cassette and each form room should have available at least one cassette-player of good quality for each pair of pupils. The cassette acts much like the pupil's slate in the old elementary school. Messages in the foreign language are regularly recorded and erased when finished with. The recordings are made by teacher and by native assistant. So far as possible they are personalised.

iii It is at level 3 also that the value of the school-to-school 'link' is greatest. The presence in the school of even a few pupils from the linked school in France or Spain makes possible the purposeful use of the foreign language. Children can talk to native speakers about things that matter to them. It would be an excellent investment for LEAs to offer scholarships to selected pupils from France, Spain or Germany, giving free tuition and help with board and lodging, to enable them to spend a term in one of the authority's comprehensive schools. The presence in each class of only one pupil who 'represents' the foreign language can transform the authenticity of the classroom dialogue. A reciprocal treaty which allowed selected pupils from schools in Britain to spend a term in a school abroad would seem to be an obvious first step towards implementing some of the hopes that were raised by Britain's membership of the EEC.

iv *Reading*
The difference between reading at level 2 and level 3 is in the degree of choice exercised by the pupil. At level 3 typical activities would be:

(a) borrowing one of the class collections of short stories and selecting one story to read and tell the class about at a fortnightly 'reporting on reading' session, at which the pupils tell each other of things that they have found worth reading

(b) browsing through an anthology of verse (e.g. *Las Cien Mejores Poesías Españolas*) and selecting 12 lines to be learnt by heart and recited to the class the following week, when the pupils will explain *why* they chose to learn this particular poem

(c) selecting one item (from the weekly edition of the newspaper taken in multiple copies in the school modern languages library) and writing a summary of it in English (about 10 lines) to hand to the class teacher at the end of the week

(d) solving (simple) crossword puzzles is an under-used activity at this stage; the discussion of the puzzle in class, after pupils have tried to solve it, stimulates the search for meaning.

Level 4: true performance (IL) (the motivation now is to achieve some effect *other than* learning the language)

Production

i   Just as at level 3 the presence of the native assistant, the existence of the linked school and the imaginative use of the cassette make it possible for the pupil to express more personal meanings as part of the rehearsal process, at level 4 the same allies are needed but now the emphasis is wholly on use of the foreign language to satisfy real needs. The best way to promote this use of language is in the 'intensive course'. The various forms that this can take were discussed in Chapter 6: day-long immersion sessions; week-ends, ideally residential week-ends, in specially prepared environments; 'reciprocal fortnights' in collaboration with the linked school, in which equally matched groups of pupils from the two countries teach and learn from each other in alternate sessions; and study courses abroad. The essential requirement is that the experience is felt as true performance. It is for this that the rehearsal has prepared. Language transactions are now meaningful; they satisfy curiosity, meet real needs; their purpose is not to get ready for some eventual survival situation in the future. Survival, in performance, is *now*.

ii Much the best intensive experience is, of course, the study visit abroad, with residence in a family, not in a hotel or hostel. Study abroad, as the great Henry Sweet justly pointed out, can be a waste of time, even counter-productive. The visit must be prepared with care; a well-planned daily programme of reading must be observed; specific topics must be selected to be investigated during the visit and written up in a journal in the foreign language which is submitted to the hosts for daily correction; a linguistic diary must be kept of all new language acquisitions based on the notebook constantly ready in the pocket; the fruits of the visit must be written up in a report immediately after returning home. A dilettante approach to the study visit to one's 'language laboratory' is no more to be tolerated than would be a tourist's off-hand saunter into the science laboratory. Again example may be better than precept: A short study visit by Fulford (York) Comprehensive School pupils in their fourth year is described in Hawkins and Howson (1977). The group planned a comparative study of the cost of living in England and France. It was decided to select 30 household articles and compare the prices charged in shops and supermarkets in York and Rouen. The shopping list was selected by the pupils' parents at a discussion in school in the evening. Before the visit to Rouen all the articles were priced in three different York shops. Then the pupils rehearsed in class and in the language laboratory the dialogues that they would have to engage in when they came to enquire the prices in Rouen. Various forms of the dialogues were practised, incorporating the different replies (some rude!) likely to be forthcoming from the shopkeepers. In Rouen the pupils worked in teams of three,

pricing each article three times. Each team was led by a graduate student training to be a teacher. On their return the pupils
wrote up their study and gave their parents an illustrated
presentation of the results using a slide and poster exhibition
with cost-of-living tables. Two lessons were learned from this
project. One was that pupils 'rehearse' with much greater
motivation when they are certain that in a few weeks they will
have to 'perform' the learned material in the foreign country.
Secondly, the consultation with the parents, in drawing up the
cost-of-living index, secured the interest and commitment, and
so the encouragement, of the homes.

iii At level 4 the pupil is using the language to express personal
meanings *for a purpose* other than simply rehearsing the language. Level 3, it will be remembered, also involved personal
meanings (not relaying meanings from text-book to teacher) but
the motivation at level 3 was still essentially that of rehearsing
language rather than expressing or finding out something of
interest in itself. If for spoken production at level 4 an extra
linguistic intention is essential, it follows that spoken language
at this level *must be addressed to a native speaker*. Any use of the
foreign language *to an English speaker* involves 'suspension of
disbelief' against which many pupils react strongly in adolescence. The challenge to teaching is therefore to create activities (as in the 'reciprocal course' or as in the Rouen project just
described) which confront the pupil with the native speaker,
and encourage him to achieve results that matter by use of
language. It must be conceded that this severely limits the
scope of level 4 use of the spoken language below the sixth
form. This must be accepted. Teachers, however, should not
look for rapid acquisition of the spoken language *until* level 4
activities do become possible. The foreign language 'apprenticeship', below 16+, is fully justified *as a preparation* or spring-
board for later rapid acquisition, even if few level 4 transactions
are possible. Such a 'preparation for learning' course should not
be sanctioned *only* by tests of *performance* however (as has often
happened in the past).

iv Written production at level 4 is in many ways easier, since the
native-speaking 'audience' does not need to be present. It is
enough that the writer intends the message to be read by a
native speaker. The linked school provides the most likely
'audience' and must be exploited imaginatively. All pupils
should write a regular personal diary in the foreign language,
describing real events and genuinely held opinions, briefly
reviewing a book recently read, a film or television programme
seen, or a visit or school event. The purpose of the writing must
be to inform the linked school, as a contribution to the wall
newspaper. The readership must be felt to be a native-speaking
readership. The contributions should on no account be corrected before being sent to the linked school as this would

inhibit spontaneity and make the exercise rehearsal rather than performance. Feedback from the native speaker in the linked school, however, is welcome and suggestions regarding rephrasing, advice on 'register', comments on idiom and slang, should be requested, on a reciprocal basis, together with reactions to the content or message, of the contributions. There seems to be no reason why the drafting of such weekly level 4 contributions to the 'wall newspaper' to be sent abroad should not constitute the major part of each fourth-year pupil's classwork.

v Another regular (written) level 4 activity could be a weekly personal question put in writing to the native-speaking assistant by each pupil. A maximum length of five lines might be set. The pupil would ask a genuine question (about the foreign country) to which he or she really wished to know the answer. The assistant would either reply in writing (perhaps simply indicating where the information might be obtained) or would reply orally in a weekly session with each class, answering questions in the foreign language as they were handed back. Any linguistic errors in the questions might be indicated, *en passant*, but the emphasis would be on the information which the pupil wished to obtain.

vi An activity that used to be universal in classics courses when pupils reached what we are calling level 4 is writing in verse in the foreign language. It has been curiously neglected in modern language teaching. (The work of Miss Ellicot, HMI, who collected examples of secondary school children's verses in French, has shown what quite average pupils can do when expressing their own meanings within a 'model' metre and rhyme scheme.) The simple economical rhythms of Prévert (or the 'assonance' of the Spanish *romancero*) provide models well within the capacity of fourth and fifth years. The subject chosen must, of course, be the pupil's own. In the level 3 activity we proposed earlier, the sentence patterns of a model poem were kept as, for example, in the line 'mis arreos son *los libros*', where only one noun was altered. In versification at level 4 the metre alone is taken from the model; the entire message, like the language, is the pupil's own.

vii Possibly the most effective and engrossing kind of level 4 activity is learning a school subject via the foreign language as in the *section bilingue* experiments described in Chapter 6. If the European Community is to make a significant contribution to foreign language learning in schools it must be by promoting more experiments in this area; this could be done most effectively by recruiting, training and financing a pool of 'European' teachers who could teach geography and history in the 'working foreign language' in secondary schools of member countries. If (say) 20 schools in each country were initially selected for carefully monitored experiment, the cost of staffing for the EEC budget would be comparatively small, and the lessons learned after, say, five years could be applied by member countries to the rapid development of this kind of teaching.

Level 4

Reception

i   In many ways it is easier to use the foreign language with *intention* in reading than in production. Production requires a native-speaking audience for the intended message. In reading, the message is there in the text waiting to be decoded. The essential thing is that the pupil genuinely wants to get at the message. The drive must be to identify with the characters in the novel or play; to share the vision of the poem's imagery and enjoy its music; to learn history from first sources; to get a French viewpoint on biology from a Nobel Prizewinner such as the late Jacques Monod, or, at a different level, to solve the mystery cunningly, wrapped by Simenon, to grasp the Astérix joke, or to read a Spanish newspaper's view of Real Madrid's chances in the European Cup. The message must come before the intention of rehearsing language and must 'distract' attention from the form of the language. Only when attention is so distracted will rapid acquisition take place. This approach to reading was proposed in Schools Council Working Paper 28 (1970). It is the opposite of the traditional 'set-book' procedure, where pupils are told which books to study and where the critical factor of intention to get a *chosen* message is absent. In Working Paper 28 the proposal was made that each pupil should select the books to be studied after a good deal of browsing and trial and error, and that the selection might be made from many kinds of writing, matching the pupil's mother tongue interests, i.e. a book in French on the hobby of fishing (in which the French have unrivalled expertise) or in Spanish on the re-emergence of democracy in Spain would be possible choices by pupils of divergent interests.

ii We have earlier observed that the 16+ examination traditionally consisted mainly of tests of level 2 (meaning-relaying) activities (i.e. comprehension exercises, guided picture, compositions, etc.). If level 3 and 4 activities are to be encouraged the 16+ examination must

(a)   give opportunities for pupils to use the language with intention to convey their own personal meanings – this is best done in face-to-face discussion.

(b)   stimulate reading with intent to get the message. As Working Paper 28 showed, the way to achieve this is to assess the pupils' reading by an individual oral interview to which the pupils take their chosen books. This way of stimulating reading with intent should (as Working Paper 28 argued) not wait until 18+ but should become part of the 16+ examination.

A number of conclusions follow:

(a) the habit of choosing reading must be learned early; already in the *first* year simple readers should be introduced, with restricted vocabularies. Many publishers have attractive lists of such short readers

(b) classrooms should be furnished with supplies of readers appropriate to each age-group to encourage real choice

(c) reporting back or reviewing sessions (in English) in which pupils give an account of their reading and recommend books to others must be a regular part of the programme, with classroom time specifically allotted to it

(d) in the fourth and fifth years periodic, brief written comments should be asked for on books chosen for private reading. These can well be incorporated in the regular written report addressed to the assistant which we have suggested in Level 4, *Production*, section v

(e) reading aloud (in which the concentration is on the form or the medium and cannot therefore be on the message) should be recognised as a level 1 activity of limited application, *not* to be confused with reading for meaning.

iii Some interesting questions arise at this level concerning enjoyment of fine writing in a foreign language. A poem can be read for its own sake, for its music and imagery (not as rehearsal), even by beginners. If suitable works are chosen such reading need not wait until the sixth form. (One thinks of Prévert's Snails going to bury their autumn leaf.)

iv Any attempt at literary evaluation, however, must be approached with care. Very few students of a foreign language, even after a year or more of residence in the foreign country, and very extensive reading, can hope to approach the educated native speaker's intuitive *Sprachgefühl* or feeling for the 'company that words keep' with each other. Most non-native speakers have not the experience of the language to tell the difference between a well-worn, 'cliché' image and an original, perceptive one, between a music that merely echoes others and a new rhythmic invention. It follows that appreciation of poetry, or of fine prose, in a foreign language by the non-native speaker must nearly always, even when quite sincere, run the risk of making value-judgements which the educated native speaker will not necessarily share. The pleasure in the reading may be intense but is no sure index of complete understanding of the author's intention still less of true 'literary quality'. This calls in question any approach to literature which does not take as its point of departure the constant danger of turning attempts at literary criticism of set-books into an apprenticeship in hypocrisy.

We conclude that both intensive and extensive reading of fine literature (as of other precise and thoughtful writing, e.g. accounts of travel, history, autobiography, scientific discovery, etc.) are essential but literary appreciation of works in a foreign language has no place in our conception of education at school level. Of course pupils will enjoy some literary works more than others. This is natural and complete honesty in expressing such preferences is the only basis on which to build. There is a place also for comparing preferences and reasons for likes and dislikes. But all such discussion must be conducted against the background of an admission that pupils still largely dependent on dictionaries to decipher the meaning of a text cannot assume that they get the nuance of meaning intended by the author and must not be encouraged in the pretentious game of comparing literary values. We can move to motivated (level 4) reading in sixth forms by scrapping the set-books paper at 'A' level and substituting for it a rigorous varied reading programme (largely of books chosen by the pupil) which is tested in individual *oral* discussion with the examiner as outlined in Schools Council Working Paper No. 28(1970). (See Appendix A.)

Language acquisition: building on the apprenticeship

We envisage an apprenticeship in foreign language learning (starting at 11+) leading to the rapid acquisition (post-16+) of the language of adult choice. Since the language ultimately to be needed for the adult job or other purposes cannot be known, the apprenticeship language is selected for its suitability as an introduction to language study. The foreign language apprenticeship and the 'language awareness' course enable the acquisition stage to be intensive and effective. It follows that the menu available, after the apprenticeship, must include all the languages most likely to be asked for. Many learners, of course, will wish to press on with further intensive acquisition of the apprenticeship language (French, Spanish, or German). Others may wish to start French, Spanish, German (if not the apprenticeship language), Italian, Russian, Arabic, Japanese, Portuguese, a Scandinavian language, Polish, Modern Greek, Turkish, Chinese (Mandarin or Cantonese), Hindi, Urdu, Swahili, and possibly others.

Merely to list these important languages is to indicate our first problem. Few institutions could offer even half of them. Foreign language provision must, therefore, be planned by regions, as the West Sussex Colloquium suggested (W. Sussex, 1976). It is probably true for other areas of the curriculum as it is true of foreign languages that school autonomy in deciding what to offer no longer has any justification. Curriculum decision must take account of regional and area provision, and curriculum planning by regions is an urgent priority for the 1980s. Students in one institution may need to follow part of their course in another one. Curriculum consortia are obviously called for, with flexible interchange of students between institutions. But interchange of students has important timetabling corollaries. It will be necessary to plan foreign language acquisition in intensive sessions, on timetables coinciding across institutions.

The programme need not wait until the wide range of languages, quoted above, can be offered. A start can be made with a limited menu: public demand must then extend the choice.

The techniques employed will be the 'immersion' methods pioneered in the services in war-time, and methods such as Dr Berger's service courses or Bryan Howson's and Mary Dalwood's reciprocal courses at York, Professor Coveney's training of interpreters at Bath, or Professor Willis' courses in language and industry at Bradford.

Such language learning cannot proceed in driblets in a gale of English. It requires uninterrupted periods of immersion. The future, therefore, is with:

   (i)   the sandwich foreign language course
  (ii)   development of *sections bilingues* – type courses
 (iii)   the practice of studying abroad for one or two terms in the course of the sixth form. (It cannot be long before the EEC and the Inspectorates of the member countries realise that no single development could do more to cement the European community than a programme of interchange, for one-term language learning attachments, of sixth formers and 17-year-olds on apprenticeship or pre-professional training courses.)
 (iv)   the reciprocal course in all its varieties for more advanced specialist needs.

What are schools for?

There is one further aspect of post-16+ language work to examine. We have seen in our discussion of 'awareness of language' (Chapter 7) that, in the verbal learning demanded by the school, many children, because of the lottery of parental ineffectiveness, are severely handicapped.

If we mean business, as a community, by our claim to offer equality of opportunity to all our children, then one-to-one dialogue (with an adult) from which awareness of language springs, and of which many children are deprived, must somehow be provided. Where are the adults to be found?

The answer can only be to mobilise older learners to tutor younger ones, on the model of Alex Dickson's 'Youth tutors Youth', the York University 'student tutoring in schools', Imperial College's 'Pimlico Connection' and many other similar learning sharing schemes (see Goodlad, 1979, Roberts, 1979).

Our post-16+ students must be trained and encouraged to take part as tutors in language awareness courses, especially with slower readers and immigrant children, for whom language is the barrier to equality of opportunity and all the enrichment that confident verbal learning brings.

This implies a new concept of the comprehensive school. It should not be just a place one attends in order to 'get' an education, to 'get' a qualification, but equally a place to which every mature learner 'gives' some learning back to others. Every member of the school, both pupils and staff, would then be seen to have a dual role: learner and (sometimes) tutor. Staff would mostly teach, pupils mostly learn, but each would have a dual role; even the lowliest learner has something to teach. The idea that learning stops at the age of 21, perhaps, and teaching then begins, that all of us are in either one category or the other, would give way to the idea of a common learning journey, some being farther along the road than others, with every traveller at the appropriate stage helping those behind over the bits of the road he/she knows and the journey being for life. This is to see school learning as a rock-climb rather than a race-track. Each climber on the rope has two equally important duties: to climb his own pitch as expertly as possible and immediately to secure the rope and give his whole attention to the next man. Hitherto, learning has been a race with a tape that someone must reach first; looking back to help others costs valuable yards: not a good apprenticeship for a member of a community! It may be that language teachers, who try modestly to serve their exacting discipline and who see some of the difficulties that verbal learning poses to many pupils, are in the best position to pioneer this new concept of a comprehensive school for the democracy we can begin to build in the 1980s.

Epilogue
Implications for teacher education and
training

The course of work required for a degree in modern languages is far from
adequate to qualify these graduates for skilled professional service [i.e.
in schools]

Board of Education Circular, 1912

the student of French is rarely brought face to face with the real problems
he will encounter as a teacher

Board of Education Memorandum on the Position of French in
Grant Aided Secondary Schools in England, 1926

It will be obvious that the way ahead that we have tried to
sketch in the later chapters of this book will be quite impossible
without big changes in the education and training of teachers.
Before we consider the changes that our new proposals call for
we should look at some deficiencies in teacher preparation that
are of long standing.

In the Board of Education Reports and Circulars beginning
with the famous pamphlet of 1912, a recurrent theme was the
need to improve teaching standards. Improvements were called
for at two levels:

   i   the content of first degrees in modern languages did not pre-
      pare teachers for work in the classroom
   ii there was a lack of professionalism in teacher training.

Nor was the criticism only from the Board and from HMI. The
Report of the Leathes Committee to the Prime Minister (1918),
the only full-scale national inquest on language teaching ever
conducted, was equally critical. It said, commenting on university degree courses in modern languages 'none of the courses
give any adequate place to the history of the life, the thought, the
institutions of the foreign countries'.

How much has the education of the future language feacher improved since 1918? How much more prepared is he (or, much more often, she) to answer the questions that will be asked in the school classroom rather than in the university examination room?

In one respect, obviously, there has been a great step forward: almost all universities have now made the year of study abroad (usually in the third year) a required part of the four-year under-graduate course. This has greatly improved the spoken mastery of most young teachers while giving them a surer knowledge of at least one region of the foreign country as well as the added maturity that comes from spending a year earning one's living as an assistant in the environment of the foreign language. It will be a tragedy if the parochial bumbledom of some LEAs endangers this vital aspect of teacher preparation. By refusing to employ assistants from European universities, some penny-foolish authorities are putting the whole scheme in jeopardy.

Long-standing deficiencies

Apart from this most important development, how well do university degree courses now prepare teachers, in the words of the 1926 report, to face the 'real problems [they] will encounter' in the classroom?

From experience of selecting graduates from almost every university in Britain for the one-year post-graduate training course over the past 15 years, it has been possible to form some idea of the suitability of the courses they had followed. At York each year some 30–35 graduate language students were selected annually from four or five times that number who applied. Over the years, therefore, some 450–500 graduates followed the York training course. As a result of that experience the following questions suggest themselves:

i   Why was it extremely rare to find a student who had made even a superficial study of phonetics in the course of the degree? (The importance of phonetics was repeatedly stressed by the early HMI reports we have examined yet many students now going into classrooms cannot even read the IPA script with any confidence, so that they are unable to check the pronunciation of a word in, say, the Robert dictionary which uses the international phonetic transcription. It was very rare to find a student who had considered the implications of the difference between 'stress time', in English, and 'syllable time', in French or Spanish e.g. for the poetry of the languages they had read.)

ii How suitable, as a preparation for teaching in secondary school, is a degree course in which the student's reading is almost entirely confined to imaginative literature and which entails no systematic study of any other register of the foreign language?

iii How justifiable is it to encourage students to engage in literary criticism in their undergraduate course when this takes the form of writing essays in English making value-judgements on works in the foreign language whose meaning even for the native speaker is often obscure? Can the undergraduate, still dependent on dictionary and grammar, really express an opinion on the force or originality of the words and images in the text? Is this emphasis on literary criticism not dangerously close to an apprenticeship in hyprocrisy in that it encourages the pretence of sharing views and tastes of native-speaking critics which the student lacks the *Sprachgefühl* to assess for himself? When the student lacks a solid historical background and is ignorant of the historical and social context of the works read, and when the course involves no study of works in English offering opportunities for comparison, on which judgement must build, the whole approach to literature in the foreign language is open to question.

iv How justifiable is it to allow students to read a four-year honours course which entails no systematic study of recent research in the grammar of the foreign language?

v Can the present emphasis on literary studies at the *research* level be justified? With so many problems in linguistics and the applications of linguistics in the classroom waiting to be solved, and with research funds cut back, can the present balance between literary research and applied linguistics (problem-based) studies be defended?

Our answer to these questions must be that in these respects the education of language teachers has scarcely improved since the Board of Education reported in 1926 (see Epigraph).

What of professional training? Sad to say, with regard to the major recommendations of the Leathes Report of 1918, there has been little or no progress. We discussed the report in Chapter 4. The following points may be recalled: the 1918 report recommended that 'each university language department should include a lecturer in linguistic pedagogy' (some university signatories did not endorse this recommendation). How remote the very thought of such a thing sounds from present practice in university language departments!

It also proposed that a phonetics laboratory should be available, common to all language departments. Here there has been slightly more progress in a few places.

The report drew attention (para. 181) to an existing Board of Education regulation, little known and seldom implemented, which allowed for the training of teachers by attachment to schools provided these were approved by HMI. 'The teachers selected to carry out the work of training should receive extra allowance.' This recommendation would have had the immense advantage of encouraging excellent teachers to stay in the classroom. The only career advancement allowed in our present structure is out of the classroom into teacher training at university or college, or into advisory or inspectorial posts. The classroom is constantly denuded of excellence *and there is no return flow.* The 1918 recommendation might have reversed this disastrous trend. It must be a first priority for the 1980s to re-examine this proposal. It would be a healthy situation for university-based training schemes to have to compete and be compared with school-based schemes.

Back to the classroom
It is difficult to defend the present system of teacher training in which the career movement is entirely from school to university. Lecturers in departments of education, once appointed, never return to schools; for the remainder of their careers they become increasingly remote from school classrooms, while lecturing with increasing authority and influence about them. The illusion is created that university work is more important than work in the classroom. What is needed is a career structure which limits the tenure of lectureships in training departments to five years, after which a period of service in the classroom becomes necessary before any further promotion or move up the salary scale is possible. This is, of course, the system adopted by the services. An army officer, in the course of his career, must alternate between spells of regimental duty (in the front line) and staff duty (training and administration). Each step up the promotion ladder entails a switch of role. Only in teaching do we encourage movement out of the classroom (front line) for good as soon as the young teacher begins to show distinction.

In making its recommendation for school-based training (and the recognition of 'master teachers' with all that entails) the 1918 report was calling for something like the training pattern that has developed in France.

Its other important recommendation was also copied from

French experience. This was that language teachers should have national certification of professional competence, *by a body independent of the universities.* This was, in fact, a recognition that it was proper for the state to remove from university faculties the control over the content of teacher education and place it in the hands partly of practitioners (as is the case with other professions) and partly of the state, which foots the bill for the schools. University faculties have had time, since 1918, to demonstrate whether or not they had any interest in what goes on in school classrooms. With a very few distinguished exceptions university teachers have treated school teachers patronisingly. How many university lecturers or professors regularly go into schools to teach classes, or attend teachers' workshops or invite sixth-form teachers to take seminars in the university or attend faculty discussions? The Leathes Committee recommendation was not made idly. It is time to take it up again.

At the same time, perhaps, the most important recommendation made by the committee must be revived. This called for higher certification after a period of five years' service in school. (Again the report suggests a close study of the French system.) Leathes proposed that this higher qualification should be an honour hard to win. 'Real practical skill would be an essential requirement' and 'there should be evidence, oral and written, of further progress in the language'. The intention was to give teachers an incentive, after starting work, to continue to improve themselves and to attain a higher status as teacher, *without leaving the classroom.*

This higher certification need not be a competition, like the French *agrégation*, but it could carry similar prestige, and could stimulate greater mutual respect and cooperation between university and school teachers.

Reform of teacher education and training must begin by correcting these long-standing deficiencies which were so apparent to the Leathes Committee and to the Board of Education in the days when central direction on teaching was less inhibited than it has become. To these reforms we must add some implications for teacher education and training that follow from the proposals made in the later chapters of this book.

Teacher education

i. *Joint degrees*

We need more joint degrees in English *language*, not literature, combined with the study of one or more foreign languages. This would enable teachers of both English and foreign languages to play their part in a coherent programme of language education. As school rolls fall in the 1980s and school staffs contract (many to two-thirds of their present establishment) there will be an obvious need for teachers to be flexible. It is required in some countries (Germany, for example) that teachers be trained to teach two subjects. If we are to make a real linguistic education in the secondary school, a 'trivium' of three closely linked elements, English, a foreign language and 'awareness of language', we shall need teachers who have studied one another's discipline and in a true sense speak each other's language.

ii. *Language teachers must diversify*

Falling rolls will also require that language teachers diversify their own language skills. The minority languages (Russian, Italian, German) will only survive in schools and other languages will only find a place in the curriculum if teachers of the commonly taught languages acquire additional languages through in-service training. Experiment over ten years at York has shown that graduates can acquire a good working knowledge of an additional language in the course of the post-graduate training year and that the learning of this additional language can be made a useful part of the method training. Rather than talking about teaching methods the tutor can demonstrate techniques while teaching the graduates a new language (see p. 94, n. 4).

iii. *Language across the curriculum*

The Bullock recommendation that teachers should, in the course of their training, study 'language in education' has not yet been implemented. It must be pressed strongly. The language education for which this book argues will be impossible unless there is a common element in the training of teachers of English and foreign languages which prepares them to expect to collaborate when they get into their schools.

iv. School and university collaboration

At the close of Chapter 9 of this book, asking 'What are schools for?', we argued that children should learn how to help those coming up the school behind them. This concept of the comprehensive school as a place where every pupil (like every teacher) has two roles, to learn and to teach, so far as each is able, will call for a special kind of teacher preparation. The training course must include experience in one-to-one tutoring. The fourth, fifth and sixth formers who will be challenged to act as tutors will need guidance. The best preparation is for graduate students to be involved themselves in such one-to-one remedial tutoring (as in one university's annual French remedial week for pupils in local schools described earlier in this book). Graduate students can also be taken into schools as a 'posse' to help with intensive immersion courses, to perform play-readings, to take part in debates, to give concerts of songs in the foreign language, etc.

A useful variation on this theme is the attachment of students in training to school parties going abroad, as leaders of small sub-groups, helping pupils in their exploration, learning with them and often from them.

v. The induction year

The James Committee's proposals (James, 1972) regarding the induction year still hang fire. It is essential that they should not be delayed further. Young language teachers especially need opportunities, by release from teaching for one day each week in their first year, to continue learning their trade, guided by advisers who know the local situation and the local needs. How else is the young teacher to observe good practice or have the time to make new materials?

Questions for the administrator

Assuming that we can put right long-standing defects in teacher education (in foreign language degree courses) and in professional training, and that the new challenges of our proposed 'way ahead' in the schools can be met, there remain some administrative matters outside the control of teachers in which we depend on the support of our colleagues in LEAs, in the Inspectorate and in the DES and the Schools Council.

Need for native speakers in school

The presence in schools of native speakers is an essential element in the strategies we have proposed and especially in our attempt to move beyond what we have called 'level 2' classroom activities towards levels 3 and 4 (the levels at which the pupil expresses personal meanings). We have argued that the foreign language does not 'stick' in the learner's mind unless it is used at levels 3 and 4, and that this largely explains the inability of even good GCE and CSE candidates to use the language.

We must therefore be assured that the native-speaker assistant scheme will be strongly backed by LEAs, not as a frill to be cut when times are hard but as a normal provision, as essential as the most basic provision in the science laboratories. Administrators must learn that to teach languages effectively the collaboration of English-speaking teacher and native assistant is essential (see p. 26, note 1).

Our strategy goes further. Pupils must feel that the use of the foreign language is necessary if level 4 dialogues are to happen. We need native-speaking pupils, therefore, in our classrooms. Scholarships must be offered to bring into every classroom at least one pupil from France or Spain or Germany for a term (and, of course, by reciprocal treaty, equal numbers of English-speaking pupils would go to spend a term in schools abroad). The pupils thus exchanged would be carefully selected. It would be an honour to be chosen. In all classroom dialogues, of the kind suggested in Chapter 9, the foreign pupil would represent the interlocutor with whom it was entirely natural to use the foreign language. This is the challenge to educational administrators and to EEC commissioners, if they mean business about a European 'community' as something more than a mere 'market'.

In-service training

We are entitled to look, also, for much more systematic co-ordination of in-service training of language teachers. At present such training is organised at three levels:

(a) national level (HMI nationally recruited residential courses, CILT symposia and a few centres with a national reputation able to attract teachers on short courses)
(b) local level (LEA courses and workshops arranged by language advisers for local teachers and courses organised regionally by universities and polytechnics, etc.)
(c) school-based workshops.

Very much of the work done at all three levels is of the highest quality. It is in in-service training that the greatest progress has been made in the past two decades. The contrast with the variety and quality of in-service opportunities available before 1960 is striking. Nevertheless it is a wasteful provision in several ways. There is a vacuum at the heart of its planning. No machinery exists to link in-service work done at the three levels. For instance, the themes chosen for HMI courses and for LEA courses are uncoordinated either with each other or with other nationally recruited courses.

A sensible pattern would be for themes studied at nationally recruited courses to be taken for further detailed study at local level and then for their implications to be worked at by each school in school workshops run by heads of department. Such sensible coordination is quite impossible at present for lack of in-service planning arrangements.

Not only is the choice of in-service priorities uncoordinated nationally and regionally but also attendance at in-service courses is haphazard. Some teachers are inveterate course-goers; others do little reading and seek no opportunity to improve their knowledge and skills. The answer, like the answers to several other questions affecting teachers' professional performance, lies with the careful reconsideration of teachers' contracts of service. A higher certification after (a minimum of) five years' teaching as proposed in the 1918 report would provide an incentive to further study. Similarly the requirement of successful completion of appropriate training before promotion to Head of Department would do something to ensure a higher level of professional commitment than is apparent, for example, in the report of HMI on the 83 comprehensive schools (HMI, 1977).

Curriculum planning

If there is a lack of coordination of in-service training nationally and locally, the vacuum where central guidelines on the curriculum should be (and were, at least in embryo, between the wars) is equally deplorable. The pre-war Board of Education, dismantled by the 1944 Act, led by presidents of the calibre of Michael Sadler and Lord Eustace Percy, was advised by a standing Consultative Committee of considerable authority which was above party politicking. The main national guidelines were set out periodically by the Consultative Committee in carefully researched recommendations of which the three great Hadow Reports were outstanding examples (Hadow 1926, 1931, 1933) as well as by national commissions reporting directly to the Prime Minister such as the influential Leathes report, *Modern Studies* (1918) already referred to. The brief given to Leathes, as to the sister committee on science education in the sixth form, was *to determine the courses that central government would be willing to sanction in the new LEA secondary schools.* To qualify for grant-aid from central government LEAs would have to follow the guidelines. This is a world away from the drift and uncoordinated muddle of responsibility of the post-war years.

Happily the 1980s have seen a swing away from the vacuum in curriculum planning. There has been a welcome lead from Ministers and from a highly respected and independent Inspectorate. The 'secret garden' of the curriculum is no longer considered a domain to which only Heads of schools (without any qualifications in curriculum planning outside their own narrow specialism) or their Governing Bodies (even less well qualified) have access.

The argument that the curriculum of our schools largely determines the kind of nation we hope to become, and ought to be the subject of a national consensus, centrally agreed and regionally administered, will, of course, always provoke opposition, as a knee-jerk reflex, of the kind that Derek Morrell's Curriculum Study Group (1962) and its successor, the Schools Council (1964) had to endure. But the price paid for lack of guidelines in wasteful, uncoordinated in-service education of teachers becomes so obvious that the argument is rapidly gaining ground. What is now needed is clear thinking about the way in which nationally agreed guidelines can be implemented regionally.

Ultimately what happens in classrooms will be determined by the quality of the teaching, and here in-service education is crucial, as we have argued above. Local, regional and national provision must be coordinated. But the other factor that determines what is taught, all too often, is the 16+ examination.

Here we face a new situation. The GCE and CSE examinations are merging to form the new GCSE. The eight GCE Boards and the thirteen CSE Boards are replaced by five regional examining groups. In the run-up to this change teachers have played a notable part in the discussions of curriculum which have led to the national 'criteria' accepted by the examiners for the new papers. But the curricula that are to be sanctioned by the new examinations must not be static. They must be constantly amended and renewed to meet changing needs. It is essential that this on-going renewal of the curriculum should be reflected in regional curriculum committees capable of standing up to the examining bodies. The latter are staffed (and generally most impressively) by professionals qualified in testing. Unless there is adquate machinery for curriculum discussion *prior to* decisions being taken by examiners, we shall again find that examinations are filling the vacuum where carefully planned curriculum guidelines ought to be. The obvious answer, since the examinations, after 1988, are to be regionally administered, is to lose no time in setting up regional curriculum committees, representative not only of teachers but of other interests such as employers, trade unions, the professions and those who select for Higher Education.

The foreign language as an ancillary skill

Post 16+ also we face a new situation. For the first time, since the debacle of the 'N' and 'F' proposals, the universities have shown a readiness to consider the needs of pupils who may not proceed to degree courses but whose education in the sixth form is strongly influenced by the demands made by university selectors. The Vice-Chancellors have welcomed the new 'Advanced Supplementary' 'AS' level papers (see Appendix A). The message of recent research into the use of foreign language skills by adults, that overwhelmingly what employers and the professions look for are school leavers with a foreign language as an *ancillary* skill, is now generally understood. But though the joint statement by the Vice-Chancellors' Committee and the Standing Conference on University Entrance describing the new papers as 'an important step in broadening the sixth-form curriculum' is welcome, much more will be needed than the publication of a leaflet expressing 'commitment to the success' of the new papers. Everything will depend on the encouragement given to schools by admission procedures of the universities. The warning given by Cambridge University in 1979 (p. 19), that in the end only central direction via the grant regulations can guarantee a broadening of sixth form programmes, is still valid.

The teacher

Throughout this book it has been a recurrent theme that reform movements may come and go, but real progress in language teaching must depend on the quality of the teachers. We saw that

Comenius' insights might inspire an outstanding schoolmaster like Hoole, but for lack of a base in teacher education and neglected by the universities, Comenius had little impact in the schools. Our review of the Great Reform in the last decades of the nineteenth century revealed how, despite the devoted efforts of a gifted group of teachers (Widgery, MacGowan, von Glehn) the universities, cold-shouldering Sweet and failing to respond to the farsighted proposals of the Leathes Committee, allowed language teaching to fall into a long period of stagnation. Exciting ways forward can be discovered by gifted individuals but the footsoldiers needed to follow the break-through must come from the rank and file and they must be well trained. The universities failed to respond to the needs of the country after the 1914–18 war. The Leathes Committee, with foresight, offered the Board of Education the means of removing from the universities the final responsibility for the content of courses of education and training for language teachers. Sadly none of the committee's important recommendations was implemented.

Much that Leathes said is still valid 60 years later, and his committee's proposals, especially regarding teachers' professional certification and higher certification, should be studied most carefully. Everything will depend on avoiding the mistakes of 60 years ago.

There are grounds for optimism. Unlike the inter-war years, we now have a number of universities where the problems of teaching languages are taken seriously. There are undergraduate courses in which the study of linguistics is taken to an advanced stage and others in which students spend a year abroad as part of their course, working in industry while studying the foreign language. Students who have followed such courses as these will be far better prepared, in the words of the 1926 report: 'to face the real problems [they] will encounter as teachers'.

There is something about the discipline of language learning that makes it excellent preparation for a professional career. The discipline is difficult and this seems to make for modesty and resilience in its teachers. Above all the discipline calls for professionalism. It is in the hope that it may make a modest contribution to maintaining standards in his chosen profession, to which he owes a great debt, that the author offers these reflections to his colleagues who have accompanied him on his journey and to those who will follow.

APPENDIX A

New examinations

The 1980s have seen a number of developments in public examinations, all encouragingly in line with the argument pursued in this book. Four of these deserve special mention.

1. At 16+: the General Certificate of Secondary Education

From 1988 the dual system of GCE 'O' level and CSE will be replaced by a single examination, the GCSE, catering for pupils across the ability range. The new GCSE papers will be set by five examining 'consortia' formed by merging the existing eight GCE Boards with the thirteen CSE Boards. The new GCSE papers in foreign languages will have the following characteristics: a substantial element of (internally assessed) course work; emphasis on 'authenticity' in the tasks set and the materials used with consequent omission of such traditional exercises as the 'prose translation'; increased attention to the spoken language; 'criterion-referenced' rather than 'norm-referenced' grading of candidates.

The last feature has important implications. To make criterion referencing possible it has been necessary for the examiners to describe in some detail the kinds of performance in the language tested at each passing grade A to E. This has meant that for the first time the language content of the 16+ examination has been set out in the syllabus (see page 161). Because the new examination caters for pupils across a wide ability range the tasks are described at two levels, 'basic' and 'higher' for the four skills of listening/reading/speaking/writing. The three 'basic' levels in listening, reading and speaking form the 'common core' obligatory for all candidates. To the core can be added further objectives (i.e. 'basic' and 'higher' writing and 'higher' levels in the three other skills). Each additional test offered beyond the 'core' raises the candidate's potential maximum passing grade by one step.

A typical syllabus, that of the Northern Examining Association (the Joint Matriculation Board plus five regional CSE Boards) describes its tests in the four skills at the 'basic' and 'higher' levels under the following heads: Settings and topics/Language tasks/ Language functions/General notions/Structures and grammar/ Communication strategies and finally Vocabulary listed both by topics and alphabetically. Settings are home/town/country/sea-side/public transport/shops/etc. Topics are personal identifi-cation/house and home/holidays/accommodation/relations with others/etc. Tasks, functions etc. are similarly prescribed. (The indebtedness of this approach to syllabus definition to the work referred to on page 169 is clear.)

The new examinations at 16+ have obvious implications for teaching. Omission of translation into the foreign language removes a practice which, however rigorous a test of language mastery it may have been, undoubtedly had an unfortunate 'backwash' effect on classroom method. The stress on authentic-ity in the tasks and materials used, especially in the spoken language and listening tests, is bound to encourage schools to build up resources such as the 'bibliothèque sonore' (see 'Use of Radio and TV', page 195). Schools will also be encouraged to offer pupils increased opportunities to make 'motivated' use of their foreign language through study-visits abroad, exchange of letters with penfriends and linked schools etc. Not the least of the welcome effects of the new examinations must be to encourage teachers constantly to refresh *their own* linguistic skills by such techniques as post-to-post exchanges with colleagues from linked schools abroad. The role of the native-speaking assistant must also assume new importance. Pupils in LEAs which have withdrawn native-speaking assistants from their schools for cheese-paring financial reasons will clearly be handicapped. There are now over 30 such LEAs. It will be for parents to exercise their new powers under the Education Act of 1987 and bring back their authorities into line with accepted good practice.

2. At 18+: Reform of GCE 'A' level

Reform at 18+ has gone less far but there have been some important gains. There is a growing consensus that changes are required. This was well expressed by Corless and Gaskell (1983): 'there is now a growing demand that the fragmentary language course, often conducted chiefly in English and largely divorced from the foreign culture, with its emphasis on translation and academic writing activities, should be replaced by something more in tune with the needs of students and the demands of the modern world' quoted in *German for A level* (CILT, 1985). (See also the comments, page 281 above, on the traditional 'set books' papers, which, with their encouragement to candidates to memorise and repeat second-hand opinions on novels and plays, came dangerously close to being an apprenticeship in hypocrisy.)

Several GCE Boards have announced new papers, notable among them the totally re-planned papers from the Associated Examining Board and the Joint Matriculation Board. These stress authentic use of the language, both written and spoken. The AEB papers include enterprising listening tasks, commentary in the foreign language on a passage in English and discussion in the Oral test of factual problems and topics prepared in advance. The JMB papers include optional course work *in the foreign language* (3 essays of 2,500 words) as well as discussion in the Oral test of one or two books chosen by the candidate (as advocated in Schools Council W.P. 28 in 1970). Both of these new 'A' levels become available in 1988 as *replacements* of existing papers, not alternatives. An even more radical development in examining foreign languages at 18+ is the Joint Statement by the Standing Conference on University Entrance and the Council for National Academic Awards *Guidelines for Written French at A Level* (SCUE/CNAA, 1986.) This paper, the work of an expert committee chaired by Professor F. M. Higman of Nottingham University, describes the content of a 'common core syllabus at A level in French', on which there was general agreement among teachers and examiners at this level. (Similar 'minimal core syllabuses' for mathematics, physics and chemistry have already been published by SCUE/CNAA.) The French syllabus follows the pattern of the Council of Europe work directed by John Trim, in particular *Un Niveau Seuil* (Coste, 1976), with its list of 'functions' ('actes de parole') applied to series of 'notions générales' and to topic areas ('notions spécifiques') with resulting language exponents (lexical and grammatical) listed. This approach to defining the language content of the 'A' level course has the further value for teachers that it is supported by an interesting series of sample marked scripts, covering a wide range of attainment, showing teachers in practical terms what the different grades at 'A' level mean in the productive use of French.

3. Advanced/Supplementary Papers

A third development of great importance is the introduction, from 1987, of new 'AS' level papers. These are to count as half an 'A' level for purposes of entry to Higher Education so, at long last, repairing the mischief done in 1949 when the Subsidiary papers were axed and non-specialists were deprived of a target that Universities would recognise as part of an entry qualification. The new 'AS' level papers have been welcomed by SCUE and by the Committee of Vice Chancellors and Principals (*AS Levels and University Entrance* SCUE/CVCP 1986). Of 38 universities quoted in the paper, some 28 state that they will, in principle, welcome two 'A' levels plus two 'AS' levels as an alternative to three 'A' levels. The encouragement that this *could* give to non-specialists not to drop their foreign language altogether in the sixth form may well be the most important single development for our subject in the last two decades, *provided that university admission tutors prove equal to their task.*

4. Vocational foreign language courses

Finally some mention should be made of the steadily growing interest in vocational courses at sixth form level, including the following: AO French and German for Business Studies, O and C Board; Foreign Languages at Work (FLAW), London Chamber of Commerce; Foreign Languages for Industry and Commerce (FLIC); Institute of Linguists Grade II; Communicative Examinations Levels I–IV, Business and Technician Education Council (BETC) and Royal Society of Arts (RSA). Developing interest in such courses as these has stimulated publication of new practically orientated materials, an excellent example being *Objectifs: Assignments in Practical Language Skills* by A. Limb and P. Bourgeois (1986).

APPENDIX B

A simplified phonetic script

The simplified phonetic script for use in the primary school 'education of the ear' programme will so far as possible (as Otto Jespersen suggested) use symbols with which pupils are familiar and which they will meet in the traditional spelling forms of the language.

The following is a suggested script. It would be preferable for each school to work out its own script and even better *to encourage pupils to devise their own version as part of the course*. In the examples below the script is adapted for French and Spanish. It could easily be further adapted (for German, for example).

French		Spanish	
a	as in *chat*	a	as in *casa*
b	as in *bon*	b	as in *Barcelona, vámonos*
c	as in *comme, caractère*	c	as in *casa, queso*
		ch	as in *orchata*
d	as in *dans*	d	as in *dar*
		ḏ	as in *Madrid*
è	as in *elle*	e	as in *el* (also as in *dedo*)
é	as in *avez*		
f	as in *fou*	f	as in *fino*
g	as in *garçon*	g	as in *gato*
		ḫ	as in *jota*
i:	as in *il*	i:	as in *fino*
j	as in *je*		
l	as in *la*	l	as in *la*
		ll	as in *llamar*
m	as in *mère*	m	as in *mozo*
n	as in *nul*	n	as in *no*
gn	as in *agneau*	ñ	as in *niño*
o	as in *pomme*	o	as in *como* (as in the Welsh
o:	as in *eau*		pronunciation of Jones)
p	as in *papa*	p	as in *para*
ʀ	as in *route* (uvular)	r	as in *pero* (tip of tongue)
		rr	as in *perro*

sh	as in *chat*		s	as in *así*
s	as in *simple*			
t	as in *thé*		t	as in *toma*
			th	as in *cerca*
u	as in *vous*		u	as in *tu*
ü	as in *tu*			
v	as in *voix*		ɏ	as in *neuve*
w	as in *oui*		w	as in *cuatro*
x	as in *accident*			
z	as in *zéro*			

Additional symbols:

ɛ̃ as in *pain* ⎫
ã as in *langue* ⎬ (*un bon vin blanc*)
õ as in *long* ⎪ œ̃ bõ vɛ̃ blã
œ̃ as in *un* ⎭
ø as in *deux*
œ as in *fleur*
ə as in *le, me*

Transcription of numerals: | Transcription of numerals:

œ̃, dø, tʀwa, catʀ(ə), sɛ̃c, si:(s/z)   uno, dos, tres, cwatro, thi:nco,

sèt, üit, nœf, di:(s/z)   seis, siete, ocho, nweɏe, dieth

'Awareness of Language' in the curriculum

The first edition of this book (1981) carried an appendix in which a suggested syllabus was set out for a course in *awareness of language* for pupils in the age range 10 to 14. This outline of learning activities in a hitherto neglected area of language study aroused considerable interest. It was, for example, quoted in the influential DES Report of the Committee of Inquiry into the Education of Children from Ethnic Minority Groups (Swann, 1985) as 'an illustration of the various aspects of language which we would wish to see incorporated into the mainstream curriculum of all schools' (p. 423). The Swann committee reprinted the proposed syllabus as an appendix to their Report.

Since 1981 interest in 'awareness of language' in the curriculum has grown rapidly and some 70 LEAs report its introduction in some form into their schools (Donmall, 1985). Approaches differ from school to school depending on the interests of the teachers responsible (and of the pupils) but most programmes include some or all of the following key themes:

Communication without words

Pupils are encouraged to explore animal communication and then to examine how much human communication is possible by non-verbal means (by 'body language' and via signs and symbols, codes, music, dance etc.). The purpose is to stimulate curiosity as to what is special about human language.

How language works

Here pupils discover that they are linguists without realising it, by detective work, in pairs and in groups, on the patterns of language that they are familiar with or that they may meet in other languages learnt in school (such as French) or spoken by their classmates. It is a novel approach to grammar, making what used to be seen as a bugbear into a voyage of discovery.

Using language

This theme explores the ways in which our use of language is constrained by factors outside language itself. If investigation of 'how language works' examines the rules of grammar, here we look at 'rules' of a different kind: the expectations of society; what the speaker thinks the hearer knows already; how the speaker sees his/her own relationship with the hearer etc.

Spoken and written language

The discussion here encourages questions about the differences between speech and writing, and about the history of our alphabetic writing system. Other alphabets are explored (Greek, Russian, Hebrew) and the alphabetic tradition is compared with other (logographic) ways of writing. The history of printing is explored, as well as proposals for spelling reform.

Varieties of language

Starting with the 'language map' of the world and the place in it of the rich variety of languages now spoken in the UK (over 150 in London alone), the emphasis is on welcoming language variety as enriching and interesting and on helping to build confidence in one's own language as a necessary basis for respecting others.

How do we learn languages?

The intention, in studying this topic, is to show how we learn our mother tongue, bringing out the vital role of the parent and helping pupils to become aware of the similarities and differences between acquiring our first language and learning languages in school.

These and related key themes have appeared in a number of publications (e.g. Aplin, 1981; Penman and Wolff, 1981; Raleigh, 1981), but the specific syllabus suggested in our first edition has been developed in the series of topic books under the title 'Awareness of Language' published by the Cambridge University Press. The pupils books are supported by a background book, for teachers and others, *Awareness of Language: An Introduction*. The first part of this book charts the explosive growth of the teaching of awareness of language in schools since the early experiments began in Hessle High School, Hull, in 1972. The book then devotes one chapter to each of the themes covered by the pupils' topic books, providing the background that teachers will need and a selected, annotated reading list.

An interesting footnote to this growing interest in the place of awareness of language in the curriculum is the announcement by Kenneth Baker, Secretary of State for Education and Science (February 1987) of a committee of inquiry, as suggested by HMI in the discussion paper *English 5 to 16* (HMI 1986), to report on the teaching of English and the implications for teacher training. The minister's decision reflects the growing realisation that far too many children at present fail to acquire the confident mastery of their mother tongue that the school process demands. Though all are 'pre-programmed' at birth (with their *language acquisition device*, Chomsky's LAD) a tragically high number are denied Jerome Bruner's equally vital LASS (*language acquisition support system*) at the vital pre-school stage (Bruner, 1983). They are 'potential song birds who never learn to sing'. The question to be addressed by the DES committee, however, touches deeper issues (though press speculation has focused narrowly on details such as the place of explicit grammar teaching). One is the question, how can the school help the future citizen of our multi-lingual democracy, with its rich tapestry of mother tongues spoken at home and with its mercantile windows wide open on the polyglot world, to see his/her own mother tongue *in perspective*, to learn to love and respect it without denigrating the many other languages equally deserving of study that will be met in school, town, UK, European Community, the world?

It is important that the new Inquiry should not repeat the mistake made by its predecessor (Bullock, 1975) of totally ignoring other languages that figure on the school timetable and which can make an important contribution to the pupil's understanding of language itself. Another question that should be faced (and in justice to Bullock this *was* faced and cogently discussed in *A Language for Life*) is: how can our future school leavers, so soon to take on the responsibility of parenthood, be helped to meet the challenges of trying to be a *good* parent (surely the hardest job any adult ever has to tackle). As Bullock showed, preparation for parenthood has an important *language* dimension. At their best 'awareness of language' discussions seek to create foundations on which later preparation for parenthood discussions of the type Bullock advocated can build. It is to these wider questions, as well as to the important but narrower issues like the place of 'grammar' in the language lesson, that 'awareness of language' teaching should be directed.

APPENDIX D

Some names of the game

1. *The names given to the 'Great Reform' of 1880–1914*
   Otto Jespersen (1904) lists the following names given to the
   'Great Reform' movement as alternatives to the 'living
   method' which he would have preferred:
   the new method
   the newer method
   die neuere Richtung
   the reform method
   the natural method
   the rational method
   the correct method
   the sensible method
   the direct method
   the phonetical method
   the phonetical transcription method
   the imitative method
   the analytical (contrasted with the constructive) method
   the concrete method
   Anschauungsmethode
   the conversational method
   the anti-classical method
   the anti-grammatical method
   the anti-translational method

2. It is interesting to compare the above list with the 15 names
   given by Mackey (1965) as being in use in various parts of the
   world:
   direct method
   natural method
   psychological method
   phonetic method
   reading method

grammar method
translation method
grammar/translation method
eclectic method
unit method
language control method
mimicry/memorisation method
practice/theory method
cognate method
dual language method

3. We might add to the above:
   audio-visual method
   audio-lingual method
   bilingual method
   cognitive-code-learning method
   active method
   oral method
   intensive method
   immersion method (IL)
   drip-feed method
   'gardening in a gale' method

Bibliography

(Place of publication is London unless stated otherwise.)

Adamson J. W. (1925) *An Outline of English Education 1760–1902.* CUP
Ager D. E. (1977) Survey 11/76. Language in an industry. Quoted in *National Congress on Languages in Education. Papers and Reports 1* (1979)
Ahn J. F. (1834) *A New Practical and Easy Method of Learning German.* German edn. 2 vols. English edn Philadelphia, 1859
Allen J. P. B. and Corder S. P. (Eds) (1973–7) *The Edinburgh Course in Applied Linguistics.* 4 vols. OUP
Annan N. (Lord Annan) (Chairman) (1962) *Report on the Teaching of Russian.* HMSO
Aplin T. R. W. et al. (1981) *Introduction to Language.* (2nd edn 1986) Hodder and Stoughton
Arnold M. (1861) *The Popular Education of France with notices of that of Holland and Switzerland.* Report to the Newcastle Royal Commission
Arnold M. (1868) *Schools and Universities on the Continent.* Vol. 6 of Taunton Commission (1868)
Ascham R. (1570) *The Scolemaster or plaine and perfite way of teaching children the Latin tong,* J. Daye
Austin J. L. (1962) *How to Do Things With Words.* (2nd edn 1975) Oxford
Bearne C. G. and James C. V. (Eds) (1976) *Modern Languages for the 1980s.* CILT
Bell A. (1865) *Visible Speech: A New Fact Demonstrated.* Hamilton Adams and Co.
Beloe R. (1960) *Secondary School Examinations other than GCE.* Report of a committee appointed by the Secondary Schools Examinations Council. HMSO
Bennett S. N. (1975) Weighing the evidence: A review of *Primary French in the Balance. British Journal of Educational Psychology* 45, 337–40
Bernstein B. (1971) *Class Codes and Control.* Vol. 1. Routledge and Kegan Paul
Bever T. G. (1981) Normal acquisition explains the critical period for language learning. In Diller K. C. (Ed.) *Individual Differences and Universals in Language Learning Aptitude.* Rowley. Mass.: Newbury House
Blackie J. S. (1852) *On the Studying and Teaching of Languages.* Two lectures delivered in the Marischal College of Aberdeen (the second lecture in Latin). Edinburgh: Sutherland and Knox
Bloom L. (1974) Talking, Understanding and Thinking. In Schliefelbusch R. L. and Lloyd L. L. (Eds) *Language Perspectives – Acquisition, Retardation and Intervention.* New York: Macmillan
Bloomfield L. (1933) *Language.* New York: Holt, Rinehart, Winston
Board of Education. Circulars: (1912) No. 797. *Modern Languages* (Re-

issued 1925); (1913) No. 826. *Sixth Form Curriculum*; (1916) *Inquiry into the Teaching of French in London Secondary Schools*
Pamphlets: (1926) Educational Pamphlet No. 47. *Position of French in Grant-Aided Secondary Schools*; (1928) Educational Pamphlet No. 70. *Report on the Position of French in the First School Certificate Examinations*. HMSO

British Overseas Trade Board (1979) Report of Study Group: *Foreign Languages for Overseas Trade*. BOTB

Brooks N. (1960) *Language and Language Learning*. (2nd edn 1964) New York: Harcourt Brace

Bruner J. S. (1975) Language as an Instrument of Thought. In Davies A. (Ed.) *Problems of Language and Learning*. Heinemann

Bruner J. S. (1983) *Child's Talk*. Oxford: OUP

Bruner J. S., Olver R. R. and Greenfield P. M. (1966) *Studies in Cognitive Growth*. New York: Wiley

Buckby M. (1976) Is Primary French really in the Balance? *Audio-Visual Language Journal* 14, 1

Buckby M. et al. (1981) *Graded Objectives and Tests for Modern Languages*. Schools Council. CILT

Bullock A. (Lord Bullock) (Chairman) (1975) *A Language for Life*: Report of Committee of Inquiry appointed by the Secretary of State for Education and Science. HMSO

Burstall C. (1970) *French in the Primary School: Attitudes and Achievement*. NFER

Burstall C., Jamieson M., Cohen S. and Hargreaves M. (1974) *Primary French in the Balance*. NFER

Business Education Council (1978) Circular No. 1/78

Butzkamm W. and Dodson C. J. (1980) The teaching of communication: from theory to practice. *International Review of Applied Linguistics* 18(4)

Cambridge University Reporter (1979) 335/109 (17 January), 223–6

Caplan D. (1972) Clause boundaries and recognition latencies for words in sentences. *Perception and Psychophysics* 12, 73–6

Carroll J. B. (1969) Psychological and educational research into second language teaching to young children. In Stern H. H. (Ed.) *Languages and the Young School Child*. Oxford: OUP

Carroll J. B. (1971) Implications of aptitude test research and psycholinguistic theory for foreign language teaching. Colloquium 15, XVIIth International Congress, International Association of Applied Psychology, Liège July 1971. Also in Research Memorandum RM 71 – 14 Princeton, New Jersey, Educational Testing Service

Carroll J. B. and Sapon S. M. (1958) *Modern Language Aptitude Test*. New York: The Psychological Corporation

Chao, Yuen Ren (1968) *Language and Symbolic Systems*. CUP

Charlton K. (1965) *Education in Renaissance England*. Routledge and Kegan Paul

Chomsky N. (1957) *Syntactic Structures*. The Hague: Mouton and Co.

Chomsky N. (1959) Review of Skinner B. F.: *Verbal Behavior* (1957). In *Language* 35, 1, 26–58

Chomsky N. (1965) *Aspects of the Theory of Syntax*. Cambridge, Mass.: MIT Press

Chomsky N. (1966) Address to 1965 Northeast Conference. In Allen and

Corder (Eds) (1973–7)

CILT (1985) *German for A Level: A Resource-Based Approach.* Centre for Information on Language Teaching and Research

Clarendon Commission (1864) Report of Royal Commission on the Public Schools

Clark H. H. and Clark E. V. (1977) *Psychology and Language.* New York: Harcourt Brace Jovanovich International

Clegg A. and Megson B. (1968) *Children in Distress.* Harmondsworth: Penguin Education Special

Clyne M. (1986) *An Early Start: Second Language at Primary School.* Melbourne, Australia: River Seine Publications

Colbeck C. (1887) *On the Teaching of Modern Languages in Theory and Practice.* (Two lectures) Cambridge: Pitt Press

Coleman A. (1931) *The Teaching of Modern Foreign Languages in the United States.* American and Canadian Committees on Modern Languages. New York: Macmillan Co.

Coleman A. (1934) *Experiments and Studies in Modern Language Teaching.* Chicago: University of Chicago Press

Comenius J. A. (1631) *Janua Linguarum Reserata. The Gates of Tongues Unlocked and Opened.* Amsterdam

Comenius J. A. (1632) *Didactica Magna.* (Trans: *The Great Didactic* 1896. Black)

Comenius J. A. (1646) *Methodus Linguarum Novissima.* (Reissued Chicago: University of Chicago Press, 1953)

Comenius J. A. (1659) *Orbis Sensualium Pictus. Picture of the Visible World.* Kirton

Corder S. P. (1974) Error Analysis. In vol. 3 of Allen and Corder (Eds) (1973–7)

Corless F. and Gaskell R. (1983) Foreign languages at the post O level stage. Paper 5 in Richardon G. (Ed.) *Teaching Modern Languages.* Croom-Helm

Coste D. (1976) *Un Niveau-Seuil.* Paris: Hatier

Coulthard M. (1977) *An Introduction to Discourse Analysis.* Longman

Council of Europe (1969) Committee of ministers: Resolution (69) 2: *On an intensified modern language teaching programme for Europe.* Strasbourg: Council of Europe

Council of Europe (1972) *The Teaching of Modern Languages in Primary Schools. CCC/EGT (72)3.* Report on the Reading (England) Symposium (1967). Strasbourg

Council of Europe (1974) *The Early Teaching of a Modern Language CCC/EGT (74)10.* Report on the Wiesbaden Symposium (1973). Strasbourg

Council of Europe (1977) *Modern Languages in Primary Education CCC/EGT(76)38–E.* Report on the Copenhagen Symposium (1976). Strasbourg

Crowther G. (1959) *15 to 18: Report of the Central Advisory Council for Education – England.* HMSO

Cyrano de Bergerac (1657) *Histoire comique des Estats et Empires de la Lune.* Paris: Le Bret Nouvelle édn *Oeuvres Complètes* (1977)

Dakin J. (1973) *The Language Laboratory and Language Learning.* Longman

Davie R. et al. (1972) *National Child Development Study.* (1958 Cohort) Longman

Davies G. D. and Higgins J. (1982) *Computers, Language and Language Learning*. CILT

Davies G. D. and Higgins J. (1985) *Using Computers in Language Learning: A Teachers' Guide*. 2nd enlarged edition. CILT (originally published in 1982 as *Computers, Language and Language Learning*)

De Laguna (1972) *Speech: Its Function and Development*. Bloomington, Ind.: Indiana University Press

DES (1983) *Survey of the Use of Graded Objectives and their Effect on the Teaching and Learning of Modern Languages in the County of Oxfordshire*. Report of HM Inspectors

DES (1985) Assessment and Performance Unit. *Report on 1983 Survey of French, German and Spanish*. Department of Education and Science

DES (1986a) Assessment and Performance Unit. *Report on 1984 Survey of French*. Department of Education and Science

DES (1986b) *Foreign Languages in the School Curriculum. A Draft Statement of Policy*. Department of Education and Science/Welsh Office

Dickson A. (1972) Each one, Teach one. *Frontier* (June) 99–103

Dickson A. (1975) Tutoring – Service within the community of the school itself. *Community Development Journal* (January) 44–9

Dodson C. J. (1967) *Language Teaching and the Bilingual Method*. Pitman

Dodson C. J. (1978) *Bilingual Education in Wales*. Schools Council

Dodson C. J. (1985) Second language acquisition and bilingual development: a theoretical framework. *Journal of Multilingual and Multicultural Development* 6(5)

Donaldson M. (1978) *Children's Minds*. Fontana

Donmall B. G. (Ed.) (1985) *Language Awareness*. NCLE Papers and Reports 6. CILT

Donnison D. V. (1967) Education and Opinion. *New Society* (26 October) Quoted in Kogan M. (1971)

Dufief N. G. (1818) *Nature Displayed in her Mode of Teaching Language to Man*. 2 vols

Dunning R. (1970) Alternative exercise to prose composition. In Schools Council (1970)

EEC (1974) *Education in the European Community*. Bulletin of the European Communities. Supplement 3/74. Brussels

Emmans K. A., Hawkins E. W., Westoby A. (1974) *Foreign Languages in Industry and Commerce*. York: Language Teaching Centre, University of York

Estacio C. I. C. (1971) A Cognition Based Programme of Second Language Learning. In Pimsleur P. and Quin T. (Eds) *The Psychology of Second Language Learning*. Cambridge: CUP

Eton College (1979) Modern Languages as a Career Qualification. Broadsheet. Slough: Modern Language Department, Eton College

Eysenck H. J. (1947) *Dimensions of Personality*. (Reprinted 1961) Routledge and Kegan Paul

Federation of British Industries (1962) Report of Working Party. *Foreign Languages in Industry*. (1964) Report of Second Working Party (same title)

de Fivas V. (1836) *The New Grammar of French Grammars*. (57th edn 1905) Crosby Lockwood and Son

Fodor J. A. and Bever T. G. (1965) The psychological reality of linguistic segments. *Journal of Verbal Learning and Verbal Behaviour* 4, 414–20

Forster K. I. (1979) Levels of processing and the structure of the language processor. In Cooper W. and Walker W. (Eds) *Sentence Processing: Psycholinguistic Studies Presented to Merrill Garrett.* New York: Halstead Press

Francke F. (1884) *Die praktische Spracherlernung auf Grund der Psychologie und der Physiologie der Sprache.* Leipzig

Furth H. and Wachs H. (1974) *Thinking goes to School.* New York: OUP

Gamble C. J. and Smalley A. (1975) Primary French in the Balance: Were the scales accurate? *Modern Languages* vi, 2, 95

Gardner R. C. and Lambert W. E. (1972) *Attitudes and Motivation in Second Language Learning.* Rowley, Mass.: Newbury House

Gattegno C. (1972) *Teaching Foreign Languages in Schools: The Silent Way.* New York: Educational Solutions, Inc.

Geschwind N. (1964) The Development of the Brain and the Evolution of Language. *Monograph Series on Languages and Linguistics* 17, 155–69

Geschwind N. (1972) Language and the Brain. *Scientific American* 226, 76–83

Gilbert M. (1953, 1954, 1955) The Origins of the Reform Movement in Modern Language Teaching in England (Parts i, ii and iii). Three articles in *Research Review* 4, 5 and 6

Goldschmidt E. P. (1950) *The Printed Book of the Renaissance.* CUP

Goodlad S. (1979) *Learning by Teaching.* Community Service Volunteers

Gougenheim G. et al. (1965) *L'Elaboration du français fondamental.* Paris: Didier

Gouin F. (1880) *L'Art d'enseigner. The Art of Teaching and Studying Languages.* (Trans. 1894) Philip

Green P. S. (Ed) (1975) *The Language Laboratory in School: Performance and Prediction:* The York study. Edinburgh: Oliver and Boyd

Guberina P. and Rivenc P. (1961) *Voix et Images de France.* St Cloud: Crédif

Hagboldt P. (1940) The teaching of languages from the middle ages to the present: a historical sketch. In *The Teaching of German.* Boston: D. C. Heath and Co.

Halliday M. A. K. (1975) *Learning How to Mean.* Edward Arnold

Halliday M. A. K., McIntosh A. and Strevens P. (1964) *The Linguistic Sciences and Language Teaching.* Longman

Hamilton J. (1823) *The Hamiltonian System*

Hans N. A. (1951) *New Trends in Education in the Eighteenth Century.* Routledge and Kegan Paul

Harding A. and Page B. (1974) An alternative model for modern language examinations. *AVLA Journal* 12, 3

Hartnoll J. H. (1823) *Exposure of the Hamiltonian System*

Hartog P. J. (1907) *The Writing of English.* Oxford: Clarendon Press

Hawkins E. W. (1970) The A level examination syllabus. The problem of definition. In Russell (Ed.) (1970)

Hawkins E. W. (1981) *Modern Languages in the Curriculum.* Cambridge: CUP

Hawkins E. W. (1984 Revised ed 1987) *Awareness of Language: An Introduction.* Cambridge: CUP

Hawkins E. W. and Howson B. (1977) *Le français pour tout le monde.* Book 4. Edinburgh: Oliver and Boyd

Hawkins E. W. and Perren G. (Eds) (1978) *Intensive Language Teaching in Schools.* CILT

Hawkins E. W. and Howson B. (1979) *Revision French*. Edinburgh: Oliver and Boyd

Hayter W. (1961) University Grants Committee, Report of Sub-committee on Oriental, Slavonic, East European and African studies. HMSO

Her Majesty's Inspectorate (1977) *Matters for Discussion 3: Modern Languages in Comprehensive Schools*. HMSO

Her Majesty's Inspectorate (1978) *Curriculum 11–16: Modern Languages. A working paper of the ML committee*, HMI. DES

HMI (1986) *English 5 to 16*. Curriculum Matters series no. 1. DES

HMI (1987) *Modern Foreign Languages to 16*. Curriculum Matters series no. 8. DES

Holmes D. T. (1903) *The Teaching of Modern Languages in Schools and Colleges*. Paisley

Hoole, C. (1660) *A New Discovery of the Old Art of Teaching School*. Reissued 1913. Campagnac E. T. (Ed.) Liverpool

Howson B. (1978) A French Remedial Course. In Hawkins and Perren (Eds) (1978)

Hoy P. H. (1977) *The Early Teaching of Modern Languages*. Nuffield Foundation

Huttenlocher J. (1974) The origins of language comprehension. In Solso R. L. (Ed.) *Theories in Cognitive Psychology*. Potomac, Md: Lawrence Erlbaum Associates

Illich I. (1971) *Deschooling Society*. New York: Harper and Row (Penguin edn 1973)

Incorporated Association of Head Masters (IAHM) (1963) *Modern Languages in the Grammar School*. (Revised edn 1966) Nuffield Foundation

Ingram M. (1975) Psychology and language learning. In vol. 2 of Allen and Corder (Eds) (1975)

Jacotot J. (1826) *Manuel de l'enseignement universel*. Louvain: H. de Paul

James C. V. (1979) Foreign languages in the school curriculum. In Perren (Ed.) (1979)

James E. (Lord James of Rusholme) (1949) *An Essay on the Content of Education*. Harrap

James E. (Lord James of Rusholme) (Chairman) (1972) *Teacher Education and Training*. Report of a Committee of Inquiry appointed by the Secretary of State for Education and Science. HMSO

Jespersen J. O. H. (1904) *Sprogundervisning: How to Teach a Foreign Language*. Swan Sonnenschein & Co.

Johnson M. R. (1966) Tape-Recorder versus Non-Record Laboratory. Baltimore: *French Review* 39, 899–906

Jones B., Daly F. and Brodzki W. (1986) *Granville. Quelle tête! Jeu des ménages*. Three programs from Cambridge Micro Software. CUP

Journal of Education (1890) Review of Cheltenham Conference XII, 335ff.

Kamenev V. Y. (1955) *Cours audio-visuel préliminaire de français*. Paris: TAVOR Aids

Kavanagh J. F. and Mattingley I. G. (1972) *Language by Ear and Eye*. Cambridge, Mass.: MIT Press

Keating R. F. (1963) *A Study of the Effectiveness of Language Laboratories*. Columbia University Institute of Administrative Research. New

York: Teachers' College

Keith G. R. and Glover M. (1987) *Primary Language Learning with Computers*. Croom Helm

Kelly L. G. (1969) *Twenty Five Centuries of Language Teaching*. Rowley, Mass.: Newbury House

Kennedy G. (1969) Conditions for Language Learning. In Oller and Richards (Eds) (1973)

King A. (1978) Haygrove Comprehensive School. In Hawkins and Perren (Eds) (1978)

Kinsbourne M. and Smith W. L. (Eds) (1974) *Hemispheric Disconnection and Cerebral Function*. Springfield, Ill.: Charles C. Thomas

Kogan M. (1971) *The Politics of Education*. Harmondsworth: Penguin Education Special

Krashen S. D. (1977) The Monitor Model for Adult Second Language Performance. In Burt, Dulay and Finocchiaro (Eds) *Viewpoints on English as a Second Language*. New York: Regents

Krashen S. D. (1979) A Response to McLaughlin. The Monitor Model. *Language Learning* 29, 1

Krashen S. D. (1981) *Second Language Acquisition and Second Language Learning*. Oxford: OUP

Krashen S. D. (1983) The din in the head. Input and the language acquisition device. *Foreign Language Annals* 16, 41–4

Labov W. (1970) The Logic of Nonstandard English. In Williams F. (Ed.) *Language and Poverty: Perspectives on a Theme*. Chicago: Markham

Lado R. (1957) *Linguistics Across Cultures*. Ann Arbor, Michigan: University of Michigan

Lado R. (1964) *Language Teaching. A Scientific Approach*. New York: McGraw Hill

Lazaro C. M. (1963) *Report on Foreign Language Teaching in British Primary Schools*. (January – March) Nuffield Foundation Foreign Languages Materials Project. Reports and Occasional Papers, No. 1

Learned W. S. and Wood B. de K. (1938) The student and his knowledge. New York: Carnegie Foundation for the Advancement of Teaching, *Bulletin* 29

Leathes S. (Chairman) (1918) *Modern Studies*. Report to Prime Minister of Committee on the Position of Modern Languages in the Educational System of Great Britain. HMSO (Cd. 9036)

Lenneberg E. H. (1967) *Biological Foundations of Language*. John Wiley and Sons

le Page R. B. (1964) *The National Language Question*. Oxford: OUP

le Vert C. (1826) *An Analytical, Comparative and Demonstrative Mode of Tuition*

Lévy J. (1878) Open letter to L. Sauveur. Boston. Quoted in Kelly (1969)

Limb A. and Bourgeois P. (1986) *Objectifs: Assignments in Practical Language Skills*. Cambridge: CUP

Littlewood W. T. (1975) Role performance and language teaching. *IRAL* XIII, 20

Locke J. (1690) *Some Thoughts Concerning Education*. T. Basset

Lopato E. W. (1961) An experiment to determine the effect of learning conversational French on academic achievement of third grade children. Unpublished Ph.D. dissertation. New York University

Lozanov G. (1978) *Suggestology and Outlines of Suggestopedy*. Sofia: Institute of Suggestology. New York: Gordon & Breach, Interface

Lupson J. (1977) The effect of training in perception of pattern in language. Unpublished M.Ed. thesis. University of Leeds

Mackey W. F. (1965) *Language Teaching Analysis*. Longman

Mackey W. F. (1967) Paper to conference on language testing. Michigan (September)

McMunn H. (1914) *A Path to Freedom in the School*. Rewritten as *The Child's Path to Freedom*. G. Bell and Sons. (Reissued 1926 J. Curwen and Sons)

Marcel C. (1853) *Language as a Means of Mental Culture and International Communication*. (2 vols)

Marcel C. (1867) *The Study of Languages Brought Back to its True Principles, or The Art of Thinking in a Foreign Language*. Paris

Marler P. (1973) Speech Development and Bird Song: Are there any Parallels? In Miller (Ed.) (1973)

Matulis A. (1977) *Language and Hope*. Detroit: National Research Institute for Psychoanalysis and Psychology

Menuhin Y. (1977) *Unfinished Journey*. Macdonald and Jane's

Mill J. S. (1867) Inaugural Address. Scotland: St Andrews University

Miller G. A. (1956) The Magical Number Seven – Plus or Minus Two. Some limits on our capacity for processing information. *The Psychological Review* 63, 2

Miller G. A. (Ed.) (1973) *Communication, Language and Meaning*. New York: Basic Books

Miller G. A. and Johnson-Laird P. N. (1976) *Language and Perception*. CUP

Milton J. (1644) *Tract on Education*

MLA/BALT (1986) *Call for the Computer. Computer Assisted Language Learning for the Modern Language Teacher*. Council for Educational Technology, London. Loughborough, Leics: Tecmedia Ltd

Mobbs, M. (1985) *Britain's South Asian Language*. CILT

Montaigne M. de (1580) De l'Institution des Enfants. *Essais*. Paris: Langlier

Morris P. D. (1984) *The Head of Department: A Guide to Good Practice*. MLA Handbook No. 3. MLA

National Congress on Languages in Education. See Perren (Ed.) (1979)

Newcastle Commission (1861) Report of Royal Commission on Popular Education in England. 6 vols

Newmark L. and Reibel D. A. (1968) Necessity and Sufficiency in Language Learning. *IRAL* vi 145–61

Nicholson D. (1975) Final Report on the French Pilot Scheme. (Mimeograph) York: Micklegate House

Nuffield Foundation (1964–75) Modern Language Materials: *En Avant* E. J. Arnold and Son. *Adelante* Macmillan. *Vorwärts* E. J. Arnold and Son. *Vperyod!* Macmillan/Lund Humphries

Ogden C. K. (1932a) *Basic English: A General Introduction*. Kegan Paul, Trench Trubner and Co. Ltd

Ogden C. K. (1932b) *The Basic Words*. The Orthological Institute

Ollendorf H. G. (1783) *A New Method of Learning to Read, Write and Speak a Foreign Language in Six Months*. Frankfurt. (Adapted to the French 1843)

Oller J. W. Jr (1972) Cloze tests of second language proficiency and what they measure. *Proceedings of AILA Congress 1972 Copenhagen*

Oller J. W. Jr (1979) *Language Tests at School*. Longman

Oller J. W. Jr and Conrad C. A. (1971) The cloze technique and ESL proficiency. *Language Learning* 21, 183–96

Oller J. W. Jr and Richards J. C. (Eds) (1973) *Focus on the Learner*. Rowley, Mass.: Newbury House

Oller J. W. Jr and Nagato N. (1974) The long term effects of FLES: An experiment. *The Modern Language Journal* LVIII, 1, 2, 15–19

Ollion H. (1912) *Lettres inédites de Locke*. The Hague

Olson G. M. (1973) Developmental changes in memory and the acquisiton of language. In Moore T. E. (Ed.) *Cognitive Development and the Acquisition of Language*. New York: Academic Press

Page B. W. (1974) An Alternative to 16+. *Modern Languages* 55 (March 1974)

Palmer H. E. (1917) *The Scientific Study and Teaching of Languages*. Harrap. (Reissued, Harper D. (Ed.) 1968, OUP)

Palmer H. E. (1921) *The Principles of Language Study*. Harrap. (Reissued 1964, OUP)

Parker W. R. (1966) The National Interest and Modern Languages. In *The Language Curtain and Other Essays on American Education*. Baltimore: Modern Language Association of America

Passy P. (1886) *Le Maître Phonétique*. Monthly Journal of International Phonetic Association

Pemberton R. (1857) *Report of the Proceedings at the Inauguration of Mr Pemberton's New Philosophical Model Infant School for Teaching Languages, Native and Foreign, on the Natural or Euphonic System*

Penfield W. and Roberts L. (1959) *Speech and Brain Mechanisms*. OUP (Reissued in paperback 1966, New York: Atheneum)

Penman T. and Wolff A. (1981) *Web of Language*. Oxford: OUP

Perren G. (Ed.) (1979) National Congress on Languages in Education, 1978, Papers and Reports 1 and 2. CILT

Perren G. See Hawkins and Perren (Eds) (1978)

Peters R. S. (Ed.) (1973) *The Philosophy of Education*. OUP

Pienemann M. (1985) Learnability and syllabus construction. In Hyltenstam K. and Pienemann M. (Eds) *Modelling and Assisting Second Language Acquisition*. Avon: Clevedon Printing Co.

Pimsleur P. (1966) Testing Foreign Language Learning. In Valdman A. *Trends in Language Teaching*. New York: McGraw-Hill

Plötz K. (1865) *Elementarbuch der französischen Sprache*. Berlin

Plowden B. (Lady Plowden) (Chairman) (1967) *Children and their Primary Schools*. Report of the Central Advisory Council for Education, England. 2 vols. HMSO

Powell B. (1986) *Boys, Girls and Languages in School*. Information Guide 24. CILT

Prendergast T. (1864) *The Mastery of Languages or The Art of Speaking Foreign Languages Idiomatically*. (12 editions by 1879)

Pringle M. L. K. (Ed.) (1969) *Caring for Children*. Longman

Pringle M. L. K. (Ed.) (1980) *A Fairer Future for Children*. Macmillan

Quick Reverend R. H. (1875) *Some Account of Celebrated Methods*

Raleigh M. (1981) *The Languages Book*. ILEA English Centre

Rees F. (1986) The wrong gender? *Times Educational Supplement* 31.10.86
Reibel D. A. See Newmark and Reibel (1968)
Reibel D. A. (1969) Language learning analysis. *IRAL* vii/4
Reimer E. (1971) *School is Dead.* Harmondsworth: Penguin Education Special
Richards I. A. (1935) *Basic in Teaching: East and West.* Kegan Paul, Trench, Trubner and Co. Ltd
Richterich R. (1972) *A Model for the Definition of Language Needs of Adults Learning a Modern Language.* Strasbourg: Council of Europe. Reprinted in Trim et al. (1973)
Riddy D. C. (1966) Modern Language Teaching Today. In Schools Council (1966)
Riddy D. C. (1972) Where are the teachers to come from? *Times Educational Supplement* (2 February)
Rivers W. (1964) *The Psychologist and the Foreign Language Teacher.* Chicago: Univ. of Chicago Press
Rix D. (1978) Intensive Russian. In Hawkins and Perren (Eds) (1978)
Robbins L. (Lord Robbins) (1963) *Higher Education.* Report of the Committee appointed by the Prime Minister. HMSO
Roberts D. J. (1979) The Deployment of Sixth-Formers in Modern Language Lessons *Audio-Visual Language Journal* 17, 2, 125–6
Robertson T. (1845) *Nouveau Cours pratique, analytique, théorique et synthétique de langue anglaise.* (Trans: *The whole French language comprised in a series of lessons.* 2 vols. Paris and London. 1853)
Rowell S. (1980) Graded Objectives in Modern Languages. *GOML Newsletter* 3. CILT
Royal Society of Arts (1979) *Journal*
Russell C. V. (Ed.) (1970) *Post O-level Studies in Modern Languages.* Oxford: Pergamon
Rutter M., Maughan B., Mortimore P., Ouston J. (1979) *Fifteen Thousand Hours.* Open Books
Salter M. V. (1980) Arguments for and against graded tests. Inner London Education Authority, *Bulletin* (Spring Issue)
Sanderson D. (1982) *Modern Language Teachers in Action.* York: University of York Language Teaching Centre
Saussure F. de (1983) *Course in General Linguistics* (trs. and annot. by Roy Harris). Duckworth (lectures given in 1914)
Sauveur L. (1874) *Introduction to the Teaching of Living Languages Without Grammar or Dictionary.* New York: Holt
Sayce A. (1879) How to learn a language. *Nature* 20, 93
Schools Council (1966) Working Paper No. 8. *French in the Primary School.* HMSO
Schools Council (1970) Working Paper No. 28. *New Patterns in Sixth Form Modern Language Studies.* Evans/Methuen Educational
Schools Council (1973) *Concept 7 – 9.* E. J. Arnold for Schools Council
Schools Council (1981) *Language other than French in the Secondary School.* Schools Council
Schools Council Modern Languages Project, York (1970) *Reports and Occasional Papers* No. 35. York: Micklegate House
SCUE/CNAA (1986) *Guidelines for Written French at A Level.* SCUE
SCUE/CVCP (1986) *AS Levels and University Entrance.* SCUE
Searle J. (1969) *Speech Acts.* CUP

Shaw B. (1916) *Preface to Pygmalion*. Constable

Sinclair H. (1969) Developmental Psycholinguistics. In Elkind D. and Flavel J. H. (Eds) *Studies in Cognitive Development: Essays in honour of Jean Piaget*. New York: OUP

Skelton R. B. (1957) The effect of High School foreign language study on freshmen test scores at Alabama Polytechnic Institute. *School and Society* LXXXV, 203–5

Skinner B. F. (1957) *Verbal Behavior*. New York: Appleton Century Crofts

Slobin D. I. (1979) *Psycholinguistics*. Glenville, Ill.: Scott Foresman and Co.

Slobin D. I. and Welsh C. A. (1973) Elicited imitation as a research tool in developmental psycholinguistics. In Ferguson C. A. and Slobin D. I. (Eds) *Studies of Child Language Development*. New York: Holt Rinehart and Winston

Smith P. D. Jr (1970) *A Comparison of the Cognitive and Audiolingual Approaches to Foreign Language Instruction*. The Pennsylvania Foreign Language Project. Philadelphia Center for Curriculum Development. Harrap

Smith F. (1983) *The Promise and the Threat of Microcomputers in Language Teaching*. Reading: University of Reading Centre for the Teaching of Reading

Spicer A. J. and Riddy D. C. (1974) *The Initial Training of Teachers of Modern Languages in Colleges and Departments of Education*. Colchester: Language Centre, University of Essex

Stack E. M. (1960) *The Language Laboratory and Modern Language Teaching*. New York: OUP

Stern H. H. (1963) *Foreign Languages in Primary Education*. Hamburg: UNESCO Institute for Education

Stern H. H. (1976) Optional age: Myth or reality? *Canadian Modern Language Review* 32, 3, 283–94

Stern H. H. (1983) *Fundamental Concepts of Language Teaching*. Oxford: OUP

Stevick E. W. (1976) *Memory, Meaning and Method*. Rowley Mass.: Newbury House

Stubbs M. (1980) *Language and Literacy: Sociolinguistics of Reading and Writing*. Routledge and Kegan Paul

Swan H. (1894) *The Systematic Teaching of Languages*

Swann M. (Lord Swann) (Chairman) (1985) *Education for All*. The Final Report of the Committee of Inquiry into the Education of Children from Ethnic Minority Groups. HMSO.

Sweet H. (1899) *The Practical Study of Languages*. (Reissued 1964 OUP)

Sweet H. (1874, 1876) *Papers to the Philological Society*

Tacke O. (1923) *Der Sprachunterricht muss umkehren*. Leipzig

Taunton Commission (1868) Report of the Royal Commission on education given in schools in England. 21 vols

Taylor W. L. (1953) Cloze procedure: a new tool for measuring readability. *Journalism Quarterly* 30, 415–33

Ticknor G. (1832) *The Best Methods of Teaching the Living Languages, Lectures*. Harvard University

Tizard J. et al. (1981) Collaboration between teachers and parents in assisting children's reading. *British Journal of Educational Psychology* 52, 1–15.

Trim J. L. M., Richterich R., van Ek J. A. and Wilkins D. A. (1973) *Systems Development in Adult Language Learning*. Strasbourg: Council of Europe. 1980 Pergamon Press

Trinity College (1979) *Examination Syllabuses*: Spoken English as a Foreign or Second Language and Written English (Intermediate). Revised edn Trinity College, London

Turner J. D. (1965) *Language Laboratories in Great Britain*. (3rd edn) Univ. of London Press

Valette R. M. (1967) *Modern Language Testing*. New York: Harcourt Brace

Van Buren P. (1974) Contrastive Analysis. In vol. 3 of Allen and Corder (Eds) (1973–7)

van Ek J. A. (1972) *Proposal for the Definition of a Threshold Level in Foreign Language Learning for Adults*. Strasbourg: Council of Europe

van Ek J. A. with Alexander L. G. (1980) *Threshold Level English*. Oxford: Pergamon

van Ek J. A., Alexander L. G. and Fitzpatrick M. A. (1980) *Waystage English*. Oxford: Pergamon

Viëtor W. (1882) *Der Sprachunterricht muss umkehren*. Published under pen name: 'Quousque tandem?' Published 1886 under author's name, Heilbronn

von Wittich B. (1962) Prediction of Success in Foreign Language Study. *Modern Language Journal* 46, 208–12

Vygotsky L. S. (1962) *Thought and Language*. Cambridge, Mass.: MIT Press. (First issued, posthumously, 1934; suppressed 1936)

Watson F. (1909) *The Beginnings of the Teaching of Modern Subjects in England*. Pitman (Reissued 1971. Wakefield: S. R. Publishers)

Webster J. (1654) *Examination of Academies*

Wells G. et al. (1981) *Learning Through Interaction*. The study of Language development. Cambridge: CUP

West M. (1926) *Learning to read a foreign language and other essays on Foreign Language Teaching*. (2nd edn 1955) Longman

West Sussex Education Authority (1976) West Sussex/CILT Colloquium. In Bearne and James (1976)

West Sussex Education Authority (1978) Report of County Working Party: *Modern Languages 11–18*. West Sussex Education Department

White J. P. (1973) *Towards a Compulsory Curriculum*. Routledge and Kegan Paul

Widdowson H. G. (1973) Directions in the teaching of discourse. In Corder S. P. and Roulet E. (Eds) *Theoretical Linguistic Models in Applied Linguistics*. Paris: AIMAV/Didier

Widdowson H. G. (1978) *Teaching Language as Communication*. OUP

Wilkins D. A. (1972) *An Investigation into the Linguistic and Situational Content of the Common Core in a Unit/Credit System*. Strasbourg: Council of Europe

Wilkins D. A. (1976) *Notional Syllabuses*. OUP

Williams R. (1961) *The Long Revolution*. Chatto and Windus. (Penguin edn 1965)

Winter R. F. (1977) A Redundant Resource? *Times Educational Supplement* (15 April)

Wynburne S. B. (1960) *Vertical Translation and the Teaching of English*. Macmillan

Index

ability 26, 41
agrégation 153, 289
Annan Report 5, 6, 63, 70, 150, 182, 190
apprenticeship x, 49, 58, 68, 71, 72, 77, 92, 93, 238, 278, 282–4
Arnold, M. 114
assimilation and accommodation (Piaget) 178
Audio-Visual Language Association 6
Austin, J. L. 217, 218, 220

balance of language provision 68, 94
Basic 156–8
BBC language broadcasting 195–8
Berger, T. 94, 190, 283
Berlitz, M. D. 129, 130
Bernstein, B. 49, 50
bilingual dialogue 49, 166
Board of Education
    Circular 797 (1912) 132, 133–7, 140, 141, 142, 152, 153, 285; Circular 826 (1913) 144; Circular (1916) 137, 141, 142, 152; Pamphlet 47 (1926) 137, 141, 142, 153; Pamphlet 70 (1928) 149
    Consultative Committee 149
brain growth 183, 184
British Overseas Trade Board 37–40
Brooks, N. 8, 154, 215
Bruner, J. 51, 52, 55, 56, 174, 231
Buckby, M. 171, 189
Bullock Report 33, 34, 52, 85, 228, 239
Burstall, C. 9, 11, 12, 56, 59, 78, 185–90
Butzkamm, W. 222, 259, 271, 273, 274

CILT 5, 8, 59, 251, 292
Carroll, J. B. 12, 229, 236
Central Bureau 7
Chao, Yuen Ren 32, 33, 48
Charlton, K. 102, 115
Cheltenham conference 7, 122, 124, 125
Chomsky, N. 9, 10, 122, 154, 162, 177, 178, 179
Clarendon Commission 62, 111, 113, 114, 121, 151
classroom activities: level 1 256, 262–8; level 2 256, 268–70; level 3 257, 270–6; level 4 258, 276–82
cloze tests 224, 236–7
Coleman, A. 151, 189
Comenius, J. A. 102–9, 112, 114, 115, 116, 131, 213, 214, 295
computers and language learning 199–202
concept formation and language 214, 215, 228
Coulthard, M. 168, 169, 220
Council of Europe 48, 59, 169, 181
Crédif 159, 160, 173
critical age for language acquisition 182–4
Crosland, A. 20
Cross, D. 191, 275
curriculum: administrative constraints 69; autonomy of school Head 61, 62;

decisions 29, 68; freedom of the individual 29; 'hidden' 28; 'middle-class' 28, 50; Study Group (1962–4) 6, 61–2, 294; vacuum in planning 61, 62, 293, 294

Dakin, J. 167, 168
Dalwood, M. 194, 283
departmental support of teachers 252
deschooling 27
dialogue: with adult 53, 229; one-to-one 245, 283
discourse (*v.* text) 220, 255
Dodson, C. J. xiv, 152, 215, 221, 222, 224, 256, 259, 271, 273, 274
Donaldson, M. 50, 51, 52, 55, 213, 220, 221, 231, 236
drop-out figures (modern languages) 10, 16, 23, 171

EEC ix, 5, 10, 28, 37, 63, 283
ETML 180–90
education of the ear xii, 57, 239–46, 264
Eldon judgement (1805) 111
Emmans, K. A. 36, 72, 74, 75, 76
empathy in language learning 43, 188, 205
enactive learning 174
English: teachers of 228, 252; as world vehicle language 26, 38, 47, 86
ergons (*v.* etymons) 167
erosion of language skills 4, 41
errors: inter-language (transfer) 78, 79; intra-language (analogical) 78, 82, 83
ethnic minorities xi, 28, 58, 189, 248, 305
examinations
    'AS' level 300
    CSE 6, 8, 65, 153, 161, 170, 172, 262, 294, 297–300
    GCE 8, 15, 19, 34, 62, 65–7, 70, 90, 166, 170, 222, 294
    GCSE 294, Appx A
    Higher School Certificate 5, 67, 90, 138, 143, 145, 149, 153
    School Certificate 66, 138, 149
examinations: boy:girl entrant ratio 23; mode III 161; oral test 122, 143, 149, 150, 153; proliferation of 149; SSEC 62, 68, 148, 149, 150, 153; stress on grammar 112; written test 149
examining boards 149; Associated Examining Board (AEB) 150; Joint Matriculation Board (JMB) 150; Oxford and Cambridge Joint Board (O and C) 150
exchange of teachers 8

FL *v.* IL 98–9
Federation of British Industries 4, 36, 182
'force' *see* speech acts
français fondamental, le 155, 159, 173
Francke, F. 124, 130, 140, 152, 198, 222
functions 219, 220
Furth, H. and Wachs, H. 239, 240, 241

£9.50